I0126621

Templeton

THE TEMPLETON COAT OF ARMS

The following is a description of the Templeton Coat of Arms as found in Burke's General Armory, world authority on heraldry, and also in Burke's Encyclopedia of Heraldry. (The explanations of the terms used were taken from a dictionary of heraldry and are given in parentheses.)

"Templeton. A. (azure, or blue) A fesse, or. (A fesse is formed by two horizontal lines drawn across the field, comprising the escutcheon. It is emblematic of the military girdle worn around the body over the armor.) ("or" means gold or yellow.) In base a church ar. ("Ar" means white or silver.) Crest: a holy lamb reguard ar., ("reguard" means watchful) sustaining over the shoulder a banner gu ("gu" means red).

Translated into modern English, this means:

"Blue background with a gold fesse; a white or silver church in the base; a white or silver holy lamb in a watchful position, holding a red banner over the shoulder."

The following is also taken from Burke's General Armory:

"Templeton, Scotland, 16th century: Gu. a temple ar. on a chief sa. a star or."

In modern English, this means: "Templeton, Scotland, 16th century; red, with a white or silver temple on a black chief (upper third) a gold or yellow star."

From these descriptions it would appear that there were two Templeton coats of arms, one in England and one in Scotland.

"The surname was undoubtedly adopted by the Templeton family because of their residence near a temple, a place of worship, as was the ancient custom when surnames were first assumed. The coat of arms of the Templeton family indicated they were deeply religious and it was, no doubt, because of the zeal and heroism of some early ancestor participating in the Holy Wars that the arms was awarded. A great many of these staunch crusaders embodied in their personal name, or bore on their coat armor, some allusion or symbol proclaiming their allegiance to the Christian faith.

Regarding the significance of the heraldric bearings: azure (blue) denotes sincerity; gold indicates great generosity and elevation of mind; the paschal lamb and the pennant which it carries are symbolical of the Pilgrim, particularly one who engaged in the Holy Wars during the Crusades.

The absence of a motto on the Templeton coat of arms shows it to be a most ancient one, as mottoes were adopted somewhat later than the beginning of the decoration of coat of armor.

Templeton
Family History

RECORDS AND DESCENDENTS OF THE
TEMPLETONS WHO FIRST SETTLED IN WHAT IS
NOW LAURENS COUNTY, SOUTH CAROLINA
TOGETHER WITH BRIEF SKETCHES OF OTHER
TEMPLETONS WHO SETTLED IN OTHER PARTS
OF SOUTH CAROLINA AND OTHER STATES

WITH A
NEW APPENDIX
BY RON TEMPLETON

COMPILED BY

L. B. Templeton, Jr.

HERITAGE BOOKS
2014

HERITAGE BOOKS

AN IMPRINT OF HERITAGE BOOKS, INC.

Books, CDs, and more—Worldwide

For our listing of thousands of titles see our website
at
www.HeritageBooks.com

A Facsimile Reprint
Published 2014 by
HERITAGE BOOKS, INC.
Publishing Division
5810 Ruatan Street
Berwyn Heights, Md. 20740

Copyright © 1953 L. B. Templeton, Jr.

*This edition includes an appendix by Ron Templeton
and an updated index.*

— Publisher's Notice —
In reprints such as this, it is often not possible to remove blemishes from
the original. We feel the contents of this book warrant its reissue despite
these blemishes and hope you will agree and read it with pleasure.

International Standard Book Numbers
Paperbound: 978-0-7884-5563-6
Clothbound: 978-0-7884-9031-6

LEUMAS BASCOM TEMPLETON, JR.

To

The many Templetons and Templeton descendents who have so generously assisted in this work by furnishing valuable data;

To

Miss Ruby Templeton, in particular, whose leadership, enthusiasm and assistance have been so encouraging;

and, finally

To

My daughter, Mary Ellie Templeton Simpson, without whose untiring and efficient help in typing, this work could never have been completed

This History is

Gratefully Dedicated

INTRODUCTION

The work on this history, begun some twenty-five years ago as a hobby, has grown into a career of almost a lifetime. The descendents of the early Templetons of what is now Laurens County, S. C., became scattered over such a wide area that few of the present generation knew much about the Templetons except thir close kin. About 1927 the writer began to contact all of the Templetons that he could find in and around Laurens County. In 1929, he invited them all to a Templeton reunion at the home of L. B. Templeton, Sr., at Cross Anchor, S. C. This "get-acquainted" meeting was attended by some 175 people and proved to be of such interest that the Templeton Clan was organized then and there with Mr. Scott Templeton of Laurens, S. C., as the first president. Enthusiastic reunions have been held each year since then. In 1948 the Clan was incorporated and chartered by the Secretary of State, Columbia, S. C.

Two of the first Templetons who settled in what is now Laurens County were Robert and John Templeton, brothers. They left South Carolina in 1802 and moved, with theirs and other families, to southwestern Ohio and, in 1804, when Indiana was opened up to immigrants, were among the first settlers in that territory. Due to the great distance away the writer has been limited in securing data on these two Templeton families and their descendents.

The records of the Templeton women who were among the early settlers of Laurens County, S. C., seem to have faded into oblivion, although hundreds of their descendents are doubtless living in Laurens and other counties of South Carolina as well as elsewhere, awaiting the labors of some capable genealogist to establish their Templeton lineage.

To say that the writer has spent a "poor man's fortune" in travel and research in the effort to collect accurate information and to organize it into systematic form is only a moderate claim. There are surely hundreds of names of more recent descendents of Templetons that are not listed because the writer could not obtain them with his limited means. For these omissions and for the errors that may be found in the data the writer offers his humble apologies.

EXPLANATION OF NUMBERS

Each Templeton and each Templeton descendent has been given an identification number.

David Templeton, Sr., is given the number 1 on the assumption that he was the oldest of the Templetons listed, since his first child was born a good many years before the known birth date of the children of the other Templetons. James Templeton, Sr., is given the number 2; Robert Templeton, Sr., No. 3; John Templeton, Sr., No. 4, etc.

The first child of 1 David Templeton is No. 11 (11 David Templeton, Jr.); first child of 2 James Templeton is No. 21 (21 William Templeton); first child of 3 Robert Templeton is No. 31 (31 William Templeton); first child of 4 John Templeton is No. 41 (41 Mary Templeton), etc. The second child in each family has the number 2 annexed to the number of his or her parent. The third child has the number 3 annexed to the number of his or her parent, etc.

In cases where there are ten or more children, letters a, b, c, etc., are used instead of numbers.

Example 1: The number, 14g672, given to Mary Frances Templeton, shows by the digit "2" that she is the second child of 14g67 Ewell Hood Templeton who, as the digit "7" shows, was the seventh child who, as the digit "6" shows, was the sixth child who, as the letter "g" shows, was the seventh child who, as the digit "4" shows, was the fourth child of No. 1, David Templeton.

Example 2: The number 27a12g, given to Catherine Asbil Rogers, shows by the letter "g" that she was the seventh child of her parent, 27a12 Mary Lula Templeton Rogers, who, as the digit "2" shows, was the 2nd child of her parent, who, as the digit "1" shows, was the first child of his parent, who, as the letter "a" shows, was the first child of the parent who, as the digit "7" shows, was the seventh child of No. 2, James Templeton.

The number of digits, or of digits and letters combined, in any identification number shows the generation of that person.

Example (1) 111d121 Frances Caroline Boggs belongs to the eighth generation, since there are eight digits (and letters combined) in her number.

Example (2) 25518 Joseph B. Templeton has five digits in his number, and, therefore, he belongs to the fifth generation.

Templetons of Laurens County South Carolina

The earliest records we have of those Templetons who settled in what is now Laurens County, S. C., are in the form of land grants. In the office of the Secretary of State, Columbia, S. C., we find the records of land grants to 2 James Templeton, 3 Robert Templeton, 5 Martha Templeton, and 6 Agnes Templeton, all on Duncan's Creek and Enoree River, and all dated March 17, 1775. In 1786 and again in 1793, 1 David Templeton was given grants of land on Duncan's Creek and joining the land of 3 Robert Templeton. Although we find no record of land grants to 4 John Templeton we have other records to indicate that he lived in Laurens County, along with these others, until he migrated, in 1804, to Indiana, with 3 Robert Templeton.

Although we have no positive proof that all of these six Templetons were brothers and sisters, we do have strong indications that they were. In the first place, we see that they all settled in the same immediate vicinity about the same time. In the next place, we have photostat copies of papers that indicate a very close association in their business transactions. For instance: on September 23, 1785, 2 James Templeton and 3 Robert Templeton signed a joint paper authorizing Robert Hanna to collect their pay for military services in the South Carolina Militia during the War for Independence. On September 26, just three days later, 1 David Templeton signed a similar paper. In the next place, the descendants of 3 Robert Templeton and 4 John Templeton claim to have authentic records that these two were brothers. (See their line for these records). Then we have the family tradition among later generations that these descendents were kinfolks. For example: in 1927-28, and before he had ever heard of 1 David Templeton, one of his descendents, 111j2 Lucius Langdon Templeton, said that he had always heard that his great grandfather, 11 David Templeton, Jr., (who was the oldest child of 1 David Templeton, and who was still living when 11j2 Lucius Langdon Templeton's grandfather was 20 years old) WAS A "SECOND COUSIN TO 255 OLIVER TEMPLETON," who was a grandson of 2 James Templeton. If this family tradition is true, it verifies the assumption that 2 James Templeton and 1 David Templeton were brothers, as can clearly be seen by observing the line of descendents of these two men.

1 David Templeton, 2 James Templeton, and 3 Robert Temple-

ton all served in the South Carolina Militia during the Revolutionary War. These services are recorded in the South Carolina Historical Commission office in Columbia, S. C.

Of 5 Martha Templeton we have no further record.

The 100 acres of land granted to 6 Agnes Templeton in 1775 was sold by her husband, Robert Taylor, to Eleanor Craig on June 22, 1784. This land deed, recorded in the office of Clerk of Court, Laurens, S. C., is the latest authentic information we have of 6 Agnes Templeton, although we do find the following information that may indicate the same 6 Agnes Templeton Taylor and her husband, Robert Taylor:

(1) In the office of Probate Judge, Laurens, S. C., we find one Robert Taylor listed as one of the legatees of William Taylor, Sr., in the final return of the estate of William Taylor, Sr., dated May 15, 1809. In this same return we find also: "—legatees of Agnes Taylor, deceased, $33.70" (paid).

(2) On the rolls of Rocky Springs Church, Laurens County, S. C., we find: "Robert Taylor, Sr., died 1851." Also: "Agnes Taylor deceased." Her name is listed after his which might mean that the information about her was written after 1851.

1 DAVID TEMPLETON
—— - 1817

Although we have no positive proof that 1 David Templeton was living in what is now Laurens County, S. C., prior to the Revolutionary War, the indications are that he settled there along with the other Templetons. He took an active part in the War for Independence as is shown in Fig. 1 by the photostat copy of part of his military record found in the office of the South Carolina Historical Commission, Columbia, S. C.

The next record we have of 1 David Templeton is in the form of land grants recorded in the office of the Secretary of State, Columbia, S. C., where we find the following:

Book 12, page 367: "____David Templeton one hundred and fifty acres in the district of Ninety Six on a small branch of Duncan's Creek, bounded on all sides by vacant lands.—three pounds sterling.
Sixteenth September, 1784.
Robert Hanna D. S.   Ephriam Mitchell Surveyor General."

Also:

Book 32, page 333: "—I do hereby certify for David Templeton

Fig. 1

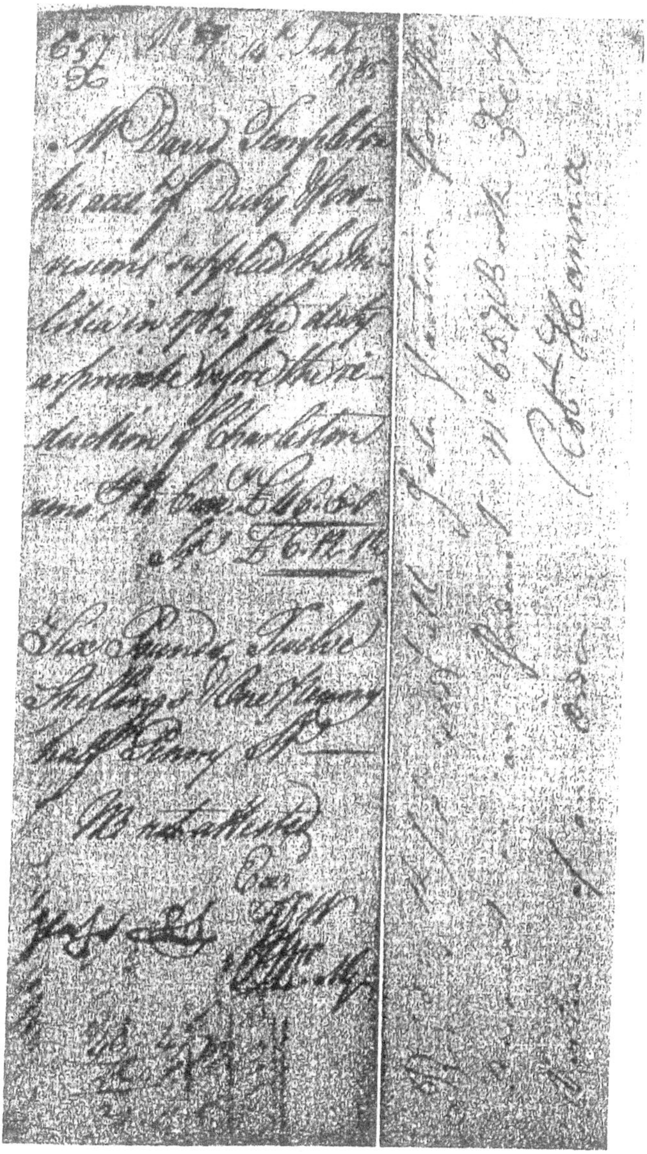

Reproduction of part of the Revolutionary War record of 1 David Templeton,
as found in the office of the South Carolina Historical Commission, Columbia, S. C.

a tract of land containing sixty seven acres surveyed for him the 8th of February, 1793, situate in the District of 96 in Laurens County on a branch of Duncan's Creek and hath such form marks buttings & boundings as the above plat represents.
Given under my hand this 7th of May 1793.
Robert Hanna Dist Surv   F Bremar Surv Genl.

—To David Templeton 67 acres in the district of Ninety-Six, Laurens County, on a small branch of Duncans Creek, bounded by a line running S. E. by Robert Templeton's land; E. & S. by David Templeton's land; E. by Richard Holland's land; N. by Jno D. Kern's and N. by Dr. Ross.——"

The U. S. Census of 1790 shows only seven Templetons as heads of families in South Carolina. Two of these, 7 James Templeton and 8 Margaret Templeton, were in York County, while 9 Aaron Templeton was in Spartanburg County. The remaining four were 1 David Templeton, 2 James Templeton, 3 Robert Templeton, and 4 John Templeton, all in Laurens County.

By comparing the ages of the children of 1 David Templeton as shown by this census report with the birth dates as shown by the family birth record every child can be precisely accounted for. For example, there were in the household of 1 David Templeton, "Males 16 years and upward, including heads of families, 2." These were 1 David Templeton, the father, and 11 David Templeton, Jr., who was born (as shown by the family record and also by his tombstone) March 6, 1772, and who was, therefore, 18 years old in 1790. This census report also shows in this same family "Males under 16,—3." These are accounted for by: 13 James Templeton, born June 10, 1778, and who was, therefore, 12 years old in 1790; 14 Robert Templeton, born Nov. 26, 1784, who was six years old in 1790; 15 John Templeton, born March 19, 1787, who was three years old in 1790. Again, the census shows: "Females—2." These were Mary Templeton, wife of 1 David Templeton, and 12 Elizabeth Templeton born Oct. 14, 1774.

In like manner, the members of the family as shown by the census reports of 1800, 1810, and 1820, can be precisely accounted for by the family record, even for the absence of 1 David Templeton, from the census report of 1820, because he died, as shown by family records, April 20, 1817.

All we know about his wife is found in the meager family record which says, "Mary Templeton, wife of David Templeton Cenr. departed this life March 11, 1803." Where their graves are is still unknown.

The next record we have of 1 David Templeton is that of his will, which is still in the office of Probate Judge, Laurens, S. C.

WILL OF 1 DAVID TEMPLETON

"In the name of God, amen. I David Templeton Senr. of So. Car. Laurens District being of sound & deposing mind & memory, but weak in body & calling to mind the uncertainty of life and being desirous of disposing of all such worldly estate as it hath pleased God to bless me with do make this my last will in manner following. That is to say

I desire that all my lawful debts and funeral expenses to be paid out of the sum of Eleven hundred dollars to be paid for from four negroes sold to Doct. Ross at two installments in the course of two years, viz Liley Tom Matilda and Henry, the remainder of the money to be equally divided between my four children David Templeton James Templeton John Templeton & Robert Hanna my heir. I give all my land and property and my household and plantation furniture, (except one dutch plow and furniture belonging to it for Robert Templeton) all my stock that is cows and hogs (except one heifer and shoat it being belong to my negro girl Lotty), be equally divided between my other two heirs viz Robert Templeton and William Templeton for them and their heirs and the balance of the money due on the negro girl Cyntha sold to Doct Ross be equally divided between the said two heirs Robt and William Templeton. I will my black man to my grandson David Hanna for his property to do as he may think proper with. I desire that my negro woman Lotty and her future offspring may be free so long as they may live and that Doct Ross acts as a guardian for her or them.

And lastly I do constitute and appoint my two friends, Doctor George Ross and Creek William Craig Executors of this my last will and Testament hereby revoking all other and former wills and testaments by me heretofore made in testimony whereof I have hereunto set my hand and affixed my seal this the 19th day of April 1817.

Seal   David Templeton

Legima. seald publisht and declared as and for the last will and testament of the above named David Templeton in the presence of us

William Craig ER
James Templeton Senor
Hezekiah Rice

The will of David Templeton deceased recorded in admtion Book D Page 390 by me David Anderson (Seal) 1817."

("Laurens, S. C., March 31, 1928. The tracing on this page is from the will of David Templeton, Sr., recorded in this office under date of June 2, 1817. O. G. Thompson, Probate Judge.")

In this will we find the names of all of 1 David Templeton's children except that of 12 Elizabeth Templeton who had evidently married and had died before the will was made. Her two sons, 122 David Hanna and 121 Robert Hanna, were named as heirs. It is interesting to note that 1 David Templeton was probably on his death bed when he made his will, as he died the next day, April 20, 1817, according to an item of family record found in a note book belonging to 14g Benjamin Clark Templeton, 1/17/1817 —7/4/1872, which reads as follows: "David Templeton Cenr Departed this life April the 20th 1817."

Fig. 2

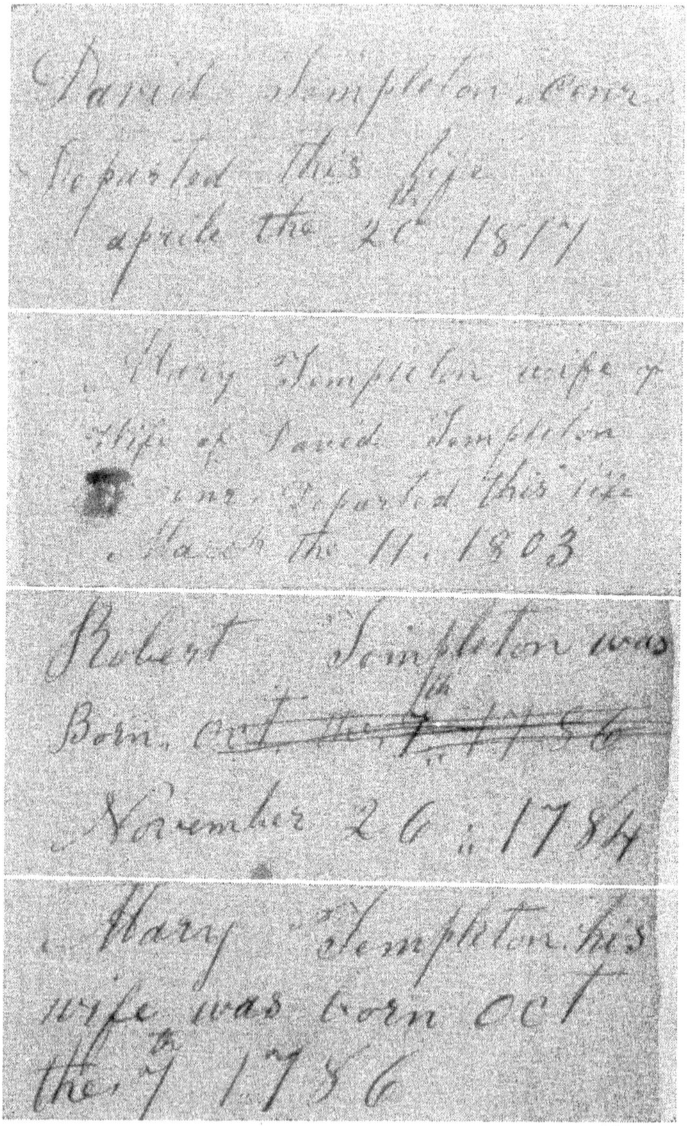

David Templeton Senr
Departed this life
aprile the 20th 1817

Mary Templeton wife of
Wife of David Templeton
Senr Departed this life
March the 11. 1803

Robert Templeton was
Born ~~Oct the 7th 1756~~
November 26 1784

Mary Templeton his
wife was born Oct
the 7th 1786

Reproduction of Part of Family Records Taken from Old Daybook of 14g Benjamin Clark Templeton 1817-1872 as Written by Him About 1850-1856.

Fig. 3

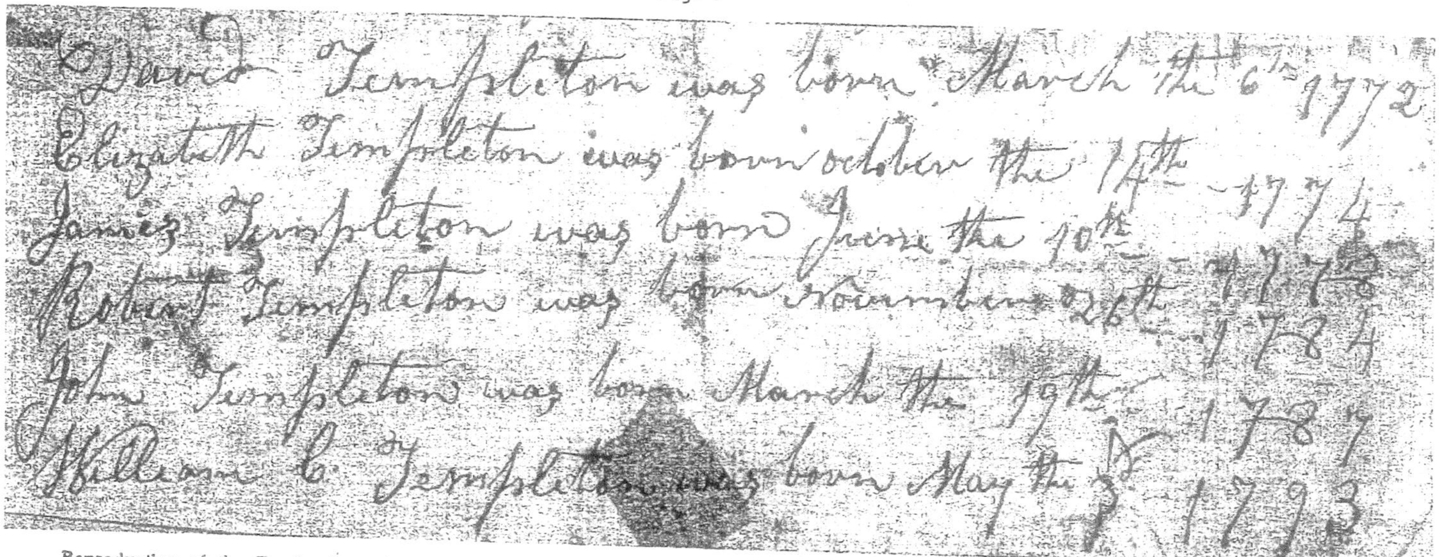

David Templeton was born March the 6th 1772
Elizabeth Templeton was born october the 14th 1774
James Templeton was born June the 10th 177[illegible]
Robert Templeton was born November 26th 1784
John Templeton was born March the 10th 1787
William C. Templeton was born May the 3d 1793

Reproduction of the Family Record of Births of Children of 1 David Templeton, given the Writer by 1561 Priscilla Garrett Who was Reared by her Grandfather, 15 James Templeton 1787-1872, Who Probably Wrote or Gave the Records.

11 DAVID TEMPLETON, JR., 3-6-1772—2-6-1860

This Daguerreotype of 11 David Templeton was sent to the writer on August 27, 1933, by Mrs. Mollie Martindale of Rochester, Texas, whose husband, 11312 James Augustus Martindale (1855-1932), was a great-grandson of 11 David Templeton. In letters dated September 10, 1932, August 27, 1933, and September 10, 1933, Mrs. Martindale says: "—We are in possession of a picture of one of the Temple men. The old gentleman—was my father-in-law's grandfather.—I believe now that I could be positive in telling you that Mr. Templeton—whom I sent the picture of is Mr. David Templeton.—I am sure Mr. Templeton's picture was made in S. C. and this picture was carried to Ark. in 1859 by either his son-in-law, grandfather Martindale.—This picture of Mr. Templeton was given to my husband as well as other gifts and it does seem to me like I remember his name was David."

On November 8, 1952, when the frame was torn open in order to have a zinc etching made from the picture, there was written on the back of the inside packing, "David Tempellton." Thus the identity of the picture seems certain.

Judging from the record of land deeds in the office of the clerk of court, Laurens, S. C., it is evident that 11 David Templeton spent practically all of his life on or near Duncan's Creek. He was very probably one of the two deacons of Bethany Presbyterian Church, elected in 1849, according to Howe in his history of the Presbyterian Church in S. C. He was a prosperous man, as is indicated by the records of his real estate and by his will, the administration of which shows that he left an estate valued at $17,000.00, which must have been considered somewhat of a fortune in those early days.

Mrs. Mollie Martindale writes: "—I have often heard him (her father-in-law) tell how his grandmother (wife of 11 David Templeton) picked seed out of cotton as she would go to the spring for water, spin thread from that cotton, weave cloth and sell that cloth for $1.25 pr yd."

WILL OF 11 DAVID TEMPLETON
Filed February 8, 1867, Box 136, Bundle 7,
Office of Probate Judge
Laurens, S. C.

"State of South Carolina
Laurens District.
In the name of God. Amen.

I, David Templeton, being weak in body, but of sound mind and memory and understanding, do make and ordain this my last will and testament in manner and form following:

First: I desire all my just and legal debts paid.

2nd: It is my desire and I instruct by Executor herein named, after my death to sell all my estate personal and real and out of the proceeds to give to my son William L. Templeton, $200. and to each of my granddaughters, Elizabeth and Jane Stewart, $50., and the residue equally divided between all my children, the child or children of a deceased child to receive what their parent would if living.

3rd: I give to my friend, W. D. Byrd, in trust for the use and benefit of my daughter Elizabeth Martindale a tract of land lying in the above state and district on waters of Warrior Creek containing 40-1- acres adjoining land of William Robison, John Pool and others, said trustee to have the right to change this and all other property left him in trust of said daughter, whenever he thinks fit and to her interest to do so with and by her consent. I desire that my daughter Elizabeth account for this land at the price I gave for viz. 1078 dollars and 67c and further I have given to my grandson James (see note below) L. Martindale a deed of trust or gift to a negro girl for the use and benefit of his mother Elizabeth that I desire her to account for at $300. as a part she the said Elizabeth may be entitled to under the 2nd clause of this will and the balance she may be entitled to under said clause I give to my friend W. D. Byrd in trust for her use and benefit with the privilege stated above.

4th: I do hereby nominate and constitute and appoint my son William L. Templeton Executor to this my will and testament in witness whereof I do hereby affix my hand and seal this 16th day of May, 1858.
David Templeton."

Signed sealed and acknowledged in our presence.
George Byrd
N. W. Prather, Sr
D. C. Templeton

(Note: The name, "James" M. must have been an error in the original will. "Geo." M. was the name actually receiving the inheritance when the will was executed.)

11 David Templeton married Massie Laird (1778-1857), daughter of Captain Robert Laird, a Revolutionary patriot. They were buried side by side in Bethany Presbyterian cemetery near Clinton, S. C. They had six children:

111 John Templeton 5/13/1797-6/17/1841
112 Sarah Templeton 12/29/1799-2/14/1842.
113 Elizabeth Templeton, b about 1803; d_____.
114 James Templeton, July 2, 1804—July 11, 1846
115 Eunice Templeton, 1814—May 16, 1851, buried, Bethany Church, Clinton, S. C.
116 William Livingston Templeton, 1814—6/30/1881

111 JOHN TEMPLETON, oldest child of 11 David Templeton and Massie Laird Templeton, was born near Bethany Presbyterian Church. After he was grown he moved to Liberty, S. C. He was married February, 5 1824, to Catherine Fairburne, 12/11/1800 —2/28/1885. They are buried at Carmel Presbyterian Church in Pickens County, S. C. They had eleven children:

    111a Louise Templeton
    111b Martha Elizabeth Templeton, 1/21/1826—3/18/1854, buried Carmel Church, Pickens County, NM.
    111c William Andrew Templeton, 11/4/1827—8/5/1852.
    111d Jane Sabema Templeton, 10/31/1829—10/1/1854-5.
    111e James Dickson Templeton, 8/24/1831—12/25/1831.
    111f John Templeton, 12/28/1833—5/22/1863, a Confederate veteran, NM.
    111g Letitia Frances Templeton, 3/13/1835— _____, buried Carmel Church.
    111h Esther Catherine Templeton, 1/3/1837-7/..../1919.
    111i Mary Eunice Templeton, 5/24/1838—_____, buried Carmel Church.
    111j David Humphries Templeton, 3/13/1840—3/15/1912.
    111k Samuel F. Templeton, 3/7/1842—_____, buried Carmel Church.

111a Louise Templeton married Rice Moore. Their two children were:
    111a1 Mae Moore.
    111a2 John ("Bud") Moore.

111c William Andrew Templeton lived near Liberty, S. C. He married, 10/17/1849, Mary Hamilton.

111d Jane Sabema Templeton married, 12/25/1850, Joseph Addison Boggs, 2/11/1825-1/10/1894. They were buried at Carmel Church, Pickens County, S. C. They had seven children:
    111d1 John Thomas Boggs, b. 11/11/1851.
    111d2 Ella Catherine Boggs, 7/10/1853-6/15/1854, buried Carmel Church.
    111d3 George Leland Boggs, 3/11/1855. He went to California.

111d4 Walter Lewers Boggs, 12/21/1862—1936.
111d5 Sarah Ada Boggs, 4/12/1866—5/15/1894.
111d6 Louise Florence Boggs, 4/12/1868—9/19/1869, buried Carmel Church.
111d7 Corrie Addison Boggs, 3/6/1872—11/8/1911.

111d1 John Thomas Boggs lived at Harleton (?) Harlingen (?), Texas. He married first, Ann Welborn. They had five children:
111d11 Oscar Boggs, b. 8/9/1874.
111d12 Flora Boggs, who lived with Miss Louise Berdie, Greenville, S. C.
111d13 Frank Boggs, who lived at Jacksonville, Fla.
111d14 Herbert R. Boggs, who was reported, 7/7/1939, Jacksonville, Fla., as deceased.
111d15 Dora Boggs, living at Ortega, Fla.

111d11 Oscar Boggs m._____. Their children were:
111d111 Eleanor Lucile Boggs, 9/25/1903—3/11/1925.
111d112 Howell Willie Boggs, b. 8/29/1906.
111d113 Vernon Addison Boggs, b. 8/9/1908.

111d111 Eleanor Lucile Boggs m. 6/7/1924, Millard E. Reynolds.
111d12 Flora Boggs m. _____Berdie. They had one child:
111d121 Willie Berdie.

111d112 Howell Willie Boggs m._____. They had one child:
111d1121 Frances Caroline Boggs, b. 8/31/1928.

111d1 John Thomas Boggs m. 2nd, Melvina Hutchinson. They had no children.

111d4 Walter Lewers Boggs m. 12/27/1897, Maggie Eloise Neely. They lived at Liberty, S. C., where he was buried. They had one son:
111d41 Lewers Addison Boggs, b. 7/19/1894.

111d5 Sarah Ada Boggs was buried at Liberty, S. C. She m. Julian Wertz. They had two children:
111d51 James Claudine Wertz who m._____Crow.
111d52 Julian Wertz, Jr.

111d7 Corrie Addison Boggs was buried at Liberty, S. C. She m., 11/13/1906, T. H. Galloway. They had one daughter:
111d71 Pauline Galloway, b. 7/13/1910. She lives in Greensboro, N. C.

111h Esther Catherine Templeton was educated at old Thalien Academy, Laurens, S. C. She m., 11/11/1866, 1127 Samuel Dixon Stewart, her first cousin. They had five children:
111h1 Thornwell Stewart, 1/8/1869—9/27/1871, buried, Carmel Church.

111h2 Eugene Lowerey Stewart, 9/11/1871—8/3/1873, buried, Carmel.
111h3 Adger Stewart, 3/30/1875—10/27/1877, buried at Carmel.
111h4 William Addison Stewart, b. 3/28/1877.
111h5 Samuel Converse Stewart, b. 3/21/1881.

111h4 William Addison Stewart m. 1st., Ethel Folger. He lived at Portland, Ore., where he was a postal telegraph operator.

111h5 Samuel Converse Stewart was graduated from Clemson College, S. C., in 1902. He was a structural engineer for the American Bridge Co., in Pennsylvania for six years, and for the Virginia Bridge and Iron Co., Roanoke, Va., from 1909 until 1918, Since 1918 he has been an orchardist at North Wilkesboro N. C. He m., 12/22/1907, Irene M. Faulconner. They have three children:

111h51 Louise Marguerite Stewart, 4/29/1910.
111h52 Esther Catherine Stewart, 8/15/1912.
111h53 Dorothy Jean Stewart, 11/23/1914.

111j David Humphries Templeton was born in Pickens County, S. C. He was a corporal in Co. I, 14th Regiment, S. C. Volunteers, and served during the entire Civil War. He was wounded seven times. After the war he moved to Laurens County, S. C. He married, 3/13/1866, Sarah Stoddard, 1844—·12/12/1924, of Owings, S. C., where he lived as a successful farmer the remainder of his life. He and his wife were buried at Liberty, S. C. They had four children:

111j1 Ida Templeton, 3/19/1868—9/27/1923.
111j2 Lucius Langdon Templeton, 4/15/1870—11/17/1951.
111j3 Leonora Templeton, 1/2/1873.
111j4 Edgar Templeton, 9/9/1875-7/1/1903, buried Liberty, S. C. NM.

111j1 Ida Templeton was born and reared in Laurens County, S. C. She was a teacher in the public schools for several years. She married Dr. W. A. Sheldon and moved to Liberty, S. C., where she lived until her death. She was buried at Liberty. They had two sons:

111j11 William Garrett Sheldon, now a druggist at Apopka, Fla.
111j12 Eugene Sheldon, who coaches athletics at Burnell, Fla.

111j2 Lucius Langdon Templeton was born and reared in Laurens County, S. C., where he was a successful farmer practically all of his life. He died 11/17/1951, and was buried at Owings Presbyterian Cemetery. He married, 12/18/1895, Ellen Stewart. They have five children all of whom are well educated:

    111j21   Ralph Templeton, 10/24/1896.
    111j22   Lilla Templeton, 2/26/1899.
    111j23   Ross E. Templeton, 1/19/1903.
    111j24   Sarah Louise Templeton, 12/2/1906.
    111j25   David Samuel Templeton, 9/18/1909.

111j21   Ralph Templeton lives at Owings, S. C. He is married and has one son:
    111j211   Ralph Templeton, Jr., 10/15/1937.

111j22   Lilla Templeton was graduated from Due West Woman's College in 1920, and lives at Woodland, N. C.. She married, 6/19/1924, Roy Griffin. They have one daughter:
    111j221   Jane Ellen Griffin, b. 10/29/1928. She m. 9/2/1950, Walter Gay Wells, Jr. They have one son:
    111j2211   Walter Gay Wells III, b 8/27/1952.

111j23   Ross E. Templeton attended Presbyterian College, Clinton, S. C. For a great many years he has been a successful salesman for the World Book Company (encyclopedia). He is now Division Manager for that firm with offices in Charlotte, N. C. He m 8/17/1939 Frances Engenia Stuart.

111j24   Sarah Louise Templeton was graduated from Due West Women's College in 1928. She was, for several years, a successful teacher in the public schools of South Carolina. She m 12/18/1935 Horace N. Foy. They have one adopted son:
    Lucius Barrington Foy, b 1/31/1944.

111j25   David Samuel Templeton was graduated from Presbyterian College, Clinton, S. C., in 1932. Since his graduation he has been teaching and coaching athletics in South Carolina. For several years he was a teacher and athletic coach in the Ninety Six, S. C., High School where he developed some state championship teams in basketball. He now lives at Clinton, S. C., where he is principal of Academy Street Elementary School. In Clinton he has organized an extensive recreation program for the city. His program includes the Pony League, Little League and Small Fry baseball teams for boys of 12 years old and under. One of these teams recently won the national championship in baseball. In 1952 the Clinton Lion's Club named him the "Citizen of the Year." He m. 8/6/1937, Miss Marjorie Cash of Simpsonville, S. C. They have one son:
    111j251   David Samuel Templeton, Jr., b 9/14/1946.

111j3   Leonora Templeton lives at 706 Crescent Ave., Greenville, S. C. She m. .... Champ H. Parkins. They have four children:

111j31   Hortense Parkins, b 12/2/1898, a teacher in the Greenville City Schools.
111j32   D. Frank Parkins, b 3/13/1900.
111j33   Catherine Parkins.
111j34   Willie Parkins, 1910-8/—/1911, buried at Liberty, S. C.

112   Sarah Templeton, second child of 11 David Templeton and Massie Laird Templeton, was born and reared near Bethany Church, in Laurens County, S. C. She married Walter Stewart 1797-5/28/1842. Both were buried at Bethany. They had seven children:

1121   William Clark Stewart, b....., d. 12/12/1863, buried, Carmel Church, Pickens County, NM.
1122   Elizabeth Ann Stewart, 8/20/1825-4/27/1858, buried at Bethany Church, NM.
1123   Eunice Pauline Stewart, 12/21/1828-4/19/1900.
1124   James Lewers Stewart.
1125   Louise Jane Stewart, b..........., d. 9/6/1861, buried at Carmel Church, Pickens County, NM.
1126   John Preston Stewart, 2/9/1837-2/14/1874, a Confederate veteran, buried at Carmel.
1127   Samuel Dixon Stewart, b........, d. about 1923, buried at Carmel. He married, 11/11/1866, his first cousin, 111h Esther Catherine Templeton. Their descendents are listed under her name.

1123   Eunice Pauline Stewart was buried at Liberty, S. C. She married, 12/22/1857, Joseph Addison Boggs, 2/11/1825-6/10/1894, the widower of Jane Sabema Templeton Boggs (111d). They had two children:
11231   Lizzie Jane Boggs, 4/15/1859-9/23/1899.
11232   Mary Josephine Boggs, 6/25/1861-3/10/1902.

11231   Lizzie Jane Boggs was buried at New Harmony Church, Laurens County, S. C. She married J. W. Dupree but they had no children.

11232   Mary Josephine Boggs was buried at Liberty, S. C. She married D. J. Greer. They had four children:
112321   Zula Greer, who died young and was buried at Carmel Church.
112322   Palmer Greer, who lives at Kannapolis, N. C.
112323   Alliene Greer.
112324   Ethel Greer.

112323   Alliene Greer m. W. H. Cheney, a superintendent for Southern Railway and lives at Spartanburg, S. C. They have four children:

14

1123231   Mary Eugenia Cheney, b. 1/2/1906.
1123232   Willoughby Greer Cheney, b. 8/18/1907.
1123233   Donald Richard Cheney, b. 3/8/1909.
1123234   John William Cheney, b. 10/5/1917.

1123232   Willoughby Greer Cheney is married and has one son:

       11232321   Willoughby Greer Cheney, Jr., b. 1/13/1937.

1123233   Donald Richard Cheney is married and has three children:

       11232331   Patsy Jean Cheney, b. 6/26/1933.
       11232332   Donald Richard Cheney, Jr., b. 9/10/1935.
       11232333   Wallace H. Cheney, b. 6/26/1946.

1123234   John William Cheney is married and has one son:
       11232341   Jonathan L. Cheney, b. 11/29/1946.

112324   Ethel Greer married Samuel Leeper Graham. They live at 1506 S. 12th St. Birmingham, Ala., where she is connected with Smith Cullom Real Estate and Insurance Company. They have three children:

       1123241   Samuel Leeper Graham, Jr.
       1123242   John Wagner Graham, b 11/17/1924.
       1121243   Mary Josephine Graham, b about 1929.

1124   James Lewers Stewart was a Confederate veteran. He died in Arkansas. He married Mary Louise Chamblin. They had two children:

       11241   Bessie Stewart.
       11242   James Stewart.

113   Elizabeth Templeton, third child of 11 David Templeton and Massie Laird Templeton, married Captain James Martindale. They must have lived near Bethany Church, near Clinton, S. C., since their youngest child, 1133 William D. Martindale, was buried there. Mrs. Mollie Martindale (who lives at Rochester, Texas, and whose husband was 11312 J. A. Martindale, a grandson of Captain James Martindale and 113 Elizabeth Templeton Martindale) thinks that 113 Elizabeth "died in, or near Laurens, S. C.," but neither her grave nor her husband's can be found. In the will of 11 David Templeton, dated 5/16/1858, he gives, among other properties, in care of his friend, W. D. Bird, "to my daughter, Elizabeth Martindale 41 acres of land on the waters of Warrior Creek, Laurens County, S. C." She died after her father's death but before his will was executed (1867) with the result that her two surviving children were given their mother's share of the estate ($3,104.01). They had three children:

1131 George L. Martindale, b. 12/25/1827.
1132 Louis B. Martindale, d. .... 1865.
1133 William D. Martindale, 12/26/1829-10/9/1837, buried at Bethany, near Clinton, S. C.

1131 George L. Martindale was born Dec. 25, 1827, in Laurens County, S. C., where he taught school for many years and where he married, 12/21/1852, Martha Minerva Hutchinson (b. 6/30/1833), daughter of Squire Alexander Simpson Hutchinson and his wife, Isabella J. Hitch. They were said to have been living "within a stone's throw" of Laurens Court House when their first son was born. After two children were born they moved, in the fall of 1858, to Arkansas. He died there, in Howard County, in 1905. They had seven children:

11311 Emma Elizabeth Martindale, b. 3/22/1854.
11312 James Augustus Martindale, 12/3/1855-8/18/1932.
11313 Frederick Lewers Martindale, b. 7/19/1861—.
11314 Minerva Cornelia Martindale, 9/26/1864-11/15/1928, buried Nashville, Ark., married George Grover.
11315 George Hicks Martindale, 7/24/1867-1937.
11316 Ada Kathleen Martindale, 6/13/1869—.
11317 Adolphus Simpson Martindale, b 4/11/1871—.

11311 Emma Elizabeth Martindale was born in Laurens County, S. C. She was carried to Arkansas in 1858 by her parents. There she married Walter Stuart. She was living at Nashville, Ark., at the time of her death.

11312 James Augustus Martindale was born in Laurens County, S. C. He moved, in 1858, to Arkansas with his parents who made their home at Nashville in 1859. At the age of 18 James Augustus, or "Gus" as he was affectionately known, was converted and joined the Methodist church. Some fourteen years later he joined the Presbyterian church. In 1883 he married Miss Mollie Merrill in Center Point, Ark. They moved to Texas in 1892, settling in Fannin County, near Trenton. Later they moved to Covington, Texas. Then, in 1903, they moved to Rochester, in West Texas. Here they made their happy home and proudly watched their nine children grow into manhood and womanhood. Not until August, 1932, was the family chain broken by death. For the first time in 28 years all of the children had come together for a surprise to the parents and for a re-union, when the father was unexpectedly stricken with bronchial pneumonia. After a few days, on August 10, 1932, death came to his relief and he passed on to his Christian reward. The next afternoon the funeral services were held in the Presbyterian Church, after which his body was taken to the local cemetery and buried with Masonic honors. His widow continues to make her home at Rochester, Texas. Through her generosity the Templeton Clan is now in possession of a picture (Daguerroetype) which, she is certain, is that of 11 David Templeton. Their nine children were:

113121   Dr. Lee Martindale of Oakland California.
113122   Simpson Martindale of Dallas, Texas.
113123   Luther Martindale of Dallas, Texas.
113124   Mae Martindale of Dallas, Texas, married _____ Hedgepath.
113125   Minnie Martindale of Oakland, Cal., married _____ Frederickson.
113126   Mamie Martindale of Rochester, Texas, married A. S. Lambert.
123127   Ruth Martindale of Fort Worth, Texas, married ____ _____ Stoker.
113128   Lottie Martindale of Rochester, Texas, married M. W. Michael.
123129   Hicks Martindale of Rochester, Texas.

11313   Frederick Lewers Martindale married Mary Sheppard. They live at Maysville, Okla.

11315   George Hicks Martindale was buried at Hope, Ark. He married, first Nannie Nelson, and second, Ida Copper Adkin. They had one son:
113151   James G. Martindale, a physician, married and living at 614 West B. Street, Hope, Ark.

11316   Ada Kathleen Martindale married James Rowe. She was living at Nashville, Ark., at the time of her death.

11317   Adolphus Simpson Martindale married, 7/15/1903, Hattie Musser. They lived at Nashville, Ark., where he was a doctor and where he died. They had six children:
113171   Venus Martindale, b. 4/28/1904.
113172   Frances G. Martindale, b. 1/14/1908, of 302 Lee St., Chickasaw, Ala.
113173   Nadine Martindale, 3/22/1910-4/17/1912, buried at Nashville, Ark.
112174   Lois Martindale, b. 7/11/1912, of Nashville, Ark.
113175   Kathryn Martindale (twin), b. 8/21/1916, of Nashville, Ark.
112176   Kelsie Martindale (twin), b. 8/21/1916, of Nashville, Ark.

113171   Venus Martindale married, 3/3/1926, John Glasgow. They live at DuQueen, Ark.

114   JAMES TEMPLETON, fourth child of 11 David Templeton, and his wife Massie Laird Templeton, was probably born and reared near Bethany Church, Laurens County, S. C. Rev. S. B.

17

Lewers, realizing the need for a church in the community, began early in 1833 to hold services in a school house. Within a few months he had organized Bethany Presbyterian Church, with some 26 members. 114 James Templeton and Dr. Samuel Farrow were chosen elders. By October of the same year 31 additional members had been admitted and the church determined to proceed immediately to build a house of worship. Mr. Templeton was the ruling elder and represented the church in October, 1833, at the Presbytery. His zeal for the young church, no doubt, was an important factor in its growth. He died 7/11/1846, and was among the first to be buried in the church yard. He married, 1/29/1829, Margaret ("Peggy") Anderson Smith, 5/1/1807-9/1/1865, daughter of Joshua A. Smith. To this union were born four children:

 1141 Nancy Carolyn Templeton, 12/8/1829-2/10/1906.
 1142 Mary Ann Templeton, b. 12/26/1831.
 1143 George Martin Templeton, 4/21/1835-1/8/1863.
 1144 William Cater Templeton, 5/17/1843-2/16/1923.

1141 Nancy Carolyn Templeton was buried at Lanford Station, S. C. She married first, 1/22/1852, 153 William Craig Templeton, 1828-9/27/1864. They had one child who died in infancy. She married, second, 11/23/1865, John H. Lyles, 11/11/1833-3/1/1877. They had one child:

 11411 William Perry Lyles, b. 10/20/1866. He m. ....
Lawrence. He lived at Draper Mill, Spartanburg, S. C. They had eleven children:
  11411a John Thomas Lyles, b. 7/6/1895.
  11411b Nannie Belle Lyles, b. 8/25/1896.
  11411c Addie Lue Lyles, b. 8/14/1898.
  11411d Sara Rosa Lee Lyles, b. 1/3/1900.
  11411e Clara Mae Lyles, b. 4/17/1902.
  11411f William Laurens Lyles, b. 1/10/1904.
  11411g Ora Dell Lyles, b. 3/9/1907.
  11411h Mary Lucia Lyles—
  11411i James Luther Lyles (twins), b. 11/16/1908.
  11411j Lillie Genelle Lyles, b. 5/10/1911.
  11411k Everett Bernell Lyles, b. 10/1/1915.

11411a John Thomas Lyles lives at Drayton Mill, Spartanburg, S. C. He married October 27, 1914, Ada Louise Bobo, b. 8/2/1894. They have four children:
  11411a1 Wilton Lyles, b. 1/26/1917.
  11411a2 Perry Lyles, b. 10/1/1921.
  11411a3 Virginia Lyles, b. 3/10/1925.
  11411a4 Helen Lyles, b. 2/15/1927.

11411b Nannie Bell Lyles married William Coker. They live at Spartan Mills, Spartanburg, S. C., and have seven children.

11411b1 Genelle Coker.
11411b2 William Coker.
11411b3 Annie Mae Coke!
11411b4 Lucile Coker.
11411b5 Mildred Coker.
11411b6 Virginia Coker
11411b7 Charles Coker.

11411c Addie Lue Lyles married J. C. Rush. They live at Lando, S. C. They havë three children:
11411c1 Claude Rush.
11411c2 Sarah Lou Rush.
11411c3 George Rush.

11411d Sara Rosa Lee Lyles married Ben Franklin Oxley and lives at Enoree, S. C. They have eight children:
11411d1 Sam Oxley, b. 11/7/1921.
11411d2 Joe Oxley, b. 12/20/1922.
11411d3 Mary Oxley, b. 1924.
11411d4 Margaret Oxley, b. 11/22/1925.
11411d5 Dorothy Oxley, b. 8/3/1926.
11411d6 Edwin Oxley, b. 7/2/1928.
11411d7 June Oxley, b. 4.../1929.
11411d8 Joyce Oxley, b. 2/28/1933.

11411e Clara Mae Lyles married Chaney H. Hughes. They live at Drayton Mill, Spartanburg, S. C. They have one child:
11411e1 Myrtle Hughes.

11411f William Laurens Lyles married Frances Duckworth. They live at Anderson, S. C., where he is connected with the Bigby Pharmacy. They have no children.

11411g Ora Dell Lyles married Wales Knight. They live at Lyman, S. C. They have three children:
11411g1 Wendell Knight.
11411g2 Mary Dell Knight.
11411g3 Betty Carolyn Knight.

11411i James Luther Lyles married, 1/7/1933, Essie Mae Tesner, b. 9/15/1914. They have one child:
11411i1 Carolina Joyce Lyles.

11411j Lillie Genelle Lyles married James Arthur Wofford. They live at Saxon Mill, Spartanburg, S. C.

1142 Mary Ann Templeton married, 2/21/1856, her father's first cousin, 152 Turner Templeton, whose first wife and whose first cousin, 14h Leah A. M. Templeton, had died. 1142 Mary

Ann Templeton and her husband 152 Turner Templeton, had five children:

11421 Rufus Smith Templeton, 12/19/1856-5/17/1904.
11422 Joseph Young Templeton, b. 4/17/1859.
11423 Harrison Briggs Templeton, 10/27/1862-1867, buried at Bethany Church, near Clinton, S. C.
11424 Hilliard H. Templeton, b. 10/27/1863.
11425 Bernard Allison Templeton, b......... d. 9/14/1890, buried New Cannon Church, Crossville, Ala., NM.

11421 Rufus Smith Templeton married Callie Stone. He was buried at New Cannon Church, Crossville, Ala.

11422 Joseph Young Templeton married, 1/6/1880, Mary Susan Davis. They live at Crossville, Ala. They have nine children:

114221 Ora Sophia Templeton, 1/17/1881-10/5/1902, buried New Cannon Church.
114222 Oliver Ervin Templeton, b. 11/6/1883.
114223 Callie Vesta Templeton, 1/15/1886-8/9/1887, buried New Cannon Church.
114224 Lizzie Lemon Templeton, b. 6/17/1889.
114225 Joseph Young Templeton, Jr., b. 2/23/1892.
114226 Whitt Anderson Templeton, b. 4/5/1894.
114227 Floyd Zerdie Templeton, b. 2/16/1896.
114228 Benjamin Archie Templeton, b. 2/5/1899.
114229 Rafe Orbey Templeton, b. 1/26/1901, who lives in Chicago, Ill.

114222 Oliver Ervin Templeton married, 11/5/1905, Maggie Sue Graham. They live at 2339 Long St., Chattanooga, Tenn. They have four children, the first two being:

1142221 Borman Templeton.
1142222 Shellie Templeton.

114224 Lizzie Lemon Templeton married, 8/12/1906, H. Oscar Hendrix. They live at Pisgah, Ala., Rt. 2 They have four children:

1142241 Carl Hendrix, b. 3/31/1909.
1142242 Hoyt E. Hendrix, b. 6/14/1913.
1142243 Ila B. Hendrix, b. 2/16/1915.
1142244 Opal S. Hendrix, b. 10/1/1919.

114225 Joseph Young Templeton, Jr., married, 4/11/1920, Effie Gregory.

114226 Whitt Anderson Templeton married, 12/2/1923, Toxie Stanfield.

114227 Floyd Zerdie Templeton married, 12/26/1915, Cleo

Medders. They live at Albertville, Ala., Rt. 1. They have three children:

    1142271   Troy Floyd Templeton, 7/25/1920-1/5/1921, buried, Beulah Church, Alabama.
    1142272   Berry J. Templeton, b. 7/14/1922.
    1142273   Luther Doyle Templeton, b. 1/9/1925.   He m. Gwen Wells and lives at Albertville, Ala., where he is employed by Hern Motor Co.

1142   Hilliard H. Templeton married, 12/18/1881, Susan T. Beasley. They live at Crossville Ala. They have six children:
    114241   Mamie Templeton, who died in infancy.
    114242   Margaret Templeton, who died in infancy.
    114243   Samuel Cleveland Templeton, b. 9/15/1885.
    114244   John J. Templeton, b. 8/2/1890.
    114245   Sylvester Templeton, b. 8/18/1895.
    114246   Alma May Templeton, b. 8/30/1908.

114243   Samuel Cleveland Templeton married, 9/28/1902, Mary Green. They have nine children:
    1142431   Dan Templeton.
    1142432   Louis Templeton. She lives at 508 Chester St., Gadsden, Ala.
    1142433   Tommie Templeton, b. 4/24/1906.
    1142434   J. B. Templeton, b. 2/7/1908.
    1142435   Joe Green Templeton, b. 10/26/1911.
    1142436   Livy Riller Templeton, b. 9/5/1915.
    1142437   Ernest Templeton, b. 11/6/1916.
    1142438   Briggs Templeton, b. 11/9/1919.
    1142439   Chester Templeton, b. 11/21/1925.

114244   John J. Templeton married, 12/18/1910, Julia Clark. They live at Crossville, Ala. They have three children:
    1142441   Lula Templeton, 3/26/1912-12/15/1912, buried at Clark Cemetery.
    1142442   Blondell Templeton, b. 6/16/1924.
    1142443   Oneal Templeton, b. 2/6/1929.

114245   Sylvester Templeton married Emmie Mintzie. They live at Crossville, Ala., Rt. 3, and have two children:
    1142451   Lucile Templeton.
    1142452   Vernea Templeton.

114246   Alma Mae Templeton married, 6/3/1917, Rufus Gallman. They live at Crossville Ala., Rt. 3. They have four children:
    1142461   Buron Gallman b. 9/16/1918.
    1142462   Sybil Gallman, 8/4/1921-2/3/1923, buried at Mt. Vernon, Ala.

1142463   Eva Gallman, b. 8/1/1923.
1142464   Geneva Gallman, 5/25/1925-2/4/1926, buried at Mt. Vernon Ala.

1143 George Martin Templeton served in Company F, 14th Regiment S. C. Volunteers, during the Civil War. He was in the same company with his brother, 1144 William Cater Templeton, and 14g3 Benjamin Preston Templeton, Ellie Dendy, and others. He was wounded in the Battle of Richmond. He was stricken with measles and died in Lynchburg, Va., 1/8/1863. His brother, 144, William Cater Templeton, made three trips to Lunchburg trying to find his grave. Finally, in 1921, the grave was identified. The scene must have ben a touching one when the 78 year old, gray-haired Confederate veteran, after 58 years of searching, came upon the long-lost grave of his older brother and comrade. 1143 George Martin Templeton married, 12/12/1858, Martha Ann Snead, 4/27/1829-2/20/1862. They had one son:

    11431 James David Templeton, 9/12/1859-2/28/1901, who died single.

1144 William Cater Templeton, fourth child of 114 James Templeton, and his wife, Margaret Anderson Smith Templeton, was in Company F, 14th Regiment, S. C. Volunteers during the Civil War. He served under the command of Brigadier General Samuel McGowan, Wilcox's Division, A. P. Hill's Corps, in the Army of Northern Virginia. He was with Lee and Jackson in the seven days' battle of Richmond. He was with Stonewall Jackson at Chancellorsville. He fought under General Wade Hampton in the Wilderness; was in the bloody battle of Spottsylvania Court House in May, 1863. At the surrender he was taken and imprisoned on Hart's Island, N. Y., until June 22, 1865, when he was released by the exchange of prisoners.

After the war he returned to his native community near Clinton, S. C.

"Bill" Templeton as he was better known, was keenly interested in religious, civic and political affairs. He was Superintendent of the Sunday School at Bethany Presbyterian Church, near Clinton, S. C. He was also Secretary of Campbell Lodge No. 44, A.F.M., at Clinton. In 1890, he moved to Asheville, N. C., where he died Feb. 16, 1923, in his eighty-first year. He was buried in Riverside Cemetery at Asheville.

On Nov. 5, 1868, 1144 William Cater Templeton was married to Cornelia Emmaline Compton (Jan. 22, 1843 - June 26, 1922) daughter of Charles Compton and Nancy Poole. They were married by Rev. Toliver Robertson. To them were born eight daughters:

    11441 Margaret Elliott Templeton, b. 8/13/1869.
    11442 Nancy Estelle Templeton, b. 4/24/1871.
    11443 Martha Eliza Templeton, 10/25/1872-7/27/1936.
    11444 Orra Augusta Templeton, 10/28/1875-9/11/1886.

11445   Laura Tallula Templeton, b. 4/17/1878.
11446   Minnie Cornelia Templeton, b. 8/3/1880.
11447   Emma Templeton, who died in infancy.
11448   Alice Deveaux Templeton, b. 1/21/1883.

11441   Margaret Elliott Templeton married, 1911, James Clifton Williams.

11442   Nancy Estelle Templeton married, 4/24/1890, Milton Harding of Norfolk, Va. They live at 2307 Green St., Philadelphia Pa. They have three children:
    114421   Theodore Harding.
    114422   Milton Harding.
    114423   Estelle Elliott Harding, who married Charles Disbrow. They live in New York City and have one daughter:
    1144231   Sybil Disbrow.

11443   Martha Elizabeth Templeton was buried at Cedar Hill Cemetery, Washington, D. C. She married, 1/22/1896, James Day Dumphy, of New York. They had one daughter:
    114431   Lydia Dumphy who married Lt. Henry H. Karp, U.S.N.

11445   Laura Tallula Templeton, better known as "Lulie" was born in Laurens County, S. C. She attended school near Tylersville, in her home county. She attended Bethany Presbyterian Church until her parents moved to Asheville, N. C., in 1890. After finishing in the Asheville public schools she entered Asheville Female College, majoring in piano and voice. She is a past president of the Asheville Chapter, U. D. C., custodian of the Confederate Memorial Hall, and a member of the Asheville Club for Women.

On April 2, 1902, she was married to Dr. Daniel Edward Sevier, a descendent of John Sevier, the first governor of Tennessee. For twenty-nine years, Dr. Dan Sevier was a physician and surgeon of note and active in public health work. He was Asheville's city health officer for eleven years, until his death, which came on December 4, 1934. At his death The Asheville Citizen said, "Asheville has never had a more devoted son. Dr. Sevier's loyalty to the mountain country matched his loyalty to his family and his friends."

Mrs. Sevier lives in "Possom Trot" cottage, Albemarle Park, Cherokee Road, Asheville, N. C.

11445   Tallula T. Sevier and Dr. Dan Sevier have one daughter:
    114451   Mary Virginia Sevier, b. 6/23/1911.

11446   Minnie Cornelia Templeton married, 11/14/1900, Stephen Warland Rhoades, Jr., of Charleston, S. C. He died 5/21/1921, and was buried at Asheville, N. C. She lives at 133 Annadale, Asheville, N. C. They had five children:

114461 Genevieve Rhoades, b. 10/30/1901, who married Harry Matthew and lives at Lake View Park, Asheville, N. C.

114462 Stephen W. Rhoades, Jr., b. 7/12/1906, married Mildred Davis, lives at 58 Cherry St., Asheville, N. C.

114463 Lottie Rhoades, b. 7/6/1909, married Earl Donnahoe, lives at Bartlesville, Okla.

114464 William Cater Rhoades, b. 12/2/1911, lives with his mother.

114465 Charles Wells Rhoades, b. 10/16/1913, lives with his mother.

11448 Alice Deveaux Templeton married, 1901, LeRoy Ball. They live on Patton Ave., Asheville, N. C. They have seven children:

114481 LeRoy Ball lives in New York City, married Gertrude Towe, has three children; names unknown.

114482 James Ball, U. S. Navy.

114483 Margaret Ball, married and has one daughter.

114484 Cornelia Ball, who lives with her brother, LeRoy Ball, in New York City.

114485 David Edward Ball of Chermill Hotel, Asheville, N. C.

114486 Joseph Ball, living with his parents, Patton Ave., Asheville, N. C.

114487 Charles Ball, living with his parents, Patton Ave., Asheville, N. C.

116 William Livingston Templeton, the sixth child of 11 David Templeton, and his wife, Massie, was born near Clinton, S. C. In 1843 he married Sarah Marcelle Griffin (1825-1877) of Abbeville County. To this union were born six children:

1161 Ira Griffin Templeton, 1844-9/14/1862.

1162 William Augustus Templeton, 6/17/1846-3/24/1914.

1163 James David Templeton, 7/19/1848-9/3/1849.

1164 Susan Emma Templeton, 7/6/1850—.

1165 Alexis Holtzclaw Templeton, 9/26/1852-2/1/1908.

1166 Lilly Templeton.

116 William Livingston Templeton was, emphatically, a self-made man. While still a young man he was teaching school in the village of Anderson, S. C., earning the means with which to attend the Charleston Medical College, where he was graduated in 1841.

(This information about 116 William Livingston Templeton was given by his son 1162 William Augustus Templeton. He—116 William Livingston Templeton—was evidently the teacher of the first school known to have existed in the village of Anderson, referred to on page 110, "Traditions and History of Anderson County," by Louise Ayer Vandiver, published in 1928 by the Anderson Daily Independent.)

Soon after his marriage he settled at Ninety-Six, S. C., and later moved to Greenwood. About 1857, he moved to Columbia, where he spent many years of his life and where he had a large and lucrative practice as a physician. All of his savings were swept away, however, during the Civil War when Sherman burned Columbia. When Dr. Templeton had nothing left but his watch a Yankee soldier stopped him and demanded that of him. After the soldier had gone a short distance with the watch, Dr. Templeton called him back and gave him the key, telling him that the watch would be of no use to anyone without the key.

The end of the war found him penniless, but with indomitable energy and renewed vigor he commenced, again, the practice of medicine at Abbeville Court House in 1870, and was enjoying a large practice at the time of his death.

Dr. Templeton was a deep student and possessed a read medical mind. He was a skilled physician and was successful in the treatment of diphtheria years before the discovery of antitoxin. A number of his prescriptions are still being used today.

He always wore a beaver hat and was very dignified in his appearance.

He was a man of religious conviction and practical true charity. He joined the Presbyterian Church at Abbeville in 1869.

When he died, the Abbeville Press and Banner said: ". . . none has been a more sorrowing task to us than to inform our readers of the death of Dr. W. L. Templeton—he always had the respect, esteem and affection of his patients.—He was a kind and gentle nurse, sympathetic and indulgent with his patients, and did his utmost to relieve suffering humanity."

He and his wife were buried at Long Cane Cemetery near Abbeville.

1161 Ira Griffin Templeton was living in Columbia with his parents when the Civil War began. In August, 1861, he volunteered and joined Company A, known as the Columbia Rifles, and composed principally of boys between the ages of sixteen and twenty. This company was placed in the 15th Regiment under command of Col. W. D. DeSsausure.

He was killed in the battle of Boonesboro (Turner's Gap), Sept. 14, 1862.

25

1162 William Augustus Templeton, second child of 116 William Livingston Templeton and Sarah Marcelle Griffin, was born in Greenwood, S. C., then in Abbeville County. He attended the village school until he was eleven years old, when his parents moved to Columbia, S. C. There he was a student at the preparatory school of Benjamin R. Stewart at the outbreak of the Civil War. The martial spirit gripped everybody and he was no exception. Although only fourteen years of age, he organized a company of fifty boys who had a great time playing at war, using wooden guns and sticks for swords. His father, in the effort to quell the lad's military spirit and to discourage him from enlisting too young, took him to the coast near Charleston, where his older brother was already a real soldier, and kept him there for about six weeks, thinking that this contact with the life of soldiers would satisfy the lad. On the contrary, it did not.

On March 28, 1862, while he was still under sixteen years old, he volunteered and enlisted in Company A, 15th S. C. Regiment. His Company, under command of P. T. Bean, after about four months, left for Virginia, arriving just after the Seven Days fight around Richmond. There the lad got his first glimpse of real warfare, the killed men lying unburied on the battlefield.

He had his first "charge" experience at Second Manassas. After the Yankees had been driven away the young soldier was asked how he felt and he replied: "I was never so glad in all my life." When asked why, he answered, "Because I did not run away."

When Lee's army followed the Yankees across the Potomac, young Mr. Templeton was one of those barefooted boys who were forbidden to "go into enemy territory unshod" and was marched into camp at Winchester where he watched the army return from Maryland, bringing the sorrowful report that his older brother had been "killed at Boonsboro."

In December, 1862, his outfit, in Lee's Army, was hurried to intercept Burnside's Army at Fredericksburg, wading streams with their clothes frozen on them, and where the experience of one man, who, overcome by sleep, froze to death, proved that they had to keep moving or freeze.

At The Wilderness he received his first battle wound by a piece of shell. Although ordered to the rear by his captain, he got up and marched on.

He was in the thick of the fight at Gettysburg. At Chicamauga, as a courier to General Kershaw, he was mentioned in the general's official report for conspicuous gallantry. He was also in the battle at Bean's Station, Tennessee.

In May, 1964, at Gordonsville, Va., he was given a furlough but before he reached home was pressed into artillery service at

Petersburg. Here he was one of seven men who, Col. E. B. Mobley, of Rock Hill, S. C., says, held the City of Petersburg by keeping up a rambling fire deceiving the enemy until reinforcements came up.

After this engagement, when he finally started home on his furlough, his pants were so badly torn that he had to pay $75.00 for another pair, leaving him so strapped that he had to beg his way home.

At Strausburg, Va., in October, 1864, when he had been ordered by General Kershaw to attend a wounded comrade, and after he himself had been shot through the hand, he proceeded, under the most galling fire from the enemy, to rejoin his brigade. Here again he was mentioned for gallantry in the official report of the brigade commander.

His wounded hand sent him home to Columbia, where he witnessed the burning of that city by Sherman's Army.

1162 William Augustus Templeton was a studious man and deeply interested in education. He was chairman of the board of school trustees for twenty-five years. He was also an elder in the Abbeville Presbyterian Church. For many years he was a merchant in Abbeville.

(For a more complete account of the life of 1162 William Augustus Templeton, the reader is referred to a rare paper, "Personal Experiences of W. A. Templeton In The Civil War" in possession of 11621 Mrs. Lilly Templeton Barksdale of Abbeville, S. C. This is not only her father's autobiography, but an accurate, instructive and thrilling account of the war as seen by an exceptionally well informed veteran who spent more than three years in the thick of the conflict and who was still in his teens when Lee surrendered. This paper is, in reality, so rich that it has been difficult to condense the account for this sketch.)

On November 4, 1871, 1162 William Augustus Templeton married Elizabeth Ann Giles who was born February 20, 1848, and who died May 22, 1929, surviving by 15 years her husband. Both are buried at Long Cane Cemetery, Abbeville, S. C. To them were born five children:

11621 Florence Templeton, b. 7/6/1873.
11622 Lilly Templeton, b. 9/17/1876.
11623 William Giles Templeton, b. 7/22/1879.
11624 William Livingston Templeton, b. 8/30/1881.
11625 James Patterson Templeton, 3/12/1886 - 9/7/1890, buried at Long Cane Cemetery at Abbeville, S. C.

11621 Florence Templeton was graduated in 1892 from Due West Female College and taught in Abbeville graded schools for a number of years. She took special lessons in Old English and

27

German in Atlanta one year, language being her special favorite. She is a Bible student and had a large class of young women in the Maxwell Street Presbyterian Church at Lexington, Ky. She married, Dec. 10, 1902, John McClintock Thorn. They live at 811 E. Main St., Lexington, Ky., and have four children:

116211 Sarah Templeton Thorn, b. 11/6/1903, a graduate of University of Kentucky with an M. A. Degree.

116212 Mary Giles Thorn, b. 10/22/1906.

116213 John McClintock Thorn, b. 10/12/1910.

116214 William Templeton Thorn, b. 5/4/1914, a graduate of University of Kentucky.

116212 Mary Giles Thorn attended the University of Kentucky for three years. She married, 1931, Estill Price Houston, and they have one son:

1162121 Estill Price Houston, Jr.

116213 John McClintock Thorn was graduated from the University of Kentucky and has an M. A. Degree. He married, 1937, Virginia..............

11622 Lilly Templeton, second child of 1162 William Augustus Templeton and Elizabeth Ann Giles, was graduated from Abbeville High School and attended Winthrop College for one year. She also took a business course and was bookkeeper and manager for the Fancy Grocery Store at Abbeville, S. C., for a number of years. She married, Oct. 7, 1914, William Dale Barksdale. They live at Abbeville, S. C.

11623 William Giles Templeton, third child of 1162 William Augustus Templeton and Elizabeth Ann Giles, was graduated from Clemson College in 1902. He married, Dec. 17, 1914, Mabel Stimson. They live at Statesville, N. C., where he has been a representative for a number of manufacturing concerns.

11624 William Livingston Templeton was graduated from Clemson College in 1904. After graduating he held a position in the engineering department of the New York Telephone Company for eighteen years. On Nov. 6, 1916, he married in New York, Jean Bostick. They live at 1787 16th St., S. W., Miami, Fla.

1164 Susan Emma Templeton married, Nov. 5, 1872, James Mason Giles, brother of Elizabeth Ann Giles who married 1162 William Augustus Templeton, making their children double first cousins. James Mason Giles died and was buried in Silver Brook Cemetery, Anderson, S. C. 1164 Susan Emma Templeton Giles and James Mason Giles had six children:

11641 William Templeton Giles, 5/16/1876-1/26/1930.

11642 Josiah Patterson Giles, 8/14/1878-7/6/1937.
11643 Ira Alexis Giles, b. 9/18/1880.
11644 James Mabry Giles, 9/26/1882-7/28/1884.
11645 Sarah Wilson Giles, b. 12/2/1884.
11646 George White Giless, 4/24/1887-1/18/1912, buried, Silver Brook Cemetery, Anderson, S. C. N.M.

11641 William Templeton Giles married, April 23, 1902, Owen Crawford. He died in Birmingham, Ala., where he was buried and where his widow still lives. Their children are:
    116411 Ellen Emeline Giles, 3/30/1903, married 3/30/1929, James M. Rittenburg.
    116412 Mary Graham Giles, b. 8/3/1905—married, 9/1930, Frank Hollis.
    116413 William Templeton Giles, Jr., b. 12/16/1905, who attended Princeton University and is now living in New York where he has a position and is doing well.

11642 Josiah Patterson Giles was buried at Danville, Va. He married, March 25, 1907, Willamena Glenn Phifer.

11643 Ira Alexis Giles graduated with honors from The Citadel, Charleston, S. C., and was with the Government in Panama for a number of years. He now lives in Greenville, S. C., where he has a position in the post office. He married, Jan. 22, 1905, Lucile Muckenfus of Charleston, S. C., born June 10, 1882. They had four children:
    116431 John Archie Giles, b. 3/17/1911.
    116432 Ira Alexis Giles, Jr., b. 9/18/1916.
    116433 Lucile Giles, b. 8/21/1921—d. 1/19/1922.
    116434 George Wesley Giles, b. 12/14/1922.

11645 Sarah Wilson Giles married, Oct. 29, 1914, Robert Stephens McCully. Their Children are:
    116451 James Giles McCully, b. 10/19/1916.
    116452 Robert Stephens McCully, Jr., b. 1/28/1921.
    116453 Josiah Giles McCully, 5/22/1922-7/19/1922.

1165 Alexis Holtzclaw Templeton, fifth child of 116 William Livingston Templeton and Sara Marcelle Griffin, married Feb. 20, 1879, Leila Ada Dickson, and moved to Miles, Miss. She died Oct. 4, 1921. He lives at Hollendale, Miss. They had seven children:
    11651 Sarah Georgia Templeton, b. 9/28/1882.
    11652 Joseph Livingston Templeton, 3/27/1885-4/3/1898.
    11653 Ira Griffin Templeton, 8/22/1887-9/9/1906.
    11654 Emma Giles Templeton, 1/29/1890-11/21/1897.
    11655 Hugh Dickson Templeton, b. 2/4/1892.

11656 Alexis Holtzclaw Templeton, b. 8/15/1895.

11657 Fred Taussig Templeton.

11651 Sarah Georgia Templeton was graduated from Whitworth College in 1903. She taught school several years before she married, Dec. 8, 1908, Walter Scott Coleman, who died July 6, 1922. Their children were:

116511 Annie Lea Coleman, b. 2/2/1910, graduated from Mississippi State College in 1930, and at that time was working in a bank at Inverness, Miss.

116512 Mildred Elizabeth Coleman, b. 10/14/1913.

116513 Lena Myra Coleman, b. 9/21/1917.

116514 Marion Templeton Coleman, b. 11/16/1921.

11655 Hugh Dickson Templeton has lived, since his father's death, with his sister, 11651 Sarah Georgia Templeton, where he has become the man of the house on the farm, after her husband's death.

11656 Alexis Holtzclaw Templeton was graduated from college in 1918. He married, May 2, 1920, Corrie Mae Green. They live at Hollendale, Miss., where he is manager of a large wholesale grocery. Their children are:

116561 Caroline Templeton, b. 3/21/1921.

116562 Alexis Everette Templeton, b. 12/21/1926.

1166 Lilly Templeton, sixth child of 116 William Livingston Templeton and Sarah Marcelle Griffin, died while a young child, from diphtheria, it is thought. Her death stimulated her father's efforts to combat this disease. She is buried at Ninety Six Cemetery. A marker was supposed to have been sent to her grave but whether it was put up or not is unknown. 11621 Mrs. Lilly T. Barksdale, of Abbeville, S. C., was named for her.

12 ELIZABETH TEMPLETON

12 Elizabeth Templeton, second child of 1 David Templeton and his wife, Mary, was born Oct. 14, 1774. 1561 Priscilla Garrett said she married Robert Hanna. She evidently died before her father, since she is not mentioned in his will, although her two sons, 121 Robert Hanna and 122 David Hanna, were. 1561 Priscilla Garrett told the writer that there was a daughter, Mary Ann Hanna, who married Alexander Jeans. However, after years of searching for some living descendents, the writer finally contacted Mr. Rush Nabors near Clinton, S. C., who says his grandmother was Mary Ann Hanna Jeans. Mr. Lewis Hanna of Cross Hill, S. C., and his first cousin, Mr. Larry Todd, near Clinton, S. C., both claimed that Mary Ann Hanna Jeans was a sister to their grandfather, John Hanna. They also named several other brothers and sisters of their grandfather, John Hanna, but neither of them knew of 121 Robert Hanna or 122 David Hanna. This leads the writer to believe that, either (1) 1561 Priscilla Garrett was in error by claiming that Mary Ann Hanna Jeans was the daughter of 12 Elizabeth Templeton Hanna, or, (2), 12 Elizabeth Templeton's widower married a second time, the children of this marriage being half brothers and sisters to 121 Robert Hanna and 122 David Hanna. In either case it seems that these descendents of John Hanna and Mary Ann Hanna Jeans are not descendents of 12 Elizabeth Templeton.

(Note: 1561 Priscilla Garrett was a small child when her mother died so that she was taken to her grandfather, 15 John Templeton, with whom she lived until his death when she was 25 years old. It is probable that she learned from him some of the facts about his sister, 12 Elizabeth Templeton Hanna and her husband. 1561 Priscilla Garrett was in her 80's when she gave this information to the writer.)

13 JAMES TEMPLETON

13 James Templeton, third child of 1 David Templeton and his wife, Mary, was born June (18—Bible and tombstone), 1778 in Laurens District, S. C. He died Jan. 25, 1839, and was buried at Rehobeth Methodist (now abandoned) Church near Clinton, S. C. He married Esther Laird, daughter of Capt. Robert Laird and sister of Massie Laird who married 11 David Templeton. Esther Laird Templeton was born, 1788, died Oct. 22, 1833, and was buried beside her husband at Rehobeth. The children of 13 James Templeton and Esther Laird Templeton were double first cousins of the children of 11 David Templeton and Massie Laird. They were:

131 Mascy Templeton, b. 12/7/1808, died, single, 7/31/1826, and was buried at Rehobeth.
132 David Clarke Templeton, 3/5/1810-5/29/1877.
133 Mary G. Templeton, 1/5/1812-4/4/1886.
134 Sarah A. Templeton, b. 8/29/1814 (tombstone)) 4/29/1814 (Bible), d. 3/10/1855.
135 Elizabeth D. Templeton, 12/23/1816-7/22/1879.
136 Nancy Templeton, 8/9/1818-6/13/1859.
137 James O. Templeton, b. 2/23/1821, died, single, 1/25/1839, and was buried at Rehobeth Methodist Cemetery near Clinton, S. C.

13 James Templeton died intestate and his son 132 David Clarke Templeton was appointed administrator. The amount paid May 4, 1840, to each legatee was: Esther Templeton, widow, $2,594.14; 133 Mary G. Templeton, $1,037.45; 136 Nancy Templeton, $1,037.45; 135 Elizabeth D. Templeton, $1,037.49; S. D. Glenn, (husband of 134 Sara A. Templeton) $1,037.45; 132 David C. Templeton, $1,037.45. Two children had already died—131 Mascy Templeton and 137 James O. Templeton.

132 David Clarke Templeton, second child of 13 James Templeton and Esther Laird Templeton, was born in Laurens District, S. C. He grew to be a handsome man, six feet two inches tall with deep blue eyes. In later years he was better known as "Colonel David Templeton" from the fact that he was a colonel of militia before the Civil War. He was deeply interested in public affairs, being a candidate for Sheriff of Laurens County, in 1856.

His patriotic spirit is shown by the fact that, even though he was 51 years old when the Civil War began, that struggle had barely begun when he volunteered and enlisted April 14, 1861, at Clinton, S. C. He was mustered into Co. I, 3rd Regiment of Infantry, South Carolina Volunteers, where he was first sergeant. He was transferred to Co. G, 3rd Regiment, May 25, 1861. While at Fredericksburg, Va., he was stricken with pneumonia and was sent home. On Feb. 3, 1862, he was discharged on the surgeon's certificate because of old age and general debility.

His zeal for the welfare of his state, down-trodden in 1871, was exhibited too much to suit some of the scalawags and carpetbaggers, particularly during the riot on election day of that year. When a warrant was issued for his arrest he decided it was the part of wisdom to move away. Accordingly he left his old home near Musgrove Mill in Laurens County and moved about two miles north of Greenville, on the Rutherford Road. From there he moved to Huff's Mill on Reedy River, near Fountain Inn, where he had charge of the mill and where he died. He was buried at Fairview Presbyterian Church in this same section.

On Nov. 23, 1860, at the age of 50, he married Adaline Day, who was 23 years old. To this union were born five children:

1321 James Kemper Templeton, 8/16/1861-11/9/1926.
1322 Masby M. Templeton, 6/1/1863-7/30/1897, NM.
1323 Mary E. Templeton, 8/24/1865-1/4/1947.
1324 Frances Templeton, b. 8/20/1868, a nurse in Atlanta, Georgia.
1325 Esther Templeton, b. 1/14/1873.

1321 James Kemper Templeton was buried at Rocky Springs Presbyterian Church, near Laurens, S. C. In 1889, he married Verona McQuoun, b. Aug. 16, 1861, d. Feb. 20, 1911, buried at Rocky Springs. Their children are:

13211 Niles G. Templeton, b. 2/8/1892.
13212 Amanda Templeton, b. 6/8/1894.
13213 Janie Irvane Templeton, b. 5/10/1896, unmarried, living with her sister, 13212 Mrs. Amanda Templeton Bennett, at 40 White Fawn Drive, Asheville, N. C.
13214 Danel Craig Templeton, b. 7/4/1898.
13215 Ella Templeton, b. 12/25/1900.
13216 James Kemper Templeton, Jr., b. 7/27/1907.

13211 Niles G. Templeton married, June 19, 1911, Ruth Madden, b. June 27, 1896. They lived at Dunean Mill, Greenville, S. C., and have the following children:

132111 Verona Templeton, b. 11/12/1912.
132112 Kathryn Templeton, b. 3/16/1914.
132113 Iris Templeton, b. 11/10/1917.
132114 Irma Templeton, b. 4/9/1920.
132115 Mary Ruth Templeton, b. 2/18/1923.
132116 Vivian Templeton, b. 1/23/1925.
132117 Julia Templeton, b. 6/27/1927.
132118 Jimmie Templeton, b. 8/15/1929.

13212 Amanda Templeton married, June 19, 1920, Sam Bennett, b. April 25, 1886. They live at 40 White Fawn Drive, Asheville, N. C. They have one child:
132121 Esther Bennett, b. 7/2/1921.

13214 Danel Craig Templeton, after completing grammar school in Clinton, S. C., enlisted in the U. S. Navy March 15, 1915. He served in the Navy until September, 1919, two years of which were spent in Europe during the World War. Since the World War, he has continued in the service. In 1930 he was promoted to Chief Quartermaster. By diligent study and through correspondence courses he has equipped himself to teach navigation and meteorology, both of which he is now teaching to the enlisted personnel at the Coast Guard Institute and living at 187 Lincoln Ave., New London, Conn. He married Ivy May Bilton, and they have one daughter:
132141 Ivy Irvane Templeton.

13215 Ella Templeton married Owen Andrews. They live at 12835 Terry Ave., Detroit, Mich., and have two children:
132151 Jean Andrews, b. 7/1926.
132152 David Andrews, b. 7/1931.

13216 James Kemper Templeton, Jr., is a photo engraver and lives at 11304 Marlowe Ave., Detroit, Mich. He married Gertrude Knudsen and they have one child:
132161 Meurice Templeton, b. 8/25/1934.

1322 Masby M. Templeton, second child of 132 Col. David Clarke Templeton and Adaline Day Templeton, was a devoted minister in the Presbyterian Church. He was buried at the Day family cemetery, Laurens, S. C.

1323 Mary E. Templeton, third child of 132 David Templeton and Adaline Day Templeton, attended the county schools, completing the tenth grade. She took the regular examination and secured a teacher's certificate. She taught for a time at Lanford Station. She also taught night school at the Old Mill in Laurens, S. C., about 1898. She also took a course in short hand. She lived near Laurens, S. C., and was unmarried. She was buried at Fairview Church, Greenville County, S. C.

1325 Esther Templeton, youngest child of 132 Col. David Clarke Templeton and Adaline Day Templeton, married William Burnice Parks, a contractor. They live at 402 Milledge Ave., Atlanta, Ga.

133 Mary G. Templeton, third child of 13 James Templeton and Esther Laird Templeton, was buried at Slabtown Presbyterian

Cemetery. She married, Dec. 23, 1841, Frank M. Glenn. Their children were:

1331　J. Perry Glenn, 1843-1912, buried, Anderson, S. C., who married Amanda Smith.

1232　John M. Glenn, 10/3/1845-2/9/1898.

1333　Thomas S. Glenn, 12/23/1847-6/16/1909, NM.

1334　William D. Glenn, 1851-4/10/1893.

1335　Sarah Cornelia Glenn, 8/..../1851-9/20/1906.

1332　John M. Glenn was buried at Slabtown Presbyterian Cemetery. He married Oct. 10, 1871, Anna McCown. Their children were:

13321　F. M. Glenn, 12/3/1872-1939.

13322　William Barr Glenn, b. 11/29/1874.

13323　Harrison Kennedy Glenn, b. 9/4/1876, married, Nov. 9, 1910, Mamie McCollough, and now lives 122 Hampton Ave., Greenville, S. C.

13324　Bessie M. Glenn b. 2/12/1879.

13325　Thomas Knox Glenn, 1/27/1881-..../2/1920, NM, buried, Liberty, S. C.

13326　Jessie N. Glenn, b. 2/18/1883.

13327　John Perry Glenn, b. 9/1/1885, who married, June 1915, Calla Chapman, and lives at Liberty, S. C.

13322　William Barr Glenn married, May 25, 1910, Mary Sheldon. They live at Liberty, S. C. They have one daughter:

133221　Margaret Glenn, b. 10/22/1921.

13324　Bessie M. Glenn married, March 6, 1901, W. M. Smith, who is now dead. They have one daughter:

133241　Walter Marie Glenn Smith, who is a teacher, living with her mother at Liberty, S. C.

13325　Jessie N. Glenn married, Feb., 1911, J. R. Shelor. They have one child:

133251　Marion Glenn Shelor, b. 9/17/1918, and lives, 550 Boulevard, Anderson, S. C.

1334　William D. Glenn was buried at Carmel Presbyterian Church in Pickens County, S. C. He married in 1884, Ada Gilliland Humbert. They had one son:

13341　Robert Glenn, born and died 1885, and was buried at Carmel.

1335　Sarah Cornelia Glenn was buried at Liberty, S. C. She married, Oct. 27, 1874, Jephtha Smith, brother of Amanda Smith who married her brother, 1331 J. Perry Glenn. They had five children:

13351 Mary Hester Smith, b. 7/19/1875, died single, 6/3/ 1894, and was buried at Slabtown Presbyterian Cemetery.
13352 Herbert Glenn Smith, b. 8/16/1879.
13353 Lois Amanda Smith, b. 3/25/1883.
13354 Frank Monroe Smith, b. 10/16/1887, died single, 5/1910, and was buried at Liberty, S. C.
13355 Anna Pearl Smith, b. 10/31/1890.

13352 Herbert Glenn Smith married March 2, 1905, Elizabeth Richardson. They live at 115 Forest Ave., N. E., Atlanta, Ga., and have one child:
133521 Marion Glenn Smith, 3/18/1906, who lives 27 West Church St., Bethlehem, Pa.

13353 Lois Amanda Smith married, June 7, 1911, W. C. Taylor. They live at Columbia, S. C., and have two children:
133531 Sarah Adele Taylor, b. 4/20/1915.
133532 W. C. Taylor, Jr., b. 9/25/1921.

13355 Anna Pearl Smith was graduated in 1911, at Queens College, Charlotte, N. C., in music. She has held many church offices. She is Historian and past President of King's Mountain Presbyterial; Secretary and Treasurer of N. C. Synod. She is also Regent of William Gaston Chapter, D.A.R. She married, April 9, 1913, Coit M. Robinson. They have lived at Lowell, N. C., for twenty-five years. They have three children:
133551 Marjorie Glenn Robinson, b. 6/19/1916.
133552 Jean Robinson, b. 9/2/1917.
133553 Coit McLean Robinson, Jr., b. 5/26/1920.

134 Sarah A. Templeton, fourth child of 13 James Templeton and Massie Laird Templeton, was buried at Friendship Church in Laurens County, S. C. She married Jan. 25, 1840, Simpson Dunlap Glenn, June 15, 1821-April 13 (tombstone) 26 (per Mrs. J. P. Glenn), 1896. He is buried at Slabtown Presbyterian Cemetery. Their children were:
1341 Mary Glenn, 1841-1910.
1342 Flora Glenn, who died unmarried.
1343 David Glenn, 7/4/1844-5/10/1903.

1341 Mary Glenn, married A. F. Simpson. She is buried at Friendship Cemetery. Their children were:
13411 Janie Simpson, b. 1870, who resides at the Harriett Home, Clinton, S. C.
13412 Flora Simpson, b. 1872, who, with her husband, J. Harvey Pruitt, have become widely known for their famous meals served at the Starr Hotel, Starr, S. C.

13413 L. Frank Simpson, b. 2/28/1874, of Piedmont, S. C.,
Rt. 2.
13414 Mary Perlina Simpson, b. 1879, of Starr, S. C.
13415 Tom Simpson, 1882-9/10/1926.
13416 Glenn Simpson, b. 1885, of Starr, S. C., who married Annie Yelvington.

13413 L. Frank Simpson married Sue McHugh. Their children are:
133131 Paul M. Simpson, b. 4/4/1905, of Piedmont, S. C.,
Rt. 2, who married Nita Payne.
134132 L. Frank Simpson, Jr., b. 7/29/1907, an attorney in
Greenville, S. C., who married Fannie L. Hallman.
134133 Jabez Alexander Simpson, b. 12/7/1909, of Piedmont, S. C., Rt. 2.

13415 Tom Simpson married Clara Fowler. He is buried at
Friendship Church, Laurens County. She lives at Connie Maxwell Orphanage, Greenwood, S. C. They had one son:
134151 Alexander Foster Simpson, who lives at Spokane,
Wash.

1343 David Glenn married Emma Little, who for many years
was very active in the D. A. R. and other historical and social
work. Their children are:
13431 William S. Glenn, prominent in banking affairs in
Spartanburg, S. C.
13432 Dr. J. P. Glenn, a dentist in Spartanburg, S. C., living
at 168 Oakland Ave.
13433 Tom Glenn.

135 Elizabeth D. Templeton, fifth child of 13 James Templeton
and Esther Laird Templeton, was buried at Friendship Church,
Laurens County. She married, first, Nov. 30, 1841, T. C. Simpson,
who died Oct. 28, 1845. Their children were:
1351 James A. Simpson, 1842-8/24/1861, buried at Friendship Church.
1352 Mary T. Simpson, 2/25/1844-1/10/1876, buried at
Friendship.

1351 James A. Simpson was a Confederate soldier who died
in Virginia at the post of duty and honor, a soldier of the Hampton Legion, S. C. V., having passed through the battle of July 21
(Mannassas Plains) most honorably. His remains were brought
by the Rev. C. B. Stewart to S. C., and interred at Friendship
Church, Laurens Dist., S. C., Aug. 30, 1861." (From Bible record
of Rev. J. Leland Kennedy).

135 Elizabeth D. Templeton Simpson, married second, Aug. 2, 1859, Rev. J. Leland Kennedy, the celebrated Presbyterian minister and teacher of Slabtown and whose son, "A. Ross Kennedy, married the eldest sister of President Wilson" (per Louise Ayer Vandiver, in her History of Anderson County, P. 103).

136 Nancy Templeton, sixth child of 13 James Templeton and Esther Laird Templeton, was buried at Bethany Church, Laurens County. She married, December 25, 1845, Archie Henry Smith, Sept. 13, 1819-Oct. 25, 1867.   Their children were:
    1361 Charles Butler Smith, 7/30/1848-1/10/1850, buried at Bethany.
    1362 Sarah Evaline Smith, 6/12/1849-7/19/1917, buried at Piedmont, S. C.
    1363 George David Smith, 5/5/1850-7/12/1917.
    1364 James Noah Smith, 6/20/1852-1931.
    1365 Mary Ella McCravy Smith, b. 6/5/1855.
    1366 Thomas Lewers Smith, b. 4/6/1856.
    1367 Martha Elizabeth Smith, b. 4/2/1858.

1362 Sarah Evaline Smith married, Jan. 24, 1889, William P. Morgan. They have one daughter:
    13621 Bella Morgan, b. Jan., 1890, who lives at 1320 Woodside Ave., Greenville, S. C.

1364 James Noah Smith married Mattie Hollingsworth. They have the following children:
    13641 Maude Smith who married J. W. Hass and who lives at 529 Worthington Ave., Charlotte, N. C., and who has one daughter:
        136411 Elizabeth Hass.
    13642 Jennie Smith, now of Gastonia, N. C., who married E. L. Lewis.
    13643 Minnie Smith who married J. C. Pickens.
    13644 Grace Smith of Gastonia, N. C., who married Arthur B. Howe.
    13645 Bessie Smith who married John C. Duliss, who is connected with the Tampa Brokerage Co., Tampa, Fla.
    13646 George T. Smith who lives at 401 Vail Ave., Charlotte, N. C.
    13647 Addie Hollingsworth Smith who lives at 49 East 49th St., New York City.

137 James O. Templeton, seventh child of 13 James Templeton and Esther Laird Templeton, was born Feb. 23, 1821, and died June 13, 1837.

14 Robert Templeton, fourth child of 1 David Templeton and his wife, Mary, was born Nov. 26, 1784. On May 30, 1805, he married Mary Puckett, Oct. 7, 1786-Oct. 4, 1847. To this union were born twelve children:

    14a   William A. Templeton, 4/13/1806-1883-5.
    14b   John Henry Templeton, 8/10/1807-10/9/1820.
    14c   James Frank Templeton, b. 12/5/1808—
    14d   George O. Templeton, 3/3/1811-5/28/1873.
    14e   Thomas M. Templeton, 3/3/1813-10/16/1834.
    14f   Elizabeth Templeton, 3/11/1815-10/11/1825.
    14g   Benjamin Clark Templeton, 1/17/1817-9/4/1872.
    14h   Leah A. M. Templeton, 12/14/1818—
    14i   Sarah P. Templeton, 1/24/1821-12/21/1839, married, Jan. 31, 1839, Levi Whitton.
    14j   Robert W. Templeton, 1/18/1823, went to Browningtion, Mo.
    14k   Frances Rebecca Templeton, 1/26/1826-12/7/1869.
    14L   Mary A. G. Templeton, 8/16/1829-9/29/1839.

14 Robert Templeton lived on the south side of Duncan's Creek and near the creek, on the road leading from Clinton, S. C., to Musgrove Mill. A group of large oak trees marks the site of the home. He is said to have donated the land, about 3 or 4 acres, on which Rehobeth Methodist Church was built and where he and his wife and several children are buried. The church was situated on the North side of Duncan's Creek about two miles, "as the crow flies," from his home. It was abandoned as a church as early as 1870. The cemetery all except a few graves now overgrown with underbrush, can be reached by vehicle only by a field road from the former home of Willie Meyers.

14 Robert Templeton was a farmer, teacher, carpenter, and blacksmith. He inherited no slaves, since his father in his will, ordered his slaves sold. 14 Robert Templeton's wife, however, inherited as slaves, a Negro woman and her boy, called Peter. After the Negro woman's death Peter was treated kindly by his master who taught him, among other things, to read and write. After Peter had grown up, he was sold to John Royce, who treated Peter just as the other slaves were treated. Peter resented this and ran away and returned to his former master. The law prohibiting the harboring of a run-away slave, 14 Robert Templeton turned him back over to his legal owner, Mr. Boyce, who proceeded to give him the lash as the law prescribed. Peter ran away again and again, stealing food wherever he could but mostly from his former owner, and hiding out as long as the food would last. Each time he was returned to his master he was given additional hard treatment until he became a desperado and finally, when

caught stealing food in 14 Robert Templeton's home, rather than be taken back to his owner, he murdered his former benefactor, 14 Robert Templeton.

The account of this murder on May 5, 1837, has been handed down from generation to generation. The writer, after long and tedious search, succeeded in finding a report of this murder as published by four newspapers.

The account of this murder was published by The Columbia Times, a paper not listed by the book, "The 150th Anniversary of Columbia," but which was evidently being published at the time, because the account of the murder was quoted from this paper by The Pendleton Messenger in its issue of May 12 (about), 1837. The account was also quoted ver batim by the Edgefield Advertiser of May 18, 1837, and also ver batim by The Greenville Mountaineer of May 20, 1837. The item is reproduced here (Fig. 4), together with the correction of the error.

The statement that the son only lingered two days was an error, inasmuch as he, 14d George O. Templeton, lived 36 years longer to be an old man 62 years of age. He died May 28, 1873

The following account of the murder of 14 Robert Templeton is the writer's attempt to compose the details as best he could from all additional sources available.

Robert and his son, George, age 26, were in the field. The women folks were at the nearby spring, doing the family washing. Peter, being familiar with the home, knew where to find the meat as well as the brandy. Robert and George came home unexpectedly and came upon Peter in the kitchen pantry helping himself to brandy and ham. He was using the family butcher knife, made from an old file, to carve the meat. Robert asked Peter what he was doing in there and told him that he was under arrest to be returned to his owner. The desperate negro rushed at Robert and plunged the knife into his heart, killing him instantly. George grabbed a chair and had it raised above his head in the act of striking Peter who suddenly rushed at him with the knife, sticking it into one of George's ribs, where it was left for the time being. Peter ran frantically out of the house and down by the spring where the women saw him and knew by the way he looked that something was wrong. So they hurried to the house to find Robert dead and George wounded. Their screams soon brought the other men and dogs. After several days of search and chasing on the banks and in the waters of Duncan's Creek, Peter was captured. He was given a "form of trial" at which he confessed the crime. He was taken to a spot near the scene of the murder and hanged. His head was cut off and stuck up on a pole by the side of the road as a warning to other slaves.

On May 5, 1937, the 100th anniversary of his death, a large group of his descendents met at his grave in Old Rehobeth Ceme-

Fig. 4

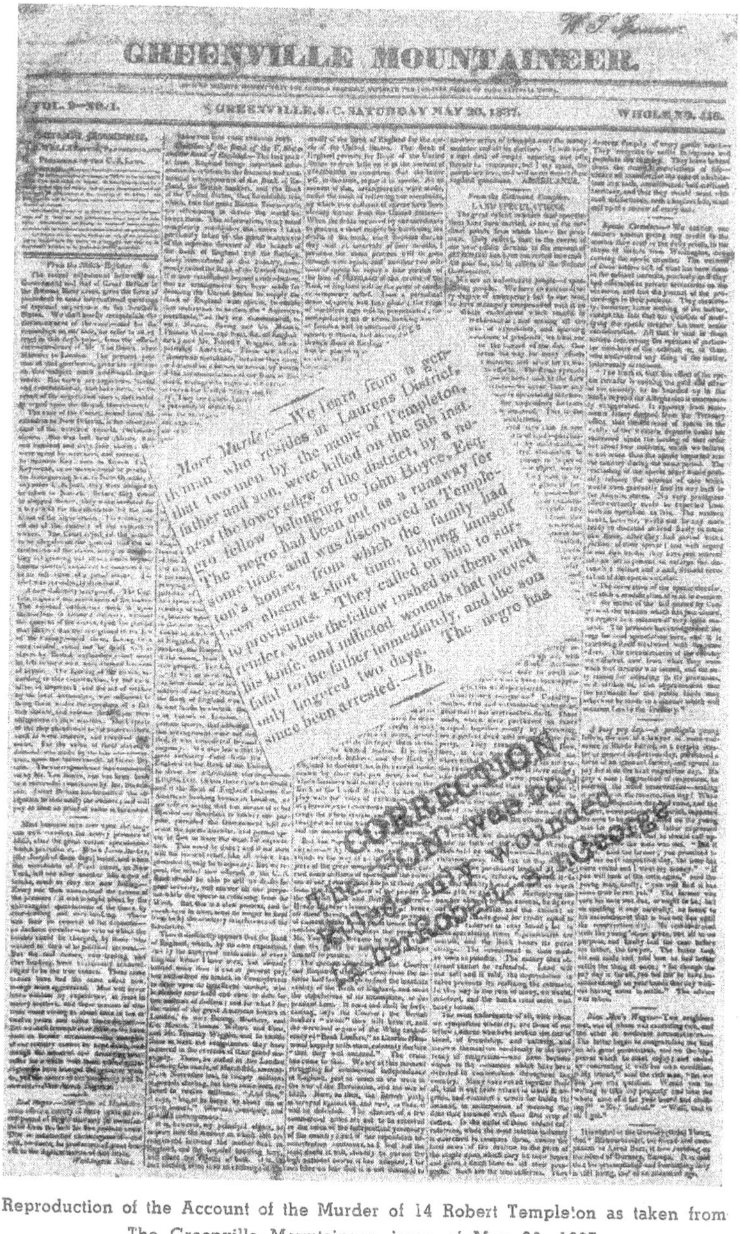

GREENVILLE MOUNTAINEER

GREENVILLE, S. C. SATURDAY MAY 20, 1837.

More Murder.—We learn from a gentleman who resides at Laurens District, that two men by the name of Templeton, father and son, were killed on the 5th inst. near the lower edge of the district, by a negro fellow belonging to John Boyce, Esq. The negro had been out as a runaway for some time, and was discovered in Templeton's house, from which the family had been absent a short time, helping himself to provisions. They called on him to surrender, when the fellow rushed out them with his knife, and inflicted wounds that proved fatal to the father immediately, and the son only lingered two days. The negro has since been arrested.—Ib.

Reproduction of the Account of the Murder of 14 Robert Templeton as taken from The Greenville Mountaineer, issue of May 20, 1837.

41

tery, and with an impressive ceremony, unveiled a small monument to the memory of 14 Robert Templeton.

DEDICATION

"Robert Templeton, third son and fourth child of the Revolutionary patriot, David Templeton and his wife, Mary, was born Nov. 26, 1784. On May 30, 1805, at the age of 20 years, 6 months and 4 days, he was married to Mary Puckett, age 18 years, 7 months and 23 days. To this union were born twelve children: William A. Templeton, John Henry Templeton, James Frank Templeton, George Osborne Templeton, Thomas M. Templeton, Elizabeth C. Templeton, Benjamin Clark Templeton, Leah A. M. Templeton, Sarah P. Templeton, Robert W. Templeton, Frances Rebecca Templeton, and Mary A. G. Templeton.

Robert Templeton departed this life May 5, 1837, aged 52 years, 5 months and 9 days. His untimely death was at the hands of one whom he had always endeavored to befriend and for whose servile race he ever held a profound sympathy.

In the name of all of his descendents, dead, living, and unborn, We now, on this the 100th anniversary of his death, dedicate this marker, sacred to his memory, forever."

His grave and those of his wife and several others are now enclosed with a strong iron fence donated by the late 14g3 Benjamin P. Templeton of Delvalle, Texas.

14a William A. Templeton, oldest child of 14 Robert and Mary Templeton, is buried at Chesnut Baptist Church on the old Chappels-Saluda, S. C., Road. He was a section foreman on the Greenville-Columbia Railroad. He was a Confederate Veteran. He married Nov. 7, 1828, Jane Hannah. Their children were:

  14a1 Katie Templeton.
  14a2 Amanda Templeton.
  14a3 Louisa Templeton.
  14a4 Fannie Templeton
  14a5 Elizabeth Templeton.
  14a6 Robert Templeton, buried at Greenville Church, Shoals Junction, S. C.
  14a7 William Templeton, buried at Greenville Church, Shoals Junction, S. C.

14a1 Katie Templeton married Dave Mack. They have one son:
  14a11 Ben Mack, living at Saluda, S. C.

14a2 Amanda Templeton married Pres. Williams. They have four children:
  14a21 Minnie Luva Williams, b. 6/30/1875, who married John Attaway and lives at Lowell, St., Ninety Six, S. C.
  14a22 Pick Williams.
  14a23 Quincy Williams who lives at Newberry, S. C.
  14a24 Annie Williams.

42

14a3 Louisa Templeton married Is Gentry. She has two children:
  14a31 James Templeton.
  14a32 Mary Templeton, who married John Duffie, a farmer living near Augusta, Ga., at the last account.

14a31 James Templeton, born about 1855, died Feb. 13, 1910, married Ella Cobb. They have the following children:
  14a311 Lee Templeton.
  14a312 Dutch Templeton.
  14a313 Will Templeton, b. 12/12/1873.
  14a314 Jess Templeton, b. 11/20/1879, who married Leo Smallwood. They had two children, both of whom died in infancy.

14a4 Fannie Templeton married Tillman Cobb. They have one daughter:
  14a41 Janie Cobb.

14c James Frank Templeton, third child of 14 Robert and Mary Templeton, married Nov. 15, 1830, Dorothy Jane Craddock. He moved to Waco, Texas, about Christmas, 1837. He was a real estate dealer. They have two children:
  14c1 John David Templeton, 8/21/1845-4/24/1893.
  14c2 Farrow Templeton.

14c1 John David Templeton married Lula C. Pope, March 19, 1858 - Aug. 12, 1918. He was Comptroller General of Texas for a great many years. They had one son:
  14c11 Pope Templeton, 12/14/1884-5/31/1885.

14d George O. Templeton, fourth child of 14 Robert and Mary Templeton, was buried at Hopewell Church, Laurens County, S. C. He was a blacksmith by trade. He was wounded at the same time his father, 14 Robert Templeton, was killed by the runaway slave. He married June 27, 1833, Nancy Luke, July 24, 1816-May 24, 1869. They had the following children:
  14da M. A. Templeton, b. 7/24/1834.
  14db John A. Templeton, 4/21/1836-8/27/1902.
  14dc M. L. Templeton, b. 10/18/1838.
  14dd M. Y. Templeton, b. 10/10/1841.
  14de P. C. Templeton, b. 12/25/1843.
  14df S. R. Templeton, b. 11/2/1845.
  14dg Margaret E. Templeton, b. 8/27/1848.
  14dh Thomas E. Templeton, 7/25/1850-10/16/1917.
  14di Robert Templeton, 5/16/1856-6/5/1927.
  14dj Ann Templeton, d. 4/11/1917.
  14dk Amanda Templeton, who married Robert Bowen.
  14dL Amelia Templeton.

14db   John A. Templeton was born in Laurens County, S. C. He married, about 1854, Henrietta Jones in Laurens County, S. C. At the beginning of the Civil War he enlisted, serving under Longstreet. He was wounded twice. On one battlefield he found a Yankee soldier with his nose shot off, in a dying condition, begging for water, and he mercifully gave the soldier water from his own canteen. After having a part in the battle of Gettysburg, he was taken prisoner by a Yankee cavalryman and remained in prison until the end of the war. Many years after the war he moved to Texas where he was a successful farmer and overseer, and where he died. He and his wife were both buried at Garrett's Bluff Cemetery, Lamar County, Texas. Their children were:

    14db1   J. Leland Templeton, 9/13/1858-1/13/1936.
    14db2   Alice Templeton, who married J. P. Martin and lives at Powderly, Texas.
    14db3   Verdie Templeton, who married Will Ellis and lives in Oklahoma.
    14db4   M. L. ("Babe") Templeton, b. 4/7/1866.
    14db5   G. E. Templeton, 4/6/1871-4/27/1896.
    14db6   Thomas G. Templeton, b. 2/19/1873.

14db1   J. Leland Templeton was born in Laurens County, S. C., and was buried in Ralls Cemetery, Ralls, Texas. On Dec. 12, 1878, he married Mary Alice Bowen. He moved to Texas, where he spent most of his life. In Dec., 1890, he made a trip to Oklahoma (which was then Indian Territory) in a wagon drawn by two yoke oxen. When they came to Red River the oxen refused to ford the cold water until he got out and waded in himself. They had the following children:

    14db11   W. D. Templeton, 11/6/1880-12/14/1900.
    14db12   Laura L. Templeton, 12/18/1882/12/15/1900.
    14db13   Whit W. Templeton, b. 5/27/1886.
    14db14   B. W. Templeton, 12/19/1888-12/19/1899.
    14db15   Etta L. Templeton, 5/25/1890-12/9/1900.
    14db16   Titus C. Templeton, b. 3/2/1893, married Sept. 22, 1912, B. E. Perkins, and lives at Ralls, Texas, Rt. 1.
    14db17   Franzie L. Templeton, 11/21/1896-9/14/1908.
    14db18   Dewey O. Templeton, 5/29/1899-12/23/1900.
    14db19   Leland C. Templeton, 11/27/1903-7/20/1907.

14db13   Whit W. Templeton of Sumner, Texas, married, June 24, 1909 Nora Allison. Their children are:

    14db13a   John Leslie Templeton, b. 6/21/1910.
    14db13b   Jewell L. Templeton, b. 6/27/1912, who married Floyd Easley.
    14db13c   Travis Templeton, b. 8/1/1914, who is a cripple as a result of infantile paralysis.

14db13d Eugenia Templeton, b. 3/7/1920, who married, 1938, Paul Smith.
14db13e James Templeton, b. 9/21/1921.
14db13f Phonice Templeton, b. 12/10/1923.
14db13g Winfred Templeton, b. 2/12/1926.
14db13h Nadine Templeton, b. 9/16/1927-6/8/1928.
14db13i Reba Templeton, b. 11/14/1930.
14db13j Pauline Templeton, b. 7/28/1934.

14db13a John Leslie Templeton married Mary Williams. They have one child:
14db13a1 Leslie Wayne Templeton.

14db4 M. L. ("Babe") Templeton married, Feb. 14, 1886, John W. McCoy, her first cousin. They live at Sumner, Texas, and have the following children:
14db41 George McCoy, b. 6/20/1886, who married, Oct., 1911, Ivy Brumby, and lives at Caviness, Texas, Rt. 1.
14db42 Grady McCoy, b. 11/15/1889, who married, 12/9/1916, Bessie Gentry, and lives at Caviness, Texas, Rt. 1.
14db43 Ray T. McCoy, b. 1/7/1895, married, 11/11/1918, Ora Wells, and lives at Sumner, Texas, Rt. 2.
14db44 Essie McCoy, b. 9/18/1904, married, Feb. 13, 1927, S. Dilday.

14db6 Thomas G. Templeton married, August 7, 1898, Laura Lillian Putman. They live at Direct, Texas, and have the following children:
14db61 Mary Etta Templeton, 6/24/1899-9/5/1905.
14db62 Leila Lee Templeton, b. 7/9/1902.
14db63 Leona Marie Templeton, b. 8/7/1907.
14db64 Stella B. Templeton, b. 6/10/1915, who married, 1933, Lee Stevens and lives at Direct Texas, Rt. 2, where they have one son:
14db641 Bobby Lee Stevens, 4/10/1934.

14db62 Leila Lee Templeton lives at Myra, Texas, Rt. 1. She taught school before she married, 2/2/1924, Carl Gimpel.

14db63 Leona Marie Templeton, living at Mineral Springs, Ark., married, 7/13/1923, Edith Parsons and has twin daughters:
14db631 Laurice Parsons, 10/4/1925.
14db632 Maurice Parsons, 10/4/1925.

14dg Margaret E. Templeton married Alf McCoy who died April 12, 1919, and was buried at Hopewell Cemetery, Laurens County, S. C. They had two children:
14dg1 John McCoy.
14dg2 Tommie McCoy, who married Ida Deason.

14dh Thomas E. Templeton was buried at Kinard Cemetery, Greenwood County, S. C. He married, first, 14L3 Mattie Hopkins, is first cousin. Their children were:

    14dh1 Joseph Calvin Templeton, 7/.../1876-8/18/1933.
    14dh2 Mamie Templeton (deceased)
    14dh3 Beulah Templeton.
    14dh4 Floyd Templeton.
    14dh5 Thomas Templeton.

14dh1 Joseph Calvin Templeton was buried at Kinard Cemetery, Greenwood County, S. C. He married Lula Connelly, 1876-12/10/1952. Their children are:

    14dh11 Earl Templeton, who married Weeber Timmerman and lives at Ninety Six, S. C., Rt. 2, where they have one daughter.
    14dh111 Guilda Templeton.
    14dh12 Madge Templeton, who married Harold Miller and lives at Ninety Six, S. C., where they have one daughter:
    14dh121 Iris Miller.

14dh2 Mamie Templeton married, first, John Connally (deceased) and second, Bud White (deceased). For many years before her death she was the beloved matron of the Goldville (now Joanna) S. C., Boarding House.

14dh3 Beulah Templeton was born Dec. 25, 1883. She married Joseph Addison who died March 15, 1934, and was buried at Ninety Six, S. C. For about 10 years they lived at Bowling Green, Fla., where he was engaged in the trucking business. Their children are:

    14dh31 Mary Emma Addison, who married T. B. Sherrell.
    14dh32 John Arthur Addison of Bowling Green, Fla.
    14dh33 James Templeton Addison, who attended Presbyterian College, Clinton, S. C.
    14dh34 Thomas Eldred Addison of Joanna, S. C.

14dh4 Floyd Templeton was born Jan. 8, 1887. He married Mary T. Jester, who was born Dec. 2, 1888. They live at Ninety Six, S. C., and have one son:

    14dh41 Wyatt Templeton, b. 6/6/1917.

14dh5 Joseph Thomas Templeton died March, 1917. His widow, Elizabeth Acker Templeton, lives at North Anderson, S. C. They have one son:

    14dh51 Joseph Thomas Templeton, Jr., b. March, 1917.

14dh Thomas E. Templeton married, second, Annie Rampey. They have one daughter:

    14dh5 Eliza ("Ez") Templeton, who married Dr. A. L. King and they live at 889 Williams Mill Road, Atlanta, Ga.

14di Robert Templeton was buried at Hopewell Cemetery, Laurens County, S. C. He married, first, Pauline Monroe. Their children are:
    14di1 Cora Templeton.
    14di2 Mattie L. Templeton, 6/1887-4/1889.

14di1 Cora Templeton married Coke Butler, who died Sept., 1932. She lives at Greenwood, S. C., with their children:
    14di11 Joseph Arnold Butler.
    14di12 James Gordon Butler.
    14di13 C. M. Butler, Jr.
    14di14 Allen Stewart Butler.
    14di15 Charles Herbert Butler.

14di Robert Templeton married, second, Mrs. Sallie Oxner Johnson. Their children are:
    14di3 Coy Templeton, b. 8/9/1904.
    14di4 Margaret Templeton, b. 3/28/1906.

14dj Ann Templeton married, first, Pomp Floyd. She married, second, Jim Martin, April 17, 1828-Feb. 7, 1877. She married, third, Lewis McCoy (brother of Alf. McCoy, who married 14dg Margaret E. Templeton.)

14dL Amelia Templeton married John Puckett. They are both buried at Hopewell Cemetery, Laurens County, S. C. Their children are:
    14dL1 Clarence Belle Puckett, b. 7/28/1876.
    14dL2 Applin Wells Puckett, b. 8/29/1878.
    14dL3 Mack Will H. Puckett, who married Ida Conn and who lives at Hazel, Okla.

14dL1 Clarence Belle Puckett married Jimmie Hazel, born Jan. 12, 1876, died Nov. 8, 1934, buried at Warrior Creek Church, Laurens County, S. C. She lives at Laurens, S. C., Rt. 1 with their children:
    14dL1a Ola Mae Hazel 6/25/1897-3/23/1914.
    14dL1b Mattie Alma Hazel, b. 5/5/1902.
    14dL1c Hugh Lawrence Hazel, 3/18/1905-12/11/1906.
    14dL1d Mary Ruth Hazel, 12/10/1906-11/1/1908.
    14dL1e Thelma Nora Hazel, b. 3/7/1909.
    14dL1f Roy Eugene Hazel, b. 8/2/1910.
    14dL1g Ora Lillian Hazel, b. 5/5/1912.
    14dL1h Lu Dee Alvin Hazel, b. 3/12/1915.
    14dL1i James Walter Hazel, b. 5/17/1917.
    14dL1j Homer William Hazel, b. 7/14/1921.

14dL1b Mattie Alma Hazel married, December, 1916, Roy Summeral. They live at Laurens, S. C., Rt. 1, and have the following children:

14dLlb1 Ruth Summeral.
14dLlb2 Hugh Summeral.
14dLlb3 Laura Bell Summeral.
14dLlb4 Robert Summeral .
14dLlb5 J. L. Summeral.
14dLlb6 Haskel Summeral.
14dLlb7 Bert Summeral.

14dLle Thelma Nora Hazel married, Feb. 2, 1929, Marvin Lindley. They live at Laurens, S. C., Rt. 1, and have two children:
    14dLle1 Nell Lindley.
    14dLle2 Patricia Lindley.

14dLlf Roy Eugene Hazel lives at Laurens, S. C., Rt. 1. He married, 1/12/1935, Gladys Jones, b. 5/23/1912.

14dLlg Ora Lillian Hazel married, 8/18/1928, Arthur Knight. They live at Fountain Inn, S. C., Rt. 2, and have three children:
    14dLlg1 Harold Knight.
    14dLlg2 Horace Knight.
    14dLlg3 Dart Knight.

14dLlh Lu Dee Alvin Hazel lives at Laurens, S. C., Rt. 1. He married, 2/26/1935, Sarah Jones, b. 4/22/1917.

14dL2 Applin Wells Puckett lives at Silverstreet, S. C. He married, first, Mattie Horn. Their children are:
    14dL21 Viola Puckett.
    14dL22 Frances Puckett.
    14dL23 Orie Puckett.
    14dL24 Rufus Puckett.

14dL2 Applin Wells Puckett married, second, Gladys Hogg.

14g Benjamin Clark Templeton, seventh child of 14 Robert and Mary Templeton, was born near Duncan's Creek, north of Clinton, in Laurens County, S. C. He was three months old when his grandfather, 1 David Templeton, Sr., died and nearly 20 years old when his father was killed by a runaway slave. He was buried at Rehobeth Cemetery. On Nov. 15, 1838, he married Mary Ann Goodwin, 12/18/1814-9/30/1882, daughter of Hiram Goodwin and Hanna Gore Goodwin. She was buried beside her husband on the same lot with his father, 14 Robert Templeton, and mother, Mary Puckett Templeton. Their children were:
    14g1 Marjorie Templeton, 9/6/1839-6/26/1925.
    14g2 Laura Ann Frances Templeton, 10/19/1841-10/25/1928.
    14g3 Benjamin Preston Templeton, 2/2/1845-12/14/1935.
    14g4 Isabella A. Templeton, 12/27/1847-3/21/1889.

14g5 Giles Goodwin Templeton, 10/24/1849-11/24/1927.
14g6 Leumas Bascom Templeton, Sr., 7/26/1856-10/6/1930.
14g7 Mary Ellie Templeton, 3/14/1857-2/6/1943.

Prior to 1857, 14g Benjamin Clark Templeton was living at the "Watty Prather Place" between the old Dr. Durrah home and Duncan's Creek. About 1857, he moved to the "Peggy Templeton" (widow of 114 James Templeton) place near Bethany Church. From there he moved to the "Billy Philson" farm, as overseer, near the old Boyce brick house, where he was living when he volunteered and entered the Confederate Army, April 1, 1864. After the close of the war he returned to his family on the Philson farm which he rented and hired ex-slave Negroes to do the farm work. In 1867 he moved to the Flat Shoals, owned by the widow of Robin Pitts, where he operated the grist mill, saw mill, etc. From there he moved to the Pitts farm near Langston church. A few years later he moved from there back to the Flat Shoals where he lived until his death in 1872.

In "South Carolina Troops in Confederate Service, Volume II, Page 540, by A. S. Salley, Secretary, South Carolina Historical Commission, The State Company, 1930," we find the following record of his military services in the Confederate Army: "Third Regiment, South Carolina Volunteers, Company I—Privates— B. C. Templeton enlisted by Colonel Preston, April 1, 1864; report on muster roll of Dec. 17, 1864, as having returned to Company Nov. 28, 1864, paroled at Greensboro, May 2, 1865." He was wounded at the battle of Cold Harbor (June 6?), 1864. In a letter to his daughter, 14g2 L. A. Frances T. Cunningham, written from the Ladies' Hospital, Columbia, S. C., and dated September 1, 1864, he says "—My wound is doing very well at present." In another letter written at "camp near Smithfield, N. C., March 23, 1865," he says: "I never have been so anxious to hear from you and the children in my life. — I have been nearly broken down several times since I came to this state—on the 16th we engaged the enemy near Averysboro and fought them all day worsting them badly. We retreated that night 15 or 20 miles, engaged them on the 19th, repulsed them again. On the 21st we engaged them again and repulsed them again and retreated to this place. I cannot tell when or where the next fight will take place. I feel like I have been favored for which I am truly thankful to the God of battles. We lost several men, three from Company I wounded, none killed. Thomas Duckett is missing. I cannot tell whether he was killed or captured. He went in the fight on the 19th and fell back with us some 200 yards from the battle line. He has not been seen or heard from since by any of our men. Whether he was killed or captured I cannot say." (Thomas Duckett was in command of the company, and, after his disappear-

49

ance 14g B. C. Templeton acted in ·his place.)

14g B. C. Templeton had fair skin, black hair and blue eyes. He was erect, had a typical military stride and commanded the profoundest respect of those around him. Late in life he was stricken with measles. · He had almost recovered and was in the field when a shower of rain came up. In ·his eagerness to reach shelter before he got wet he ran quite a distance, got over-heated and in addition, got drenched in the shower. This brought on a relapse of measles from which, it seems, he never fully recovered.

14g1 Marjorie Templeton was buried at Yarborough's Chapel, Cross Anchor, S. C., beside her husband, Calvin C. Davis, Oct. 5, 1841-Feb. 29, 1926, whom she married July 4, 1864. Her husband, Calvin C. Davis, was a Confederate veteran. He ,was a shoe maker and farmer later in life. Their children were:

    14g11 Kate Davis, 6/19/1865-4/20/1899.
    14g12 Joe Hill Davis, 10/18/1868-11/22/1890.
    14g13 Mamie Davis, 9/5/1872-7/1896, married Dec., 1895, Walter Davis.
    14g14 Florrah Davis, b. 8/6/1875.
    14g15 Pearl Davis, 8/5/1877-1/15/1934.
    14g16 Giles Jerome Davis, 6/3/1881-7/21/1881.
    14g17 Ione Davis, b. 7/5/1883.

14g11 Kate Davis was buried at Shilo Church, Cross Keys, S. C. She married Dec. 28, 1882, Robert Watkins. Their children are:

    14g111 Raymond Watkins, b. 6/24/1885.
    14g112 Irene Watkins, b. 12/1/1887.
    14g113 Christine Watkins, 8/30/1892-12/16/1930.
    14g114 Mamie Watkins, b. 8/7/1895.
    14g115 Kate Watkins, b. 4/2/1899.

14g111 Raymond Watkins is a farmer, living at Watts Mill, S. C. He married June 17, 1906,. Mattie Blakely. Their children are:

    14g1111 Ruth Watkins (twin), b. 2/9/1908, who married Lawrence Stewart.
    14g1112 Russie Watkins (twin). b. 2/9/1908.
    14g1113 Albert Watkins, b. 10/2/1910.
    14g1114 Domer Watkins, b. 4/22/1913.
    14g1115 Frances Watkins, b. 12/16/1916. She m. _____ Powers.
    14g1116 Robert Watkins, b. 9/16/1918.

14g1112 Russie Watkins married James Riddle. They have one child:

14g11121 Syble Riddle.

14g112 Irene Watkins married Sam Harrison Allen, prominent in business and fraternal circles. They live at Henderson, N. C.

14g113 Christine Watkins was buried at Bethel Cemetery, Woodruff, S. C. She married Marshall E. Riddle. Their child is:
14g1131 Roy Riddle, b. 1/2/1915.

14g114 Mamie Watkins married, first, Patton Bishop, deceased. She married, second, Rev. Charles Robinson, Baptist minister, deceased. She lives at 1014 S. Tryon St., Charlotte, N. C. Their children are:
14g1141 Roy Mugee Robinson (twin), b. 3/2/1921.
14g1142 Mamie Ruth Robinson (twin), b. 3/2/1921.
14g1143 Mary Robinson, b. 1/2/1923.
14g1144 Elizabeth Eugenia Robinson, b. 9/16/1926, who lives at 1014 S. Tryon St., Charlotte, N. C.

14g115 Kate Watkins married, Oct. 18, 1919, James Meadors. They live at 25 Jackson St., Clinton, S. C. Their children are:
14g1151 James Meadors, Jr., b. 11/20/1920.
14g1152 Ellen V. Meadors, b. 9/15/1923.
14g1153 M. Earline Meadors, b. 11/18/1925.
14g1154 Charles Ray Meadors, b. 6/25/1929.

14g14 Florrah Davis married June 5, 1895, Tom Woodruff. They live at Clinton, S. C. Their children are:
14g141 Orion Woodruff, b. 2/18/1897, who married 12/26/1921, Eva Parris.
14g142 Earl Woodruff, b. 9/13/1899.
14g143 Homer Woodruff, b. 6/16/1902, who married 6/28/1930, Kathryn Mize, b. 12/25/1910.
14g144 Marjorie Woodruff, b. 11/18/1904, married 12/19/1936, T. Earle Rice, and lives at 1002 Pendleton St., Greenville, S. C.
14g145 Crystal Woodruff, b 8/30/1908, married 8/19/1935, L. W. Rawl.
14g146 Pansy Woodruff, b. 8/17/1910.
14g147 Vivian Woodruff, b. 3/17/1914, married 10/1/1937, Russell Mize.
14g148 Ruby Woodruff, b. 9/21/1916, who married 22b318 James Bailey Arnold. They live at 34 Hill St., Greer, S. C.

14g15 Pearl Davis was buried at Clinton, S. C. She married Nov. 13, 1909, D. Marion Holman who died in 1927. Their son is:
14g151 Hugh Holman, b. 2/24/1914, at Cross Anchor, S. C. He is a graduate of Presbyterian College, Clinton, S. C. He was dean of this college for several years. He is author of several mystery stories, including "Trout in the

Milk," etc. He now teaches English in the University of North Carolina. He m. Verna McCloud. They have two children.

14g17 Ione Davis m. 6/16/1901, John J. Clark, b. 10/30/1880, who was prominent in textile work. For 30 years or more he was connected with the mill at Joanna, where he was overseer of weaving. He served two years as president of the Templeton Clan. They live at Clinton, S. C. They have six children;

    14g171   Ella Clark, b. 6/26/1902.
    14g172   Ruth Clark, b. 9/26/1904.
    14g173   Llewellyn Clark, b. 10/21/1906.
    14g174   Rolfe Clark, b. 6/..../1910.
    14g175   Sara Clark, b. 4/6/1917.
    14g176   Dorothy Clark, b. 7/6/1919.

14g171 Ella Clark m. Dock Buchanan (brother of Julia Buchanan who m. 25512 Oliver M. Templeton). He has been prominent in textile manufacturing at Joanna, S. C. They have four children:

    14g1711   Kenneth Buchanan
    14g1712   Douglass Buchanan, deceased.
    14g1713   John Clark Buchanan.
    14g1714   Linda Ruth Buchanan, b. 1/31/1939.

14g172 Ruth Clark m. 7/1/1930, P. B. Mitchell who is superintendent of Joanna Mill, Joanna, S. C. Their country home is the old Dorroh Estate near Bethany Church, and which they have restored to its original appearance, making it a most attractive place.

14g173 Llewellyn Clark m. 2/..../1926, Grace Darnell. They live at Joanna.

14g174 Rolfe Clark m., 7/1/1933, 14g418 Nonnie Belle Puckett. They live at Joanna, S. C. They have one son:
    14g1741   James Elliott Clark, b. 6/27/1934.

14g175 Sara Clark m. Walter Byars. They live at Joanna, S. C., where he is purchasing agent for Joanna Mills. They have two children:
    14g1751   Eugenia Clark Byars, b. 6/10/1943.
    14g1752   Virginia Jone Byars, b. 10/25/1947.

14g176 Dorothy Clark was graduated from Winthrop College and taught in the pubic schools of South Carolina for several years. Later she took special training in orthopedics and is now connected with the Orthopedic Hospital in Sacramento, Cal.

14g2 Laura Ann Frances Templeton was buried at Bethany Presbyterian Church, near Clinton, S. C. In 1860 she m. John Stewart Cunningham who died Nov. 13, 1860, and was buried at the Cunningham family cemetery between Rocky Springs Church and Duncan's Creek. They had one daughter:
14g21 Jonnie Cunningham, 1/2/1861-10/6/1940.

During the Civil War 14g2 Frances T. Cunningham helped nurse Confederate soldiers at the Ladies' Hospital, on the University grounds, in Columbia, S. C. After the war, she, along with the other women, gave assistance in every way possible to the Ku Klux Klan by making uniforms, etc. On one occasion, when members of this organization were being hunted down by Federal authorities, she hid some KKK uniforms in her work basket, pretending that she was going to some of the kinfolks to spin. In this way she managed to smuggle the uniforms to the meeting place of the klan.

In June, 1876, four years after the death of her father, she and her daughter, 14g21, Jonnie Cunningham, then 15 years old, made their home with her widowed mother who was then living at what is known as the Hollis place (also known as the Cunningham Place) in Union County, S. C. After her mother's death in 1882, she lived, part of the time, among her kin folks, serving as practical nurse and foster mother for her nieces and nephews. In the 1890's she went to Prof. A. G. Rembert's at Wofford College, as a practical nurse. There she so endeared herself to the family that she continued to make her home with them until the death of Mrs. Rembert. Some time after this she fell on the street and broke her hip. On account of her old age no one expected her to recover. Nevertheless she did, and became active again. A year or two later she fell and broke her other hip. She never recovered from this injury. She lingered for nearly two years, at the Cleveland Old Ladies' Home in Spatanburg, where she was making her home and where she died. She was an affectionate mother, foster mother and a devoted member of the Seventh Day Adventist Church.

14g21 Jonnie Cunningham was born Jan. 2, 1861, died Oct. 6, 1940. In 1878 she boarded with her Uncle Calvin C. Davis at Wellford, S. C., and attended the high school (or academy) under Prof. W. F. Morrison. In 1880 she took the teachers' examination and began a long teaching career of 46 years. Her first school was for three months in the spring of 1880 at what was known as Cedar Grove School on Mrs. Ray's place in what is known as Wild Cat in Union County, S. C. Her salary here was $20.00 per month which she could not collect until December. She then returned, 1880-1881, to Wellford Academy and taught the younger children in order to pay for her tuition and board. She returned to Cedar Grove School in the spring of 1883, where she taught another term of three months at $20.00 per month and again had to wait until the next winter for her pay. In 1884 she taught a third term of three months at Cedar Grove at the same salary. Her next school was at Yarborough's Chapel in Spartanburg County, a subscription term of 1½-2 months. Here she received $30.00 per month. In 1885, 1886, and 1887 she taught again at Cedar Grove, this time at $25.00 per month. She then taught two months at Rock Hill School, near Dan Yarborough's, in Spartanburg County. Next, she boarded at Murph Hill's, Cross Anchor, and taught a six-weeks' subscription school in a little house down in the field. Then she and her mother rented the old Pitts house and she taught at Langston's Church in Laurens County. Murph Hill sent his three children, Addie, Claude and Raymond, to Board with them and go to school to her. Matt Poole also sent his little girl to board with them and go to schol. The salary here was $30.00 per mnth. In 1888, she returned to the Rock Hill School where she taught 3 or 4 months. In 1889, she boarded with Mr. Cunningham and taught near Spartanburg, S. C. While teaching here she was taken ill. So serious was her illness that one old lady came to see her and asked her where wished to be buried.

In 1890, 1891, and 1892, she taught 33 months at Enoree, S. C., where she was paid $25.00 per month by the president of the mill. In 1893, 1894, 1895, she taught near Spartanburg at Cross Roads or Foster's. In 1895-96 she taught at Walnut Grove in Spartanburg County. In 1896-97 and 1897-98 she taught at Hebron in Spartanburg County. In 1898-99, 1899-1900 she taught at Todd School, near Woodruff, S. C.

In 1901, 1902, 1903, she taught at Trinity School in Spartanburg County. In 1903-04 she taught five months near Mt. Zion in Spartanburg County where her salary was $35.00 for the first time in her life. In the summer of 1905 she taught two months at Belmont School near Cross Anchor. In 1904-05, 1905-06, 1906-07, she taught at Center Point, near Spartanburg. In 1906 she also taught six or eight weeks in Oconee County. In the summer of 1907 she boarded at Tom Watsons and taught near Enoree. In the fall of 1907 she began teaching at Drayton Mill where she taught for five years.

In 1914-15, she taught at Green Point in Spartanburg County. From 1915 until 1919, she taught in Hampton County, S. C. In 1919-20 and 1920-21, she taught at Cross Anchor. From 1921 until 1924 she taught at Crescent, near Woodruff. In 1924-25 she taught at Arrowwood in Spartanburg County. Her last teaching was at Snow School, near Woodruff, in 1925-26.

She then went to make her home with, and to take care of her mother at the Cleveland Old Ladies' Home in Spartanburg. After her mother's death, she lived on South Converse Street, where she died.

14g21 Jonnie Cunningham was a devoted teacher, loyal friend, and a consecrated member of the Seventh Day Adventist Church.

14g3 Benjamin Preston Templeton was born in Laurens County, S. C. The War Between the States was only a few months old when, in the fall of 1861, 14g3 Benjamin P. Templeton, only 16 years of age, volunteered at Parks Old Field, in Laurens County. Colonel George Moseley, commander of the regiment, told him he was too young and too small, and told him to go back home with his daddy. He did so, but not for long. Within a few months he was back again. In January or February, 1862, he volunteered in Company F, 14th S. C. V., and was mustered in. His youthful vigor and zeal are shown by a letter from 1143 G. M. Templeton, dated March 29, 1862, "—Ben (14g3) is doing finely but is pretty hard to keep down but I think I can manage him. He thinks it is just a frolic, but I think he will come in after a while. I could not get him in my mess because it is full but he is in a good mess with H. Goodwin and others." In less than three months he had had a real taste of war in the Battle of Seven Pines. On June 4, 1862, he wrote, "We have been on the march for two weeks. The roads in many places nearly knee deep, had the creeks and rivers to wade and no shelter of the rainy nights. We just struck camp on the first of this month. It rained yesterday, last night and today it has been heavy and is still cloudy and will rain tonight. We have tolerable shelters made of our blankets and oil cloths.—Our great battle has been partly fought. They fought yesterday Monday took up the dead and wounded. Last Sunday and Saturday the fight raged with great fury. Yesterday which was Tuesday they had the last of it I hope. The enemy were badly beaten. We took 40 cannon and three long lines of entrenchments. Our loss was 3000 and the enemy's 17000. Some say it is not ended yet.—I got over the mumps without them hurting me. My hat and shoes are lasting fine. Tell ma to send me a jacket by Hiram if she has it made but not to put herself to any trouble."

He was wounded in the thigh at the Battle of Chancellorsville, May, 1863. After being wounded he was out of service 90 days, 60 of which were spent at home. John Gore told about 14g3 Benjamin Templeton, in the heat of battle, firing until the smoke filled his eyes so that he could not see for some time.

At the close of the war he returned home where he soon began to see the horrors of the Reconstruction. It is said that his activities in the Ku Klux Klan and the bitter fight on this organization by Federal authorities contributed, to some degree, to his decision to go West. In 1867 he went to Texas where he lived the remainder of his life as a ginner and farmer. According the the best information available, he was the last surviving member of Co. F, 14th Regiment, S. C. V.

His philosophy seems to be the best shown in a letter written by him Feb. 11, 1928, at the age of 83. He said, "—I worked hard as long as I was strong and able to work. I have lived hard, harder than any man, white or black, that ever rented land from me, to save the money I made. The only extravagance I ever indulged in was taking a few drinks of good liquor whenever I wanted it, and chewing tobacco.—I have always hated vanity, make believe, hypocrisy, and rascality. I always wanted to be myself. Whenever I caught myself imitating someone else I put the brakes down hard and pulled back the reverse lever as far as it would go."

On Sept. 13, 1871, he married Addie Harris of Bastrop Co., Texas, who died August, 1907. Both are buried at Hainey's Chapel, in Travis County, Texas. They had six children, four of whom are still living. The children are:

14g31 Emma Harris Templeton, b. 10/4/1872.
14g32 Lee Brooks Templeton, b. 3/6/1874.
14g33 Edward Giles Templeton, b. 3/13/1876, who married, 1/31/1916, Eula Sparks, and who lives at Trinity, Texas.
14g34 Marjorie Claiborn Templeton, b. 10/31/1880, who lives at Delvalle, Texas.
14g35 Ben Preston Templeton, 10/17/1877-10/18/1918, who was a U. S. soldier in World War I and died in England. His body was returned to the U. S. and was buried at Hainey's Chapel, Garfield, Texas.
14g36 David Turner Templeton, born Jan. 16, 1884, and died the next day.

14g31 Emma Harris Templeton married, Aug. 17, 1895, R. S. Young, who was born May 16, 1867, and died February, 1916, and was buried at Oliver Cemetery, Cedar Valley, Texas. She continues to live at the home place, 1021 W. 30th St., Austin, Texas. Their children are:

14g311 Agnes Young, b. 6/24/1896.
14g312 Addie Marie Young, b. 12/24/1897, who for a good many years was in the U. S. Department of State.
14g313 John Preston Young, b. 2/28/1899.
14g314 Wilson Young, b. 10/3/1906 (twin), who married 10/5/1928, Lila Hammock.
14g315 Burrelson Young, b. 10/3/1906, (twin).
14g316 Mary Lynn Young, b. 6/22/1913.

14g313 John Preston Young married, 9/15/1921, Myrtle Lee Rodes. They have one child:
14g3131 John Preston Young, Jr., b. 1/1/1927.

14g32   Lee Brooks Templeton married, Nov. 11, 1908, Susie
Starks.   They live at Delvalle, Travis County, Texas.   Their
children are:
    14g321   Lee Brooks (girl) Templeton, b. 10/17/1909.
    14g322   Tom Jones Templeton, b. 4/8/1911.
    14g323   LaRue Essie Templeton, b. 7/8/1913 (twin).
    14g324   Lucile Mary Templeton, b. 7/8/1913 (twin).
    14g325   Ben Preston Templeton, b. 12/22/1919.

14g4   Isabella A. Templeton was buried at New Hope Cemetery, Cross Anchor, S. C.   She married, Dec. 5, 1875, James Crook,
who is buried beside his wife.   Their children are:
    14g41   Narcissa ("Nonnie") Crook, b. 10/14/1876.
    14g42   Emily Crook, b. 9/5/1878.
    14g43   Ethel Crook, b. 11/7/1880.
    14g44   W. Ben Crook, 3/25/1883-2/9/1903.
    14g45   James Ed Crook, 10/23/1885-4/3/1939.

14g1   Narcissa Crook m. William Puckett, who was engaged
practically all of his life, until his death in 1946, in textile work.
For a great many years they lived at Whitmire, S. C., where he
was a magistrate and mayor of the town.   She now lives at
Greer, S. C.   They had eight children:
    14g411   Lillie Belle Puckett, 8/8/1893-4/6/19111.
    14g412   Clara Puckett, 1/18/1896-1/29/1896.
    14g413   Jessie Puckett, 4/14/1897.
    14g414   Ruth Puckett, 2/26/1900-12/16/1924.
    14g415   Carey Puckett, 2/24/1904- / /1943.
    14g416   Yancey Puckett, 9/27/1907.
    14g417   Leumas Puckett, 10/8/1910, who lives at Greer,
    S. C.
    14g418   Nonnie Belle Puckett, 1/25/1914.

14g411   Lillie Belle Puckett m. 12/9/1909, Bascom Ramsey.
She died from burns when her clothing caught on fire.   They had
one son:
    14g4111   W. Clyde Ramsey, 2/27/1911.   He m. Tessie
    Gaffney.   They live at Whitmire, S. C.   They have two
    children:
        14g41111 Iris Nellene Ramsey, 6/.../1930.
        14g41112 Charles William Ramsey, 4/30/1932.

14g413   Jessie Puckett m. 6/28/1920 Julius McKain, 12/21/1901.
They live at Greer, S. C., where he is superintendent of the Victor Mill.   They have three children:
    14g4131   Mary McKain, 5/26/1921.
    14g4132   James McKain, 11/13/1923.
    14g4133   Wilson McKain, 8/3/1925.

14g4131 Mary McKain m. Roy Livingston. They live at Taylors, S. C. They have one son:
  14g41311 Darrell Livingston, 2/11/1951.

14g4132 James McKain m. Margie Thompson. They live at Victor Mill, Greer, S. C. They have three children:
  14g41321 Michael McKain.
  14g41322 Patricia McKain.
  14g41323 Carolyn McKain.

14g4133 Wilson McKain m. Billie Margaret Few.

14g414 Ruth Puckett m. 5/18/1918, Averil Cooper of Union, S. C. She was buried at Rosemont Cemetery, Union, S. C. They had one son:
  14g4141 Billy Cooper, 6/13/1919.

14g415 Carey Puckett m. 7/17/1928 Annie Kirby. He was buried at Rosemont Cemetery, Union, S. C. They had one child:

14g4151 Joycelyn Puckett, 12/8/1929, who m. Heyward Jaco and lives at 5800 Farrow Road, Columbia, S. C. They have one child:
  14g41511 Anne Jaco, 6/15/1947.

14g416 Yancey Puckett m. 2/ .../1930 Thelma Smith. They live at Whitmire, S. C. They have one daughter:
  14g4161 Marlene Puckett, 1/18/1934.

14g418 Nonnie Belle Puckett m. 7/1/1933, 14g174 Rolfe Clark. They live at Joanna, S. C. (See his line for descendents).

14g42 Emily Crook lives at Greer, S. C. She has one son:
  14g421 Cullen Crook, 12/25/1910. He is a graduate of Wofford College, Spartanburg, S. C., and also of the Southern Baptist Theological Seminary, Louisville Ky. He lives at Greer, S. C., where he is pastor of Pleasant Grove Baptist Church. He m. Merle Brakefield. They have two sons:
    14g4211 Edward Crook, 1/28/1932.
    14g4212 Le Grand Crook, 4/18/1934.

14g43 Ethel Crook m. 1/10/1906, William Boyd Prather, 10/20/ 1883-11/2/1947. He was a farmer and lived at Cross Anchor, S. C., where she still lives except in the winter time when she lives at Charlotte, N. C. They had nine children:
  14g431 Eugene Prather, 1/11/1907, who is married and lives at Atlantic Beach, Fla.
  14g432 Earl Prather, 7/22/1908.
  14g433 Jim Boyd Prather, 9/10/1910.

14g434 Colie Prather, 7/6/1912.
14g435 Charlie Prather, 7/4/1915.
14g436 Rachel Prather, 5/12/1920.
14g437 Dora Prather, 6/18/1922.
14g438 William Horace Prather, 1/15/1925-3/24/1925.
14g439 Ethel Prather, 2/15/1927.

14g432 Earl Prather is a veteran of World War II. He m. 11/1/1944 Dorothy Smith of Union, S. C. They live at Greenwood, S. C.

14g33 Jim Boyd Prather is married and lives at 2212 Chesterfield Ave., Charlotte, N. C., where he is a uniforms salesman.

14g434 Colie Prather is a veteran of World War II, having a Surgeon's Certificate of Disability discharge. He m. Frances Cooper and lives at Myrtle Beach, S. C., where he operates a service station.

14g435 Charlie Prather m. Elizabeth Sprouse of Union, S. C. They live at Belmont, N. C., where he works at the Hatch Hosiery Mill. They have four children:
    14g4351 Charles Prather, 1/10/1941.
    14g4352 Kenneth Prather, 4/28/1943.
    14g4353 Rebecca Elizabeth Prather, 9/2/1946.
    14g4354 Patty Jane Prather, 7/28/1952.

14g436 Rachel Prather m. Bradford McCuen. They live at Arnold Drive, Charlotte, N. C. They have one child:
    14g4361 Leslie Prather McCuen, 10/5/1951.

14g437 Dora Prather m. Grover Lanford of Woodruff, S. C., where they live. They have one child:
    14g4371 Nancy Jean Lanford, 10/23/1950.

14g439 Ethel Prather m. ..../..../1950, Edwin Lanford of Woodruff, S. C., where he is an undertaker. They have two children:
    14g4391 Robert Edwin Lanford, 7/6/1948.
    14g4392 Stephen Lanford, 4/..../1950.

14g44 W. Ben Crook m. 7/..../1900, Minnie Brewington. He was buried at Rosemont Cemetery, Union, S. C. She lives at Spartanburg, S. C. They had one child:
    14g441 Bennie Celestine Crook, b. 6/16/1901. She was graduated from Union High School, Union, S. C., in 1920. She m. 2/21/1923, Chester LeRoy Langley. He is a jeweler who has been in business in Union, S. C., Kingstree, S. C., and Farmville, N. C. They have one son:
        14g4411 Chester LeRoy Langley, Jr., b. 4/19/1928. He was graduated in 1950 from East Carolina College,

Greenville, N. C., with a B. S. degree. On Jan. 4, 1950, he entered the military service and took his basic training at Camp Breckenridge, Ky. He took special training in O. C. S. at Army General School at Fort Riley, Kans., where he received his commission as a Second Lieutenant, Ordnance Corps, in 1952. He had further special training in fire control at Aberdeen Proving Ground and sailed for service in the Far East, December, 1952.

14g45 James Ed Crook m. 3/5/1905 Alma Dunaway, 3/18/1890, of Cross Anchor, S. C., where they lived most of his life. They had nine children:

    14g451 Mattie Belle Crook, 1/6/1906.
    14g452 Catharine Crook, 1/26/1908.
    14g453 Hallie Crook, 5/18/1910. She m. first, 1/6/1929, Argus Hadock and, second, Russell Howard.
    14g454 C. B. Crook, 4/25/1912, a veteran of World War II.
    14g455 Edith Crook, 8/30/1914.
    14g456 Ben Crook, 11/19/1916, a veteran of World War II who was wounded overseas. He m. Rebecca Lawson, daughter of Mansel Lawson.
    14g457 Jim Crook, 6/13/1918-2/24/1927.
    14g458 Virginia Crook, 12/19/21.
    14g459 Edna Frances Crook, b. 8/19/1924, who m. Hugh Willard, 12/19/21.

14g451 Mattie Belle Crook m. 12/29/1920, Anthony Brown of Piedmont, S. C., where they live. They have four children:

    14g4511 Leon Brown, 12/1/1921.
    14g4512 Vivian Brown, 9/29/1923.
    14g4513 Charlie Brown, 2/23/1927.
    14g4514 William Edwin Brown, 10/4/1929.

14g452 Catherine Crook m. 5/9/1926, Victor Bishop of Sedalia, S. C., now deceased. They had two children:

    14g4521 Harold Davis Bishop, 3/13/1927.
    14g4522 Bobby Joe Bishop, 10/19/1934.

14g455 Edith Crook m. Jim Hughes of Enoree, S. C. They have nine children:

    14g4551 Hazel Hughes.
    14g4552 Johnnie Hughes.
    14g4553 Barbara Hughes.
    14g4554 Edith Mary Hughes, (twin).
    14g4555 James Carey Hughes (twin).
    14g4556 Carolyn Hughes.
    14g4557 Gerald Hughes.

14g4558 Brenda Hughes (twin).
14g4559 Linda Hughes (twin).

14g458 Virginia Crook m. Ernest Ivey. They live at Cross Anchor, S. C. They have one child:
14g4581 Carol Marie Ivey, 6/24/1945.

14g5 Giles Goodwin Templeton was buried beside his wife at
the Church of the Advent, Episcopal Cemetery, Spartanburg, S. C.
While he was a young man he began work with the Southern Railway. He served that company for more than twenty years as an
engineer. Most of his life was spent as a locomotive engineer,
his last services being with the Charleston and Western Carolina
Railway. He lived at Glenn Springs, S. C., and in later years, in
Spartanburg, S. C., where he died.

He was a handsome man, loved by all the women and admired
by all the men. He was good natured, jolly and lively and every
one seemed to enjoy his company. He was not quick tempered,
but if he did get mad he did not get over it the next minute. His
generous disposition was displayed once when he was an engineer on the Glenn Springs train which operated only from Glenn
Springs to Spartanburg, S. C. One of the passengers had his hat
to blow off while looking out of the window. Mr. Templeton hap-
pened to see it, and stopped the train so the man could get his
hat, commenting that the poor fellow might, like himself, have
only one hat. He was generally considered as the best engineer
on the road.

He married Mrs. Mamie Spriggs Elford. Their two sons were:
14g51 LeRoy Spriggs Templeton, 6/29/1884-5/28/1938.
14g52 Giles G. Templeton, 1/1/1888.

14g51 LeRoy Spriggs Templeton attended Wofford College and
was for many years, director of the Spartanburg Y. M. C. A. He
was always intensely interested in art and music. His whole
soul seemed to be wrapped up in the annual music festival held
at Converse College and he enjoyed a personal acquaintance
with many of the opera personnel. He was buried beside his
parents.

14g52 Giles G. Templeton married Sallie Elliott. They live on
Glendale Road, Spartanburg, S. C., where he is a plumbing contractor. They have one adopted son.

14g6 Leumas Bascom Templeton, Sr., was born July 26, 1854,
near Clinton, S. C., between the "Yellow House" (Bird Place),
and Duncan's Creek. He died October 6. 1930, and was buried at
New Hope Cemetery, Cross Anchor, S. C. He grew up in the
section of Laurens County, S. C., where he was born. When his
father died in 1872 he moved, with his invalid mother, to the vi-

cinity of Cross Anchor, S. C., in which community he lived the
remainder of his life. On Dec. 17, 1876, he married Lucy Ann
Bobo, May 5, 1851-April 4, 1891, daughter of William and Mariah
Ray Bobo, who was buried at Padgett's Creek Cemetery in Union
County, S. C. Their children were:

14g61 Mittie Gertrude Templeton, 11/11/1877-7/24/1917.
14g62 Lillie Geneva Templeton, b. Aug. 28, 1879.
14g63 William Benjamin Templeton, b. May 15, 1881.
14g64 Walter Oliver Templeton, 3/19/1883-3/18/1951.
14g65 Grover Cleveland Templeton, b. Sept. 28, 1884.
14g66 Giles Breckenridge Templeton, Jr., b. June 10, 1887.
14g67 Ewell Hood Templeton, b. Jan. 24, 1889.
14g68 Leumas Bascom Templeton, Jr., b. Oct. 9, 1890.

14g6 Leumas Bascom Templeton, Sr., remembered the first pair
of shoes he ever had. In those days, when he was small, few
children had shoes and those were home made. Being the
youngest son he had to wait his turn until the older children had
been supplied with shoes. When his turn finally came there was
only enough leather left to make one shoe. This one, like all
home made shoes, was made on a straight last—no rights or lefts.
When the one shoe was finished he was told that he would have
to wait until more leather could be bought for the other shoe.
However, he was so proud of the one shoe that he wore it, first
on one foot and then on the other so that, when the second shoe
was finally made the first one was ready to be half soled.

It was in his early boyhood days, during the war, that Southern
people ran out of certain commodities. Among these was salt.
On one occasion when his aunt, 14k Rebecca Campbell, came to
visit them his mother prepared an extra big chicken dinner. Nat-
urally, he watched with keen delight as the dinner was being
prepared and went to the table with a good appetite. When he
began to eat, what he had expected to be a delicious chicken dinner, he found, to his dismay, that there was no salt in it. He tried
time and again but just could not relish that chicken so he left the
table and went out into the yard and cried pathetically. His Aunt
Rebecca tried to console him and promised to bring him a lump
of salt soon, which she managed to do.

When he was ten or twelve years old he wanted to take a "turn"
of corn to mill, as he said, "all by myself." So he was placed on
a mule with a bushel of corn and sent off to Musgrove Mill. The
miller helped him down with the corn, measured it, put it in the
hopper and then proceeded to take out the toll. Young Templeton watched this with consternation. He thought the miller was
stealing some of his corn, so, as soon as the miller was out of
sight, he grabbed the toll box, dipped it full out of the miller's
barrel and hurriedy dumped it back into the hopper. As soon

as he got home he boastfully related to his father how he had retrieved the corn that the miller tried to steal. His father laughingly explained that the miller always took out the toll as the charge for grinding, and later on, explained the episode to the miller and replaced the corn.

In 1873, the next year after his father died, his mother moved to the Lou Hill place in the edge of Union County near Musgrove Mill. In December, 1873, she bought the nearby John Hollis Farm (170 acres) and moved there, together with her widowed daughter, 14g2 Frances Cunningham (and grand-daughter of 14g21 Jonnie Cunningham), her other two daughters, 14g4 Isabella Templeton, 14g7 Mary Ellie Templeton, and her son, 14g6 Leumas B. Templeton. He was the only man at home to work the farm and was under the impression that he was the one who had bought the place. However, he was only 19 years of age so the title was made in his mother's name. She borrowed $450.00 from William Ray and gave him a mortgage on the farm. The payments were due to be made by Dec. 25, 1876. After working the farm for three years, he married, Dec. 17, 1876, just eight days before the payments were due to have been completed. It was about this time that he found out that the title was in his mother's name. Discord arose, so he and his bride moved about one mile to a log house in the road triangle on the Wilbanks place, where his oldest daughter, 14g61 Mittie Gertrude Templeton, was born, Nov. 11, 1877. From 1878 until 1884, he lived on the Gregory farm near Tyger River in Cross Keys Township, Union County. In 1885 he lived on what is known as the Craig place on Enoree River in Union County. In 1886 he lived at the Wilbanks place. From there he moved to the farm of Mr. Robert Hawkins, about two miles west of Cross Anchor, S. C., where he lived in 1887. From there he moved to the nearby Galdin place where he farmed in 1888, 1889, 1890, 1891, and 1892. From there he moved to the Keily place about two miles southeast of Cross Anchor where he lived in 1893, 1894, and 1895. In 1896 he lived on Mr. Tinsley's place about three miles south of Cross Anchor near Musgrove Mill. From there he moved to the Wilbanks place again where he lived in 1897. In 1898, 1899, and 1900, he farmed the Poole's Quarter place.

In December, 1900, he bought the farm near Cross Anchor known as the Hilliard Hill farm and moved there where he lived until 1919, when he sold this farm and bought the home place of Dr. W. B. Patton, where he lived until he died.

When his wife died in 1891, leaving eight children, the oldest being only thirteen years old 14g6 L. B. Templeton, Sr., in his distress, chose to re-marry rather prematurely.. This proved to be an unhappy marriage and terminated in a few months by separation. One child, 14g69, Talmage Templeton, was born of this marriage. He died at about six years of age.

Several years after his estranged wife died he married, December, 1906, the widow, Mrs. Emma Taylor Workman. She died Oct. 5, 1929, and was buried at New Hope Cemetery, Cross Anchor, S. C. They had no children.

For more than 25 years he operated a cotton gin for the Cross Anchor Oil Company and others. In the latter years of his life he was intrigued into buying worthless stock in a fertilizer firm which proved to be a fraudulent scheme that resulted in the loss of his life savings and doubtless contributed to his decline in health. He was a man of integrity and strong moral character and his reliability won for him the esteem of all who knew him.

14g61 Mittie Gertrude Templeton was born at what is known as the Wilbanks place in Union County, near Cross Anchor, S. C. She died July 24, 1917, and was buried at New Hope Cemetery, Cross Anchor, S. C.

Being the oldest child she, together with her younger sister, took over the responsibility of housekeeping when her mother died. She was keenly interested in the education of her younger brothers and did all she could to keep them in school. She continued to keep house, with the assistance of her sister, for this large family until most of them had grown up and left home. In January, 1901, she went to Enoree and worked in the mill until Christmas. When her father married in 1906 she was 29 years old. Nevertheless, she immediately made arrangements to start to school. She was classified as partly in the sixth and partly in the seventh grade. She continued in school with not one day missed until she completed the eleventh grade and received her diploma in 1911. She then attended summer school at Winthrop College. She secured a teacher's certificate and taught about three and one-half years at Belmont School and at Cross Anchor elementary school. She married, April, 1914, Adolphus Dodge Lawson. Their children were:

14g611 Annie Leumas Lawson, b. 5/24/1915.
14g612 A daughter, b. 7/6/1917, and died in infancy.

14g611 Annie Leumas Lawson was adopted by her aunt, 14g62 Mrs. Lillie T. Parham, after the death of her mother. She lived with her adopted mother almost continuously until she was grown. She attended several schools and was graduated from Cross Anchor High School in 1933. In February, 1936, she went to Panama to visit her former stepmother, Mrs. Edna Lawson Furr. She married in Panama, April 25, 1937, Herman Keepers, who was born Dec. 7, 1912. They now live at Gatun, Canal Zone. Their children are:

14g6111 Shirley Ann Keepers, b. 5/20/1938.
14g6112 Harry Keepers, b. 9/20/1940.
14g6113 William Dodge Keepers, b. 9/10/1944.

14g62 Lillie Geneva Templeton was born on what is known as the Gregory Place in Union County, S. C., near Cross Anchor. She was only eleven years old when her mother died. She promptly assumed joint management of the household with her older sister. This meant the sacrifice of her schooling. Nevertheless, she cheerfully stayed at home in order to care for her little brothers. To these duties she applied herself with unselfish devotion. Her sympathy and affection for children in need was further demonstrated by her volunteer action in twice giving a home to her young nieces and mothering them.

In 1900 she worked in the mill at Enoree, S. C., most of the year. She married Jan. 1, 1905, William J. Parham, 5/5/1886-5/26/1949. He was buried at New Hope Cemetery at Cross Anchor, S. C. Most of his life was spent in farming and merchandising. She lives at Union, S. C. Their children are:
    14g621 Bertha Frances Parham, b. 10/6/1905.
    14g622 Lucy Irene Parham, b. 11/3/1907.
    14g623 Ruby Altahlee Parham, b. 3/7/1911.

14g621 Bertha Frances Parham married, 12/23/1925, Roy P. Jennings, a mechanic and farmer. They live at Clinton, S. C., and have six children:
    14g6211 Doris E. Jennings, b. 11/28/1926.
    14g6212 Roy P. Jennings, b. 6/24/1928.
    14g6213 Betty Jean Jennings, b. 4/17/1930.
    14g6314 Laura Ellen Jennings, b. 6/21/1933.
    14g6315 William Giles Jennings, b. 6/26/1935.
    14g6216 John Carrol Jennings, b. 8/1/1939.

14g6211 Doris E. Jennings was graduated from Clinton High School and Cecil's Business College. For several years she was employed by the Spartanburg branch of Swift and Company. She also worked for Montgomery and Crawford in Spartanburg. She married, April 27, 1946, Francis Cooper. He works for the Spartanburg County Tuberculosis Association as an X-ray technician. They live on the Spartanburg-Cowpens highway. Their children are:
    14g62111 Jerry Cooper, b. 12/11/1947.
    14g62112 Terry Cooper, b. August, 1949.

14g6212 Roy P. Jennings, Jr., lives with his parents at Clinton, S. C. He works in the mill at Joanna, S. C.

14g6213 Betty Jean Jennings was graduated from Clinton High School. She married, 8/23/1948, J. D. Phillips, a loom fixer in

Spartan Mill, Spartanburg, S. C. They live at Camp Croft Apartments, and have two children:

14g62131 Lillie Carrol Phillips, b. 6/3/1950.
14g62132 Dan Phillips, b. 5/2/1951.

14g6214 Laura Ellen Jennings lives with her parents and attends Clinton High School.

14g6215 William Giles Jennings lives with his parents and attends Clinton Graded School.

14g6216 John Carrol Jennings lives with his parents and attends Clinton Graded School.

14g622 Lucy Irene Parham was graduated from Piedmont High School in 1927, and lives with her mother at Union, S. C. She is employed in Whitlock's Dry Goods Store.

14g623 Ruby Altahlee Parham was graduated from Cross Anchor High School. She married, 3/5/1932, Claude D. Watson, b. 8/21/1905. He has been a great lover of baseball for many years. For ten years he was a winning pitcher and manager for several years of the Arkwright Mill club in the Spartanburg County League. They live at Arkwright Mill, Spartanburg, S. C., where he is a loom fixer. They have three children:

14g6231 Claude D. Watson, Jr., b. 6/8/1933.
14g6232 John Parham Watson, b. 4/8/1936.
14g6233 Margaret Elizabeth Watson, b. 7/27/1938.

14g63 William Benjamin Templeton was born at what is known as the Gregory Place in Union County, near Cross Anchor, S. C. As he grew up, being the oldest of the boys, the responsibility became his for seeing that the cotton was picked and other crops harvested while his father was away operating the gin.

In 1900 he went to Enoree and worked in the cloth room and weave room of the mill. He returned to the farm but for only a short while. He then went to Spartanburg, in 1902, where he began, as a street car motorman, his long career in electrical work. In 1904, he went to Danville, Ill., and from there to Los Angeles and San Francisco where he was working as an inspector for the street railway when the great earthquake of 1906 occurred. He then returned to Spartanburg, S. C., for four more years of residence and work. He then went to the West again for about two years and then back east again. In April, 1914, he went back west to Spokane, Washington. Since then he has lived continuously in that state. He is an electrical engineer of recognized ability. He held the patent rights on a type of high voltage switch which he invented. He was later induced to release these rights to the company for whom he was working. This type of switch is now in universal use. He is now employed with the

White Pine Sash and Door Company of Spokane, Wash., where he lives. He married, May 26, 1915, Kathryn Childs, b. June 5, 1893, of Spokane. Their residence is 1111 East 18th Ave. They have two sons:

    14g631 Leumas Wendell Templeton, b. 8/10/1916.
    14g632 William Wayne Templeton, b. 11/20/1919.

14g631 Leumas Wendell Templeton married, Oct. 12, 1941, Alma Middlestadt, b. 9/14/1918, daughter of an extensive wheat farmer of near Spokane. For several years he was engaged in wheat farming and is now a building contractor in Spokane where they live. They have two sons:

    14g5311 James Dwight Templeton, b. 7/12/1942.
    14g5312 Ronald Del Templeton, b. 10/6/1944.

14g632 William Wayne Templeton was graduated from Lewis-Clark High School in Spokane in 1938. He came to South Carolina and attended Clemson College and later returned to Washington state and attended Washington State College at Pullman, Wash. He saw service in World War II, twelve months of which were in the Pacific area, including Japan. He is now connected with the Penn State Life Insurance Company and was selected as their Man-of-The-Year in 1950. He married, Nov. 9, 1940, Margaret Joyce Eichelberger, b. 12/31/1922, of Spokane, where they now live. They have two sons:

    14g6321 William Michael Templeton, b. 8/15/1941.
    14g6322 David Wayne Templeton, b. 3/10/1943.

14g64 Walter Oliver Templeton was born on what is known as the Gregory Place in Union County, near Cross Anchor, S. C. He attended school irregularly at Belmont and New Hope, both near Cross Anchor, S. C., until he was 14 or 15 years old.

He remembered the extremely cold winter of 1898-99 when many rabbits froze and some trees froze and burst open. When his father contracted to carry the mail from Cross Anchor to Enoree, Walter went with him on the first trip and liked its so well that he persuaded his father, later on, to let him carry it regularly. Among the horses used to pull the buggy, one was bad to balk. On one occasion the old horse balked several times on the trip and Walter had plenty of trouble getting him started again. When he got to the foot of the hill at Cedar Shoal Creek the old horse decided to stop again. Walter was so disgusted that he picked up the light mail bag, got out of the buggy and started walking up the hill, telling the horse to stay there. He had not gone very far when the horse came in a trot up behind him.

In December, 1902, he went to Spartanburg to work as a motorman on the street car. One day, while his instructor was still with him, he saw a horse and wagon on the track in front of the car. The instructor told him to ring the foot gong. Walter stomped his foot frantically trying to find the gong. The instructor laughed and said, "pat the other foot—it (the gong) is under one of them." After this he never denied having big feet.

After working as a motorman for a good many years he worked as a furniture salesman. In connection with this work he learned to repair furniture and to do upholstering. He gradually left the selling end and concentrated on the repairing. His high type of workmanship was evidenced by the wide area from which furniture was sent him for refinishing. He had customers from seventeen states and all the way from New York City to San Diego, California. Among the pieces of furniture re-finished were some rare antiques.

He married Dec. 22, 1910, Alma Evatt, b. Oct. 29, 1882, died Dec. 29, 1935. He died March 18, 1951, and was buried on his 68th birthday beside his wife at Sharon Methodist Church Cemetery near Liberty, S. C. They had two children:

14g641 Myrle Templeton, b. Aug. 12, 1912.
14g642 Madge Templeton, b. Aug. 11, 1914.

14g641 Myrle Templeton was born in Spartanburg, S. C., and attended the city school there, graduating from high school and also from business college. For a number of years she was employed in the office of Pacific Mills at Lyman, S. C. She married Dec. 22, 1934, Fred Thompson, Jr., of Spartanburg, S. C., a graduate of Clemson College and a veteran of World War II, having served as a lieutenant, JG, in the U. S. Navy. They now live in Brazil where he is a supervisor in a soil conservation project sponsored by the U. S. Department of Agriculture. They have one son:

14g5411 Fred Thompson III, b. Oct. 17, 1938.
14g6412 Madge Templeton was graduated from Spartanburg High School and attended the Spartanburg Junior College. She married, Jan. 12, 1935, Pat Thomas. They live in Spartanburg, S. C., where he is employed by Becker's Bakery. They have one daughter:

14g6421 Madge Thomas, b. March 5, 1942.

14g65 Grover Cleveland Templeton was born at what is known as the Gregory Place in Union County, near Cross Anchor, S. C. He grew up on the farm and gradually became his father's "right hand man." He was devoted to his parents and continued to live with and care for his father until his death. He completed the ninth grade in the Cross Anchor High School. A very unusual experience was his while enrolled as a ninth grade pupil. A prize was being offered for the best composition on a certain subject. At commencement time he was called to the platform and awarded the prize amidst all of the hand clapping. Just as this ceremony was ending Mr. J. Paul Patton, the teacher who was awarding the prize, announced that there had been a mistake and that the prize was due to be given to Hazel Rush so that he was asked to surrender the prize which was then given to the girl.

By occupation he is a farmer and painter. For a good many years he has been a fertilizer inspector under the direction of Clemson College, S. C., his territory being Spartanburg, Greenville, and Laurens Counties. He married, Dec. 12, 1933, the widow, Mrs. Lola Simmons, b. Sept. 19, 1888, of Cross Anchor, S. C. They have no children by this marriage.

14g66 Giles Breckenridge Templeton was born on what is known as the Hawkins Place two miles west of Cross Anchor, S. C. He grew up on the farm in the community where he was born. After completing the high school at Cross Anchor he won the competitive scholarship from Spartanburg County to the University of South Carolina. He received his Bachelor of Arts degree from that institution in 1915. He then taught in the Columbia High School for several years, meanwhile continuing his studies at the University where he received his Master of Arts degree in 1924.

During World War I he saw service in the U. S. Navy, being stationed at Charleston, S. C. After his discharge from the Navy he taught in Charleston for a short time. He then returned to Columbia, S. C., where he was Principal of Heathwood School and, later, for 13 years, was Superintendent of Consolidated High School No. 1 in Richland County, S. C. He was also Superintendent of Dentsville High School, Richland County, S. C. He was also Superintendent of School District No. 12 in Spartanburg County, S. C. He lives at Cross Anchor, S. C.

During the summer of 1927 he took graduate work at the University of Chicago. He has served as President of the Richland County Education Association and as Executive Committeeman for the Seventh District in the South Carolina Education Association.

In addition to his successful career in the field of education he has devoted much of his time to social service. For eleven summers he was counsellor at French Broad Camp for Boys at Brevard, N. C. He also served as scoutmaster for a troop of Boy Scouts in Columbia, S. C., for a number of years. He has always been a friend to the underprivileged and has been generous in his many acts of kindness to those in need. His hobbies are hunting, fishing, and golf. He is unmarried.

14g67 Ewell Hood Templeton was born on what is known as

the Galdin Place, about two miles west of Cross Anchor, S. C. Like his brothers and sisters, he spent his boyhood days in the little community where he was born. His attendance in school was interrupted much like that of his brothers by necessary work on the farm, but he advanced to the eighth grade before his school days ended.

When he grew up he became dissatisfied with farm life and explored a number of occupations. Among these were: chaingang guard, supervisor in the State Reform School for Boys at Florence, S. C., bookkeeper and deputy sheriff at Spartanburg, S. C., clothing salesman, ticket collector for the Southern Railway, then back to the farm for a few years, then a letter carrier in the City of Spartanburg, S. C., for 22 years where, he says, he "wore his feet out" which forced him to give up this for an occupation that was easier on his feet. He now operates the elevator in the post office at Spartanburg, S. C.

He says that the one childhood experience that stands out in his memory is that of bringing in wood and water for his uncle who promised to pay him with the next nickel he "found in a pig track." The pig track with the nickel in it was never found. He finally became reconciled. His hobbies are hunting, fishing, poetry, antiques, and cabinet work. Not only does he enjoy reading poetry but his sentiments frequently find expression in rhyming verses of his own composition, such as the following:

THE SANTA CLAUS WE KNEW

The Santa Claus we knew as boys,
Back in the olden days,
Brought little toys with mammoth joys
To suit our simple ways.
But oh! that Santa Claus is dead,
Which we all loved so dear,
And resurrected in his stead
Are Santas everywhere;
But these are all commercialized
And trek the lanes of trade;
The Santa Claus we idolized
Enjoyed the joy he made.

A nation's growth a nation's fame
Is laid in careful plan,
But Santa Claus, what e'er his name
Must not mean cash for man;
For he's an institution,
And through the centuries
His hearty constitution
Lives in our memories.

Bring back our Santa Claus of old,
With wares so freely given;
Without commercial stories told—
Whose gifts seemed dropped from heaven.

14g67 Ewell Hood Templeton married Dec. 17, 1913, Jimmie
Leila Crow of Cross Anchor, S. C. They live at 246 S. Spring St.,
Spartanburg, S. C. They have two daughters:
    14g671 Virginia Ellender Templeton, b. Sept. 6, 1914.
    14g672 Mary Frances Templeton, b. Sept. 21, 1920.

14g671 Virginia Ellender Templeton was graduated from the
Spartanburg High School and from business college. She married, Oct. 24, 1942, Andrew P. Rosco, born Oct. 24, 1910, a native
of New York State. He is a veteran of World War II, having
served as a staff sergeant. He was wounded in the Battle of the
Bulge, Belgium. They now live in Spartanburg where he is employed by the Southern Railway in their shops.

14g672 Mary Frances Templeton was graduated from the Spartanburg High School and for several years was employed by the
Southern Bell Telephone Company as supervisor of operators.
She married, Oct. 29, 1944, Terrence Carr, b. Dec. 14, 1917. He
is a veteran of World War II, having received his S. C. D. in 1943.
For several years he was City Circulation manager for the Spartanburg Herald-Journal. He was also district circulation manager
for the Greensboro Daily News, Greensboro, N. C. He is now
assistant circulation manager of the Greenville News, Greenville,
S. C. They live at 600 Overbrook Road, in Greenville, S. C.

14g68 Leumas Bascom Templeton, Jr., was born on what is
known as the Galdin Place, about two miles west of Cross Anchor, S. C. He attended the elementary schools at Belmont and
New Hope and the Cross Anchor High School where he completed the tenth grade (which was the highest grade then given in this
high school). While a pupil in the tenth grade in 1912 he attended
the State High School Athletic and Oratorical meet in Columbia
when he won first place in the 440 yard dash and first place in the
one mile run. He entered the University of South Carolina in September, 1912, and received his Bachelor of Arts degree in 1916.
While a student at the University he served as president of the
Clariosophic Society, captain of the University Track team, Chairman of the Student Body Honor Committee, Business Manager of
the Gamecock, weekly paper, student assistant librarian, member of the University Debating Council, etc. He was also supervisor of one of the Columbia City playgrounds.

During the two summer vacations, while attending college, he
canvassed in Minnesota and Iowa, selling a musical instrument

called the Mandolin Guitar Harp. In the summer of 1916, he was employed by the Jones Chautauqua System of Perry, Iowa, as a platform manager. In this capacity he worked in the Mid-Western states of Iowa, Minnesota, Missouri, South Dakota and Nebraska.

His first teaching was done at North Greenville Academy (now a junior college) at Tigerville, S. C., in 1916-17. He then volunteered for service in the U. S. Army and saw nearly two years of service in World War I as a First Lieutenant of Infantry, seven months of which were spent in France. Upon receiving his discharge from the Army he went to Washington State and was employed by the Washington Water Power Company of Spokane, Wash., where he was an associate member of the American Institute of Electrical Engineers. After two years in this work he returned to South Carolina, in 1921, and again entered the teaching profession in which he has been engaged since. From 1924 until 1942, he lived at Piedmont, S. C., where he was Superintendent of Schools. In 1927 he attended summer school at the University of Chicago. In 1931 he received his Master of Arts degree from the University of South Carolina. He now lives in Union, S. C., where he is Principal of Main Street Grammar School. While living at Piedmont, S. C., he served as President of the Greenville County Education Association, as Executive Committeeman from the Fourth District in the South Carolina Education Association, Master of Masonic Lodge, Superintendent of Sunday School and Deacon in the Baptist Church. He organized the Templeton Clan.

He has in his possession a rare Templeton heirloom, an old shot gun. One of the very first experiences he remembers was that of watching, at the age of three or four years, his father take the percussion lock off this old gun and put it on a more "modern" shot gun. When his father had completed the operation he handed the old gun, minus a lock, to the little fellow saying: "Now Son, this old gun is yours, because you are the youngest son. It has been given to the youngest son in every generation." In later years he added, "It is called a 'London Barrell' gun. It was bought in Dublin City, Ireland, by the early Templetons. In 1866 my father (14g Benjamin Clark Templeton) took this gun to Mr. Beard, a gunsmith in Laurens, S. C., who made a stock for the gun from an old walnut stump that I had helped my father dig from a gully bank. Mr. Beard took the old stock and flint lock off the gun and put the new stock and a percussion lock on. As pay for his services he agreed to accept the silver from which the mountings on the old gun were made." Family tradition said further that the gun was brought to America before the Revolution. This tradition, however, has been refuted by the Curator of the British Museum, by Captain Charles Carey, Assistant Curator of History of the Smithsonian Institution and also by H. M. Cashmore, F. L. A. City Librarian, Reference Library, Birmingham, England; through his chief assistant who reported, "Feb. 2, 1937, Mr. Templeton's gun . . . bears the mark (W. S. & C.) of the Birmingham Proof House . . . established by Act of Parliament in 1813, and the mark was not in use before that date. The probable date of the gun would appear to be after 1815 and before 1821 because . . . the firm of Woolley Sargant and Crane would appear to have existed only somewhere between those dates."

So vanished this, like many other fond traditions, when the searchlight of facts is turned on. Who bought the gun, when, and by whom it was brought to South Carolina remain unanswered questions. However, the facts do show that it is a very old one.

14g68 Leumas Bascom Templeton, Jr., married, first, June 24, 1919, his first cousin, 14g74 Frances Ryan Lockman who was born Sept. 16, 1893, died Sept. 6, 1920, buried at West Oakwood cemetery, Spartanburg, S. C. One child was born of this marriage:
14g681 Mary Ellie Templeton, b. June 6, 1920.

He married, second, June 7, 1923, Eula Permelia Waldrep, of Cross Anchor S. C., b. Feb. 28, 1891. They have one child:
14g682 Dora Louise Templeton b. Nov. 15, 1928.

14g681 Mary Ellie Templeton was born at Reardan, Wash. After her mother's death, she was brought to South Carolina and lived with and was cared for by her aunt, 14g62 Mrs. Lillie T. Parham, for about two years. When her father married the second time she was taken, at the age of three, into their home. She attended the elementary school and high school at Piedmont, S. C. While a senior in high school she was President of the Beta (honorary scholastic) Club, and valedictorian of her class. In 1937 she entered Winthrop College, Rock Hill, S. C. While a student there she was a member of the college orchestra. She received her Bachelor of Science degree from that institution in 1941. For two years after her graduation she was employed in the office of Probate Judge Guy A. Gullick, in Greenville, S. C. She married, July 27, 1943, William Van Simpson, Jr., b. Oct. 18 1920, of Greensboro, N. C. He attended North Carolina State College at Raleigh. During World War II he served as First Lieutenant in the Engineer Corps, about six months of which was in Hawaii. He was discharged in 1946 and re-enlisted in the reserve corps and put on inactive duty. For several years he was a departmental buyer for Sears Roebuck & Co. in Greensboro, N. C. In January, 1951, he was recalled to active duty and was stationed in Bordeaux, France. He was released from active duty in April, 1952, and has returned to Sears Roebuck & Co. as a departmental buyer. They have two daughters:

73

14g6811 Rebecca Ryan Simpson, b. June 5, 1948.
14g6812 Dorothy Jane Simpson, b. May 4, 1950.

14g682 Dora Louise Templeton was born at Piedmont, S. C. She attended elementary school there. She was graduated from Union High School, Union, S. C., in 1945. She then entered Winthrop College, Rock Hill, S. C., from which institution she received her degree in home economics in 1949. She married June 3, 1949, Joseph David Gault, b. Dec. 5, 1927, of Union S. C. During 1949-1950 she taught home economics in the Fairforest High School, Fairforest, S. C., while her husband attended Wofford College under the G. I. Bill. During World War II he was in the U. S. Navy and saw service in various parts of the Pacific, including Japan, China and Australia. Upon his discharge he re-enlisted in the reserves and was recalled to active duty on Feb. 12, 1951. He was stationed at the Naval Hospital, U. S. Navy Base, Charleston, S. C. He was put on inactive duty in June, 1952. They are now living at Union, S. C., where he is employed by Deering Milliken Company. They have one daughter:
14g6821 Virginia Kathryn Gault, b. Aug. 22, 1950.

14g7 Mary Ellie Templeton was buried at Oakwood Cemetery, Spartanburg, S. C. She married April 26, 1886, John Edgar Lockman, b. June 25, 1861, died June 3, 1920, and who was buried at Spartanburg, S. C. Their children are:
14g71 Louis C. Lockman, b. Jan. 28, 1887.
14g72 Howard C. Lockman, Sept. 4, 1888-May, 1945.
14g73 Charlie Lockman, Oct. 12, 1890-Nov. 28, 1892, buried, Spartanburg, S. C.
14g74 Frances Ryan Lockman, Sept. 16, 1893-Sept. 6, 1920.
14g75 Marjorie Lockman, b. June 16, 1898.

14g7 Mary Ellie Templeton was born on what was known as the Peggy Templeton (widow of 114 James Templeton) place, near Bethany Church, in Laurens County, S. C. The house was built of logs, weather boarded outside and sealed inside with very wide boards running up and down. The floor was made of puncheons—logs split and placed, flat side up, hewn smooth, and fastened to the sleepers with wooden pegs.

She went to school, among other places, at Rehobeth Church, for about two weeks. Here she learned her letters and how to spell. She always wondered how anybody could pick up a book and talk out of it. She always remembered how, when she was a little girl she longed for a doll. Her niece and playmate, Jonnie 14g21 Cunningham, had a "town doll" but she was never allowed one. After so long a time she was given a home-made doll. She was so proud of it that she practically lived with it under the house where she hid it for fear someone would take it away from her.

As she grew up she determined to earn and save everything she could. In January, 1878, she went to Glendale, S. C., where she began to work in the mill.

After her marriage, she and her husband lived in Spartanburg, S. C. In 1889 they moved to Enoree, S. C. They then moved to Spartanburg and then to Converse, S. C. From there they moved to Glendale and back to Spartanburg, where they both died. Her husband was an overseer in the mill.

14g71 Louis C. Lockman was born opposite the old Baptist church on North Church Street, Spartanburg, S. C. As he grew up he took an exceptional interest in his mill work and became proficient in loom-fixing. For many years he held a responsible position with the Draper Loom Corporation. He is a veteran of World War I, having served as a mechanic in the Air Force, including eight months in the A. E. F. He married Marie Phillips. They live at Spartanburg, S. C. They have one son:

14g711 John Edgar Lockman, b. March 5, 1926. He is a veteran of World War II. He is a graduate of Clemson College, S. C. He married Mary Frances Neighbor. They live in Atlanta, Ga., where he is employed by Lockheed Aircraft Corporation.

14g72 Howard C. Lockman was born opposite the old Baptist Church on North Church Street, Spartanburg, S. C. His boyhood days were spent mostly at Converse, Glendale, and Spartanburg, S. C. As he grew up he learned to weave in the mill and followed that work as long as he was in good health. He married May 12, 1916, Annie Lee Fuller. He died May, 1945, and was buried in the Lockman family plot, Oakwood Cemetery, Spartanburg, S. C.

14g74 Frances Ryan Lockman was born on Choice Street, now Morgan Avenue, in Spartanburg, S. C. She died Sept. 6, 1920, and was buried in West Oakwood Cemetery, Spartanburg, S. C. She married June 24, 1919, 14g68 Leumas Bascom Templeton, Jr. (See his record for record of their child.)

From early childhood she indicated a keen interest in going to school. She was graduated from Lander College in 1914, where she taught until her marriage.

Mrs. Kathleen Lander Wilson, wife of the president and daughter of the founder of the college, wrote about her as follows: "From her arrival at college she made a fine impression and before the first year ended, we had our eyes on her as a possible teacher. She was graduated in 1914, and the next year came to be a member of our faculty. Her service was well done and her spirit was always a wholesome influence. The students and fellow teachers loved her dearly. She was cheerful and sunny, neat, happy, though quiet, dignified yet full of fun. She was thoughtful and glad to do a kindness, and best of all—a dependable Christian Woman."

Among the scores of commendable traits attributed to her by her students and fellow teachers one comment serves to indicate her personality. One of her students was heard to say more than once, "I feel better now since I saw Miss Lockman."

14g75 Marjorie Lockman was born at Converse, S. C. She attended school there, as well as at Glendale and Spartanburg where she completed high school. She attended Winthrop College, Converse College and Agnes Scott College in Atlanta, Ga. She married Aug. 9 1922, Frank R. Noble of Spokane, Wash. For many years he was the proprietor of a sporting goods store in Spokane, where they now live, at 314 E. 17th Ave. They have one son:

14g751 Frank Noble, Jr., b. Jan. 8, 1924. He is a veteran of World War I, having served in the U. S. Navy in the Pacific. He married, Dec. 28, 1946, Beverley Jeanne Hubbell. They have two children.

14h Leah A. M. Templeton was born in Laurens County, S. C. She married 152 Turner Templeton, her first cousin. In 1869, he went to Georgia and in 1878 to Sand Mountain, Alabama, where he died. Their two children were:

14h1 John Templeton, a soldier of the Confederacy, who was killed, June 3, 1864, in the battle of Cold Harbor.

14h2 Lawrence Templeton, 5/16/1850-8/29/1893, who was buried at Olive Branch, Fouke, Arkansas. He married 1868, Dooley L. Dodd of Cross Keys, S. C. Their children are:

14h2a John Willie Templeton, b. 8/29/1869.
14h2b Dora Templeton, b. 12/20/1871.
14h2c Thomas J. Templeton, b. 4/20/1874.
14h2d Leora B. B. Templeton, b. 6/15/1876.
14h2e Ida Templeton, 1/10/1879-6/8/1880, buried at Sulpher Fork.
14h2f Estelle Templeton, b. 7/11/1881.
14h2g Grover Templeton, b. 9/5/1884, who lives at Doddridge, Ark.
14h2h Osker Templeton, 2/26/1888-6/27/1890, buried at Sulpher Fork.
14h2i Carl Templeton, b. 3/14/1890.
14h2j Cleala Templeton, b. 7/31/1892.

14h2a John Willie Templeton lived at Doddridge, Ark., Rt. 4.
He married, Dec. 4, 1890, Laura M. Pool. Their children are:
  14h2a1 Leonard Ivan Templeton, b. 10/8/1891.
  14h2a2 Lula Templeton, 10/4/1893-9/9/1905, buried at Mt.
  Zion, Ark.
  14h2a3 Lawrence Templeton, b. 12/20/1895.
  14h2a4 Dallas Templeton, b. 2/11/1898.
  14h2a5 Bruce Templeton, b. 10/10/1900.
  14h2a6 Cline Templeton, b. 1/4/1903.
  14h2a7 Gertrude Templeton, b. 9/5/1906, who lives at Doddridge, Ark.
  14h2a8 Iven Templeton, b. 1/10/1910, died 8/9/1910, was
  buried at Mt. Zion, Ark.
  14h2a9 Erving Templeton, b. 11/11/1913, who lives at Dod
  dridge, Ark.

14h2a1 Leonard Ivan Templeton lives at Bloomburg, Texas. He
married, 7/24/1915, Corrine Hempley.

14h2a3 Lawrence Templeton lives a 618 Jefferson St., Dallas Texas. He married, 11/21/1928, Arroane Shamby.

14h2a4 Dallas Templeton lives at 311 Show Ave., Cleburne,
Texas. She married, 12/20/1920, C. P. Hazelwood.

14h2a5 Bruce Templeton lives at 311 Show Ave., Cleburne,
Texas. He married, 11/24/1918, Connie Clemens.

14h2a6 Cline Templeton lives at Doddridge, Ark. He married,
8/27/1927, Jeannette Allen.

14h2b Dora Templeton lives at Doddridge, Ark. She married,
1891, W. W. Tidwell.

14h2c Thomas J. Templeton lives at Foulce, Ark. He married,
first, 1893, Fannie Howard; second, Minnie Lorry, and third, Callie
McBride.

14h2d Leora B. B. Templeton lives at Doddridge, Ark. She
married first, 11/9/1893, Jones Waldrop; second, January, 1901,
Scott Brown.

14h2f Estelle Templeton lives at Doddridge, Ark. She married,
first, Will Fowler, and second, 7/12/1919, Charles Jones.

14h2g Grover Templeton lives at Doddridge, Ark. He married, 12/8/1904, Murrell Adcock.

14h2i Carl Templeton lives at Doddridge, Ark. He married,
3/7/1911, Jimmie Thomas who died 11/5/1926, buried at Olive
Branch.

14h2j Cleala Templeton lives at Doddridge, Ark. She married,
first, ...Thomason, and, second, 8/1/1926, U. G. Wilbanks.

77

14i Sarah P. Templeton was born Jan. 24, 1821, died Dec. 21, 1839, married, Jan. 31, 1838, Levi Whitton.

14j Robert W. Templeton was born Jan. 18, 1823. He went from Laurens County, S. C., to Brownington, Mo.

14k Frances Rebecca Templeton was buried at Rehobeth, near Clinton, S. C. She married Wesley Campbell. Their children are:

14k1 Thomas Hilliard Campbell, 8/13/1852-8/4/1868, buried at Rehobeth.
14k2 Robert Lee Campbell, b. 12/18/1853.
14k3 Matilda Campbell, b. 1/15/1856.
14k4 Charlotte Madora Campbell, b. 1/29/1858.
14k5 John Wesley Campbell, b. 2/9/1860.
14k6 Adelia Campbell, b. 1/26/1862.
14k7 Ralph Campbell, 11/9/1864, died............ buried at Townville, S. C.
14k8 Joseph Renoriah Campbell, b. 1/5/1865, who married .... Davis, and who lived at Waxahachie, Texas (not there 6/23/39).

14k2 Robert Lee Campbell was born at Kingston, Ga., and died Feb. 17, 1917. He married, 1886, Jane Simpson Craddock, born 1860. Their children are:
14k21 Mary Estelle Campbell, b. 12/6/1888.
14k22 Frances Rebecca Campbell, b. 5/8/1890.
14k23 George Washington Campbell, b. 8/13/1891.
14k24 Robert LeRoy Campbell, Jr., b. 9/22/1892.
14k25 Willie Belle Campbell, b. 10/20/1895 at Kingston, Ga.
14k26 James Franklin Campbell, b. 4/27/1898, at Kingston, Ga.
14k27 Marvin Boyd Campbell, b. 6/28/1901.

14k21 Mary Estelle Campbell was born at Kingston, Ga. She married, 1916, Arthur Holliday of Rockmart, Ga. Their children are:
14k211 Samuel Robert Holliday, b. 12/20/1919.
14k212 James Frank Holliday, b. 4/5/1922.
14k213 Mary Jane Holliday, b. 5/24/1924 (twin).
14k214 Frances Neal Holliday, b. 5/24/1924 (twin).

14k22 Frances Rebecca Campbell was born at Kingston, Ga. She married, 1906, Luther Dewitt Broadwater. Their children are:
14k221 Luther Dewitt Broadwater, Jr., b. 9/3/1907.
14k222 Irby Hill Broadwater, b. 4/29/1912, at Rome, Ga.
14k223 Joseph Robert Broadwater, b. 1/8/1914.

14k23 George Washington Campbell was born at Kingston, Ga. He married, 12/22/1925, Zelta Martin. They have one child:

14k231 Mary Louise Campbell, b. 10/16/1926.
14k24 Robert LeRoy Campbell, Jr., was born at Kingston, Ga.
He married, 1915, Marrilla D. Pilgrim. Their children are:
  14k241 Robert Eugene Campbell, b. 1/1919.
  14k242 John Wesley Campbell, 4/20/1922.

14k27 Marvin Boyd Campbell was born at Kingston, Ga. He
married 9/25/1921 Mildred Green, Lindale, Ga. They have one
child:
  14k271 Robert Edwin Campbell, b. 12/25/1922.

14k3 Mary Matilda Campbell married, 10/1904, Jim Mullikin,
widower of 14k4 Charlotte Madora Campbell. They had no
children by this marriage.

14k4 Charlotte Madora Campbell died Oct. 1, 1899, and was
buried at Six-and-Twenty, in Anderson County, S. C. She married Jim Mullikin. Their children are:
  14k41 Delia Theodosia Mullikin, born and died 1877.
  14k42 Will Mullikin, b. 4/1879.
  14k43 Foster Mullikin.
  14k44 John Mullikin, b. 11/17/1883.
  14k45 Tom Arnold Mullikin, born and died 1886, and buried, Bartow County, Ga.
  14k46 Clarence Eugene Mullikin, b. 4/11/1889.
  14k47 Mary Irene Mullikin, 4/11/1889-7/6/1892, buried at
  Six-and-Twenty in Anderson County, S. C.
  14k48 Hill Mullikin, 2/12/1892-11/27/1916, buried at Piedmont, S. C.
  14k49 Marie Mullikin.

14k42 Will Mullikin married Ida Raney. Their children are:
  14k421 Jake L. Mullikin.
  14k422 Essie Mullikin.
  14k423 Hermon Mullikin.
  14k424 Willie Mullikin.

14k43 Foster Mullikin married Sam Mullikin (4th cousin) and
they live at Brandon Mill, Greenville, S. C. Their children are:
  14k431 Henry Mullikin, deceased and buried at Six-and-
  Twenty in Anderson County, S. C.
  14k432 Inez Mullikin.
  14k433 Roy Mullikin, 11/27/1907-8/1/1917, buried at Piedmont, S. C.
  14k434 Homer Mullikin, who graduated from Piedmont
  High School, Piedmont, S. C.

14k432 Inez Mullikin married Ed Beasley and lives at Poinsett
Mill, Greenville, S. C. They have one child:
  14k4321 Josephus Mullikin.

14k44 John Mullikin married, Aug. 28, 1910, Nannie Blakeley and lives at Chattanooga, Tenn. Their children are:
14k442 Lois Marie Mullikin, b. 11/28/1914.
14k441 John R. Mullikin, Jr., b. 10/17/1911.

14k441 John R. Mullikin, Jr., is a graduate of Wofford College, Spartanburg, S. C. Since his graduation he has been engaged in public school teaching and school administration, mostly in Spartanburg and Greenville Counties.

14k46 Clarence Eugene Mullikin married, 10/14/1914, Eva Thomson. They lived at Simpsonville, S. C. Their children are:
14k461 Mary Lee Mullikin, b. and d. March 20, 1916, buried at Piedmont, S. C.
14k462 Willie Irene Mullikin, b. 9/16/1919.
14k463 Clarence Eugene Mullikin, Jr., 5/21/1924-6/19/1924, buried at Piedmont, S. C.

14k462 Willie Irene Mullikin married Ben Duke of Piedmont, S. C. They have twin sons.

14k49 Marie Mullikin married Homer Davis, now deceased. Their children are:
14k491 Nellie Dee Davis.
14k492 James Davis.
14k493 Johnnie Davis.
14k494 Frank Davis.
14k495 Lottie Davis.
14k496 Mary Davis.
14k497 Billy Davis.

14k5 John Wesley Campbell married 11/26/1886, Cora Bell Moore. They lived at Balmorhea, Texas. Their children are:
14k51 Claude R. Campbell.
14k52 Mattie Campbell, 1890-1906.
14k53 John G. Campbell, 1892-1918.
14k54 Joe C. Campbell.
14k55 Virgil M. Campbell.
14k56 Elmer F. Campbell of Ft. Davis, Texas, who married 1927, Marion Morgan.
14k57 Sadie Campbell.
14k58 Bera Campbell.

14k51 Claude R. Campbell lives at Breckenridge, Texas. He married, 1924, Bessie Campbell.

14k54 Joe C. Campbell lives at Boling, Texas. He married Gertrude _____. They have one child:
14k541 Donna Mae Campbell.

80

14k55 Virgil M. Campbell lives at Balmorhea, Texas. He married, 5/1928, Winnie Mae Whitmire.

14k57 Sadie Campbell, of Bolmorhea, Texas, married Samuel M. Draper. Their children are:
    14k571 Samuel M. Draper, Jr.
    14k572 Cora Delia Draper.

14k58 Bera Campbell of Balmorhea, Texas, married, 12/31/1916, Lacy M. Pittman. Their children are:
    14k581 Marion Isabel Pittman.
    14k582 Clarence T. Pittman.

14k6 Adelia Campbell died 1941. She married first, 3/10/1891, John Dean (separated). Their children are:
    14k61 William Albert Dean, 5/16/1892-1932.
    14k62 James Walter Dean, b. 2/13/1895.

14k6 Adelia Campbell, married second, Marion Morris. They had no children by this marriage.

14L Mary A. G. Templeton was buried at Hopewell in Laurens County, S. C. She married Green Hopkins who was a soldier of the Confederacy, "enlisted for the war at Newberry—Feb. 22, 1862, reported on muster roll of Oct. 31, 1862, at a hospital; discharged Jan. 18 1863." Their children were:
    14L1 Lou Hopkins.
    14L2 Kate Hopkins.
    14L3 Mat Hopkins.
    14L4 Alice Hopkins.
    14L5 George Hopkins, b. 12/1/1861.

14L1 Lou Hopkins married John Carter a soldier of the Confederacy who "enlisted at Darlington March 24, 1862 transferred to Co. I sometime between March 24 and April 30, 1862; transferred to Co. I May 9, 1862; on muster roll of Dec. 31, 1864." Their children are:
    14L11 Sam Carter, b. 6/21/1874 who married Rosa Robinson, and lives at Ninety-Six, S. C.
    14L12 Cora Carter.
    14L13 Elliott Carter.
    14L14 Henry Carter.
    14L15 Annie Carter.

14L12 Cora Carter married Jess Burns. They live at Newberry, S. C., and have the following children:
    14L121 Marguerite Burns.
    14L122 James Burns.
    14L123 Evelyn Burns.

14L13 Elliott Carter married Will B. Jeter. They live at Ninety Six, S. C. Their children are:
    14L131 Lois Jeter.
    14L132 Cora Lee Jeter
    14L133 Carter Jeter.
    14L134 Douglass Jeter.
    14L135 Margaret Jeter.

14L14 Henry Carter married Kate Smith. They live at Newberry, S. C. They have one child:
    14L141 Smith Carter.

14L15 Annie Carter married Ben Glenn. They have one child:
    14L151 Arthur Glenn.

14L2 Kate Hopkins married Sump Carter (brother of John Carter who married 14L1 Lou Hopkins). Their children are:
    14L21 Leila Carter who married Mack Koon.'
    14L22 Mat Carter who married Pick Williams.
    14L23 Ekford Carter.
    14L24 Lizzie Carter.
    14L25 Bennie Carter who married .... Livingston and who lives at 1103 Nance St., Newberry, S. C.

14L3 Mat Hopkins married her first cousin, 14dh Thomas Templeton. (See his line for her descendents.)

14L4 Alice Hopkins married Pierce Connelly. Their children are:
    14L41 Beulah Connelly.
    14L42 Oleina Connelly who married Charles Jarvis.
    14L43 Mae Connelly.
    14L44 Pearl Connelly who married Hubert Sligh.
    14L45 Blanch Connelly who married Joe Ellison.

14L41 Beulah Connelly married Eugene Monroe. They live at Greenwood S. C., and have three children:
    14L411 Darnell Monroe.
    14L412 Joe Monroe.
    14L413 Daniel Monroe.

14L5 George Hopkins died May 10 1925, and was buried at Hopewell in Laurens County S. C. He married Margaret Burns. They have two children:
    14L51 Lillian Hopkins, 10/14/1888-11/28/1928, buried at Hopewell.
    14L52 Mabel E. Hopkins who married W. A. Moorehead. They lived at Goldville, S. C. where he was General Manager for the Goldville Mill. He was outstanding in the policy of liberal dealings with textile employees. He was

killed in an airplane crash, 1/13/1948, near Washington, D. C. She lives now at Clinton S. C. Their children are: 14L521 Alice Lovella Moorehead, 5/12/1911-4/24/1912, and buried at Hopewell.

14L522 William Moorehead, b. 1/9/1914.

14L523 Margaret Moorehead, 1/25/1917.

14L524 Annette Moorehead, 11/30/1924.

15 JOHN TEMPLETON

15 John Templeton, fifth child of 1 David Templeton and his wife Mary was born March 9, 1787, died September. 1872, and is buried at Bethany Presbyterian Church in Laurens County, S. C. He married Barbery Burke. Their children were:

151 James Templeton.

152 Turner Templeton.

153 William Craig Templeton, b. 1828.

154 Clark Templeton who died at the age of 21.

155 Barbery Templeton.

156 Mary Elizabeth Templeton.

151 James Templeton married his first cousin, Janie Luke (a sister to Nancy Luke who married 14d George O. Templeton). After he was married he moved to Alabama. They had three children, none of whom ever came back to South Carolina:

1511 Sam Templeton.

1512 Will Templeton.

1513 Martin Templeton.

152 Turner Templeton was born in Laurens County S. C. He moved to Bartow, Georgia, in 1869 and to Sand Mountain, Ala., in 1878, where he died, Aug. 5, 1893. He married first, 14h Leah A. M. Templeton, and second, 1142 Mary Ann Templeton. (For their descendents see descendents of 14h Leah A. M. Templeton and of 1142 Mary Ann Templeton.)

153 William Craig Templeton was born 1828, died Sept. 27, 1864. He was a soldier in the Con'ederacy. He was taken prisoner and died four hours after he was released by the exchange of prisoner at Danville, Va. He married, Jan. 22, 1852, 1141 Nancy C. Templeton. (See her line for descendents.)

156 Mary Elizabeth Templeton was born in Laurens County, S. C., and buried at Bethany, in that county. She married Joseph Garrett. They had two children:

1561 Priscilla Garrett, 8/19/1847, died about 1938.

1562 Elizabeth Garrett, 3/3/1855-10/7/1916, buried at Bethany. She m. Thomas Lynch. Their children are:

15621 Joe Lynch who married Nora Dunaway and lives at Watts Mill, S. C.

15622 Johnie Lynch who married Rosie Bobo and lives at Reno, S. C.

16523 Mamie Lynch who married Charlie Murphy and lives at Laurens, S. C.

15624 Lloyd Lynch who married first .... Riddle, and second, Jessie Odell, and who lives at Laurens, S. C., Rt. 6.

15625 Willie Lynch who married Lillian Knight and lives at Pelzer, S. C., Rt. 3.

15626 Clarence Lynch who married Kate Terry.

16 WILLIAM C. TEMPLETON

16 William C. Templeton was born in Laurens County, S. C., May 3, 1793. He inherited 142 acres of land on Duncan's Creek from his father. On Oct. 25, 1819, he sold this land for $500.00, and his wife, Mary, signed her dowry. This is the last trace we have of him.

2 JAMES TEMPLETON, SR., 1748-1824

As stated on page 1, the first record we have of 2 James Templeton, Sr., is in the form of a land grant to him as recorded in the office of Secretary of State, Columbia, S. C. In the Land Grant records, Volume 35, Class I, Page 458, we find this (abstract) record:

> "James Templeton .... 100 acres, situate in Craven County on the waters of Dunkens Creek bounded on all sides by vacant land—Seventeenth day of March anno Domino 1775 in the Fifteenth year of our reign. . . .
>
> William Bull, Esqr. Lieut."

In the Plat Book, Vol. 20 (State Records Vol. 8) Page 288, we find a copy of the plat, in the shape of a square in which a small stream (probably a spring) flows out in approximately the compass direction "N. 85 W 31.62" or "S 85 E 31.62." The plat bears the caption:

> "James Templeton, Craven County Dunkin's Creek, Bounded on all sides by vacant lands. . . Certified for 15th day of Dec. 1772 by me.
>
> Pat Cunningham." (Surveyor)

This date is about the same (Dec., 1772) as the certification of the surveys for 3 Robert Templeton, 5 Martha Templeton, and 6 Agnes Templeton, and might indicate that they were actually living there in 1772.

The next record that we have of 2 James Templeton, Sr., is that of his Revolutionary War services, part of which is reproduced here (Fig. 5).

In the office of Clerk of Court, Laurens, S. C., we find that, on Dec. 10, 1788, James Templeton "of Abbeville County" (adjoining Laurens County), S. C., sold to Samuel Flemming 180 acres of land on Warrior Creek. This was part of the 400 acres granted David Templeton of Anson County, N. C., on May 16, 1754, and referred to on page I Appendix. It was evidently this same, James Templeton referred to this time only as "in South Carolina" who, with James Adair, on April 8, 1789, sold to Elisha Attaway the remaining 220 acres of this tract. (Could this have been our 2 James Templeton?)

Meanwhile, on Feb. 21, 1789, and again on Feb. 22, 1789, we find that 2 James Templeton "of Laurens County" bought 225 acres and 225 acres more land on Little River, called the Beaverdam. One of these deeds was witnessed by William Taylor and William Taylor, Jr. (See elsewhere the possible identity of William Taylor.)

On Jan. 18, 1928, 271 Robert Scott Templeton, grandson of 2 James Templeton, stated: that 2 James Templeton was born in Ireland; that he settled about 2½ miles southeast of Laurens

(Fig. 5)

Reproduction of a Part of the Revolutionary War Record of 2 James Templeton, Sr.,
as Found in the Office of the South Carolina Historical Commission, Columbia, S. C.

Courthouse; that he was a farmer; that he had no brothers or sisters in the U. S.; that he married Margaret Taylor who came to the U. S. with him. Later on 27i Robert Scott Templeton said that he was not positive about the accuracy of some of these statements. Of chief concern are the questions of 2 James Templeton's wife and that of his brothers and sisters referred to on pages 1 and 2.

86

As to the question of whom 2 James Templeton married, we have the following information:

(a) Beside the grave of 2 James Templeton in Rock Springs cemetery, Laurens County, S. C., is the grave marked: "Jane Templeton, died Jan. 22, 1848, age 88 years, 10 months."

(b) In the office of Probate Judge, Laurens, S. C., there is recorded, Nov. 22, 1824, the settlement of the estate of James Templeton in which there was paid to "Jane Templeton, $896." This was approximately 1/3 of the estate which was the share legally allotted to a widow.

(c) Also, in the office of Probate Judge, Laurens, S. C., we find: in "A general and final return of the estate of William Tayor Senr. Decd. made May 15, 1809: . . . Jane Templeton $117.94." Other legatees received the same amount.

These data seem to show beyond a doubt that 2 James Templeton married Jane Taylor. Her full name could have been Margaret Jane Taylor.

2 James Templeton had seven children that are accounted for in family Bible records, court records, and church records. They are:

    21 William Templeton.
    22 Capt. James Templeton, 5/27/1791-1/29/1857.
    23 Mary Templeton, 7/18/1793-5/23/1864.
    24 Samuel Templeton, 11/22/1795-7/8/1888.
    25 Capt. John Templeton, 7/31/1800-10/28/1856.
    26 Jane Templeton.
    27 David Clark Templeton, 8/10/1805-4/22/1880.

He may have had other children that we have no record of.

He is one of the four Templetons in Laurens County, S. C., listed in the first U. S. Census of 1790. This census shows that he had in his household, "Free white males, 16 years old and upward, including heads of families, 2." He was evidently one of these. The other one could have been his oldest known son, 21 William Templeton, although we do not know when he was born.

This report also shows 2 males under 16. We do not know who these were. The report also shows 2 females. One of these was evidently his wife.

The Census report of 1800 shows that there were in the household of 2 James Templeton, 5 males under 10 years old. Two of these were evidently 22 James Templeton, born 1791, and 24 Samuel Templeton, born 1795. A third one could have been 25 John Templeton, born 7/31/1800. We do not know who the others were. This report also shows 2 males, 10-16 years old. The one female under 10 years old, as shown in this report, was evidently 23 Mary Templeton, born 1793. The one female of 45 years and upward was evidently his wife.

The census reports of 1810 and 1820 show some data that can

be accounted for, but all of these reports seem to indicate that, either some children were born and died that we have no record of, or that there were other persons living with 2 James Templeton.

The records in the office of Probate Judge, Laurens, S. C., show that 2 James Templeton, Sr., died intestate and that 21 William Templeton and (Capt.) 22 James Templeton were appointed administrators of his estate. These administrators paid out, on Nov. 22, 1824, in the final settlement of the estate, the following amounts to the legatees: 27 D. C. Templeton, $224.03 (signed for by 24 Samuel Templeton, guardian); 25 John Templeton, $224.03; Jane Templeton, $896.00 (this amount being the approximate 1/3 legally due a surviving widow it is evident that she was his widow); 26 Jane McDowal (signed for also by John McDowal) $224.03; I Tribble, $224.03, guardian for 22d J. C. Templeton, mute; 24 Samuel Templeton, $224.03; 23 Mary Templeton, $224.03. The administrators evidently retained their shares without necessity of receipts.

In the "History of the Presbyterian Church in South Carolina Since 1850," by E. F. Jones and W. H. Mills, we find this statement in connection with Rocky Springs Church (which was organized in 1780): "D. C. (27) Templeton and others met at the home of Z. L. Holmes in August, 1860. . . . It was distinctly recollected that the first preacher, Rev. John McCosh of Ireland, instructed old Mrs. Jane Templeton how to prepare communion bread." (This "instruction" by the "first preacher" was evidently before Jane Templeton died.)

These records of this old church show that the descendents of 2 James Templeton have been devoutly religious and staunch Presbyterians.

The oldest child of 2 James Templeton was 21 William Templeton. In addition to his record as an administrator of his father's estate, we find his name on the roll of Rocky Springs Church as "William Templeton, Sr., dismissed, 1854." 271 Mr. Robert Scott Tempelton furnished the information that 21 William Templeton married a Miss Martin, an aunt of Caroline Peden who was the wife of 27a Thaddeus McDuffie Templeton; that he lived on the west side of Little River, below Laurens, near the Captain Jimmie Davis place; and that he moved to Bartow County, near Cartersville, Ga.

The rolls of Rocky Springs Church give us a bit of valuable information about the children of 21 William Templeton. On that roll of "October 12, 1833" (and subsequently current) "of those baptized in infancy" we find:

211 "Margaret Achen Templeton, Dar. Wm.
212 "David Clark Templeton, Dar. Wm.

213 "Robert Martin Templeton, Dar. Wm. (Recd. on profession Dec. 6, 1848)."

214 Eliza Jane Templeton, Dar. Wm., Recd. July 19, 1845.

215 "James Washington Templeton, Dar. Wm., Recd. into full communion Sept. 16, 1850—dropped."

Nothing more is now known about 21 William Templeton or his children.

22 Capt. James Templeton was born May 27, 1791, and died Jan. 29, 1857. He was an elder and the clerk in Rocky Springs Church until he was dismissed, along with his daughter, 223 Mary Ann Templeton, on August 6, 1843, when he was received into Bethany Presbyterian Church near Clinton, S. C. Later on he moved to the New Harmony Church section of Laurens County, S. C., where he died and was buried. He married, March 10, 1814, Margaret Hutchison, b. Jan. 2, 1791, d. May 7, 1838, buried, Rocky Springs. Their children were: (per Bible 22g6 Dr. Anthony White)

22a William Templeton, 1/22/1816-4/17/1838.
22b Elizabeth Jane Templeton, 1/2/1818-1901.
22c Mary Ann ("Polly") Templeton, 9/27/1819-1/27/1891.
22d James Clark Templeton (mute), b. Oct. 16, 1821.
22e Samuel Taylor Templeton, b. April 16, 1824.
22f John Hutchinson Templeton, b. Sept. 11, 1826. He went to Georgia or Alabama after the War Between the States and died there. He never married.
22g Nancy Katherine Templeton, 9/4/1828-12/27/1879.
22h Robert Mitchell Templeton, b. June 2, 1830.

22 Capt. James Templeton married a second time, Nov. 10, 1842, Anne Elizabeth Hitch, b. Dec. 18, 1807 d. Oct. 26, 1879. (She was the daughter of John and Katherine Hanna Hitch, and a sister of Margaret Hanna Hitch, who m. 27 David Clark Templeton.) Their children were:

22i William Henry Templeton, b. July 3, 1844-Oct. 12, 1846, NM.
22j Isabelle Adella Templeton, Feb. 2, 1846-Jan. 18, 1918.
22k Perry Franklin Templeton, June 30, 1850-Sept. 9, 1929.
22L Clayton Walker Calhoun Templeton, March 26, 1853-Jan. 16, 1929.

22b Elizabeth Jane Templeton was buried at Mt. Zion Church, Central, S. C. She was baptized in infancy at Rocky Springs Church, according to the roll of Oct. 12, 1833. On June 1, 1843, she married W. Turner Smith. About the year 1847 they moved to Pickens County, S. C. He was a soldier of the Confederacy

and died in the Confederate Hospital in Richmond, Va., in 1863. He was buried at Carmel Church in Pickens County, S. C. Their children were:
22b1 Margaret Smith.
22b2 John Clark Smith.
22b3 Mary Catherine Smith, 7/5/1856-2/16/1915.

22b1 Margaret Smith married Joseph Rutherford. She was buried at Bethel Presbyterian Church, Oconee County, S. C. He died in Alabama. They had no children.

22b2 John Clark Smith married Elizabeth Arnold. He died in 1918 and was buried at Mt. Zion Church, Central, S. C. They had one child:
22b21 Cora Smith, who married Tom Gillespie. They have six children.

22b3 Mary Catherine Smith married Thomas Benton Arnold, b. 12/25/1852-7/6/1918. They were both buried at Mt. Zion Church, Central, S. C. They had two children:
22b31 Thaddeus Turner Arnold.
22b32 Adah Arnold, b. 1876, married, Dec. 1898, Will Oliver. They had four children, all of whom are dead.

22b31 Thaddeus Turner Arnold married, May 10, 1900, Darthula Williams, b. March 4, 1875. They live two miles east of Central, S. C., on Route 2, and have eight children:
22b311 Captain Lowndes William Arnold, b. 9/16/1901.
22b312 Thaddeus Ray Arnold, b. 4/30/1903.
22b313 Emma Lois Arnold, b. 2/28/1905.
22b314 Thomas D. Arnold, b. 12/7/1906. He married, Dec. 24, 1936, Ruth Carson, b. May, 1912. They live at Central, S. C., Rt. 2.
22b315 Marcus Wade Arnold, b. 2/24/1908.
22b316 Mary Elizabeth Arnold, b. 2/2/1910, now lives at Central, S. C., Rt. 2.
22b317 William Marshall Arnold, b. 7/30/1912, now lives at Central, S. C., Rt. 2.
22b318 James Bailey Arnold, b. 9/9/1914, who now lives at 34 Hill St., Greer, S. C., and who m. 14g148 Ruby Woodruff.

22b311 Captain Lowndes William Arnold married, June 6, 1926, Berdie Jones. They lived at Fort Oglethorpe, Ga., and have five children:
22b3111 Jack Jones Arnold, b. 2/27/1927, and lives at Royston, Ga., care Mrs. Nan Jones.
22b3112 Sallie Jones Arnold.

22b3113 Catherine Arnold.
22b3114 Tommie Arnold.
22b3115 Joel Turner Arnold.

22b312 Thaddeus Ray Arnold married, July 4, 1929, Abelia Moore. They live at 140 Monroe St., Anderson, S. C., and have two children:
    22b3121 Thaddeus Ray Arnold, Jr.
    22b3122 Lena Darthula Arnold.

22b313 Emma Lois Arnold, a sales lady in Ivey's department store, Greenville, S. C., married, Nov. 19, 1929, Dewey Hobson Bouchillon. They live at 402 Elm St., Greenville, S. C. They have two children:
    22b3131 Dewey H. Bouchillon, b. 12/19/1931.
    22b3132 Mary Louise Bouchillon, b. 7/1934.

22b315 Marcus Wade Arnold married, February, 1930, Ellen Garland. They live at Wise Court House, Va. They have two children:
    22b3151 Marcus W. Arnold, Jr., b. 12/1/1931.
    22b3152 Elizabeth A. Arnold, b. 8/1933.

22c Mary Ann (Polly) Templeton married, Oct. 13 (17?), 1843, William Washington Stewart, 12/16/1821-12/1/1864. She (and probably he) was buried at Clear Springs Baptist Church, Greenville County, S. C. They had four children:
    22c1 Laura Manderille Stewart, 7/17/1845-1910, buried at Clear Springs Baptist Church, Greenville County, S. C.
    22c2 John Thaddeus Stewart, 9/27 (29?)/1849-6/27/1899.
    22c3 James Addison Stewart, 7/16/1853.
    22c4 Margaret Linnie Stewart, 6/27/1857-9/16/1916 (1915?).

22c1 Laura Manderille Stewart m. 11/27/1866, John Westmore land Bradley, 5/18/1834-1911. They had three children:
    22c11 William Meadow Bradley, 5/12/1869-12/3/1945; m. Pauline Fortune, 2/4/1883-1947. They had no children.
    22c12 Egbert Ronald Bradley, 5/29/1873-7/30/1950; m. Evelyn Kilgore, 2/4/1883.
    22c13 Mary Effie Bradley, 2/3/1876; m. 9/23/1900, Samuel Tilden Howard, 11/22/1876-2/7/1931. She lives at Fountain Inn, S. C. They had four children:
        22c131 James Matthew Howard, 5/17/1901.
        22c132 Frank Stewart Howard, 4/17/1908, who lives at Fountain Inn, S. C.
        22c133 Eva Howard, 2/25/1913.
        22c134 Wilton Earl Howard, 6/10/1917.

22c131 James Matthew Howard m. Minnie Lookabill. They had
two children:
  22c1311 Elizabeth Ann Howard.
  22c1212 Nancy Jane Howard.

22c133 Eva Howard m. 1/16/1942, Carrol Stoddard, 9/16/1915.
They live at Fountain Inn, S. C. They have two children:
  22c1331 James Howard Stoddard, 9/30/1945.
  22c1332 Margaret Ann Stoddard, 9/9/1950.

22c134 Wilton Earl Howard m. Margaret Fletcher, 6/10/1916.
They live in Greenville, S. C.

22c2 John Thaddeus Stewart m. 11/19/1871, Mattie Jane League,
10/26/1850-11/14/1924. He was buried at Clear Springs Church.
They had thirteen children:
  22c2a William Pliney Stewart, 4/7/1874-7/13/1949.
  22c2b Mary Ann Stewart, 10/26/1875-10/15/1952.
  22c2c Nannie Hunter Stewart, 1/18/1877-8/12/1949; married
  3/1/1900, Dr. Wade D. Fowler, 7/1/1863. They had no
  children.
  22c2d Lillie Mae Stewart, 9/22/1878.
  22c2e Robert Raikes Stewart, 6/24/1881-10/13/1912.
  22c2f Hattie Stewart, 2/21/1883-2/25/1883.
  22c2g Mattie Maude Stewart, 2/18/1884.
  22c2h Thomas Thaddeus Stewart, 8/3/1886.
  22c2i Ben Price Stewart, 7/5/1888-8/13/1939.
  22c2j George League Stewart, 12/13/1890-1/10/1948, NM.
  22c2k Walter Grady Stewart, 11/5/1893.
  22c2L Maggie Grace Stewart, 12/9/1895.
  22c2m Frank Stanton Stewart, 1/31/1897-8/21/1918 (killed
  in World War I on board U. S. Destroyer Montauk.)

22c2a William Pliney Stewart m. 8/17/1897, Sallie Cummings,
2/27/1875-6/16/1920. They had ten children:
  22c2aa Edith Stewart, 2/25/1899; m. 10/11/1929, Henry
  Grady Mayfield 1/2/1900. They had no children. They
  live at Simpsonville, S. C.
  22c2ab Addie Stewart, born 1901.
  22c2ac J. Thad Stewart, born 4/6/1902. He lives at Simpsonville, S. C.
  22c2ad William Pliney Stewart, Jr., 5/14/1904-9/4/1948; m.
  Estelle Smith 8/20/1907. They live at Simpsonville, S. C.
  22c2ae Thomas Cummings Stewart, 10/15/1905.
  22c2af Wallace Stewart, 4/14/1908.
  22c2ag Helen Gould Stewart, 1/29/1910.
  22c2ah Margaret Stewart, 7/16/1912. She lives at Lyman,
  S. C.

22c2ai Mary Alice Stewart 2/24/1915.
22c2aj Frances Stewart, 2/10/1919.

22c2ab Addie Stewart m. 6/4/1924, Loy Cleland Jones, 4/26/1900. They live at 137 Capers St., Greenville, S. C. They have two children:
    22c2ab1 Sara Frances Jones, 8/12/1932.
    22c2ab2 Loy Camille Jones 4/20/1938.

22c2ae Thomas Cummings Stewart m. 10/17/1936, Katie Beauford, 2/26/1916. They live at Ridgeland, S. C., and have two children:
    22c2ae1 Tommy Stewart, 8/13/1938.
    22c2ae2 Margaret Joyce Stewart, 11/15/1942.

22c2af Wallace Stewart m. 1/28/1939, Sara Gause, 7/15/1916. They live at Simpsonville, S. C. They have one child:
    22c2af1 Patricia Frances Stewart, 12/4/1942.

22c2ag Helen Gould Stewart m. 12/1/1929, 22q41 Alvin White, 7/11/1906. They live at Simpsonville, S. C. They have four children:
    22c2ag1 John William White, 8/3/1939(?)—5
    22c2ag2 Cynthia Anita White, 4/3/1936-51?; m. A. D. Cannon, Simpsonville, S. C.
    22c2ag3 Kenneth Stewart White, 4/6/1941.
    22c2ag4 George White, 8/21/1947.

22c2ai Mary Alice Stewart m. 6/5/1936, David Donald Fowler, 8/23/1909. They live on Stewart St., Greenville, S. C. They have two children:
    22c2ai1 J. Donald Fowler, 8/16/1938.
    22c2ai2 Kathleen Stewart Fowler, 1/18/1943.

22c2aj Frances Stewart m. 9/29/1943, Eldridge C.Barnett, 3/23/1919. They live at Simpsonville, S. C. They have one child:
    22c2aj1 Robert Layne Barnett, 3/31/1949.

22c2b Mary Ann Stewart m. 12/25/1900, John Breckenridge Cook, 8/19/1875. They live at Fountain Inn, S. C. They have eight children:
    22c2b1 Nell Cook, 10/4/1901.
    22c2b2 Madge Cook, 4/2/1903.
    22c2b3 John Breckenridge Cook, Jr., 5/26/1905.
    22c2b4 Charles Stewart Cook, 3/13/1908.
    22c2b5 Frank Abraham Cook, 4/18/1910.
    22c2b6 Fred Martin Cook, 8/9/1915.
    22c2b7 Ernest Glenn Cook, 3/30/1916?
    22c2b8 Mildred Cook, 7/24/1917.

22c2b1 Nell Cook was reared on the farm near Fountain Inn, S. C., where she was graduated from high school. She also attended high school for a year or two in Washington, D. C. She attended Winthrop College, Rock Hill, S. C., for two years, after which she taught for five years in the public schools near her home. She is a member of the United Daughters of the Confederacy. She is also active in home demonstration clubs, being the Chief Prodder in her home club. She finds time to read extensively and has won many prizes for her beautiful fancy work. She has been active and efficient in compiling genealogical records in both the Stewart family and the Templeton family.

22c2b2 Madge Cook m. 6/5/1924, Fred Owings Drummond, 9/11/1903. They live at 200 N. Rose St., Kannapolis, N. C. They have three children:
    22c2b21 Charles Max Drummond, 1/17/1925.
    22c2b22 Fred Owings Drummond, Jr., 7/15/1927 (twin).
    22c2b23 Suzanne Drummond, 7/15/1927 (twin).

22c2b21 Charles Max Drummond m. Barbara Fisher. They live at Staten Island, N. Y. They have one child:
22c2b211 Deborah Irene Drummond, 11/22/1951.

22c2b3 John Breckenridge Cook, Jr., m. 5/8/1926, Lucile Jackson, 4/2/1907. They live at Woodruff, S. C. They have four children:
    22c2b31 Doris Cook, 4/1/1927.
    22c2b32 John Breckenridge Cok III, 4/9/1920; m. 8/13/1946, Celeste Morrison. They live at Norfolk, Va., where he is stationed in the U. S. Marines. They have no children.
    22c2b33 Carrol Cook, 11/7/1931 (twin). He lives at Woodruff, S. C.
    22c2b34 Carolyn Cook, 11/7/1931 (twin)

22c2b31 Doris Cook m. 9/13/1946, John Wilson Anderson, 6/4/1925. They live at 165 Anderson Drive, Spartanburg, S. C. They have two children:
    22c2b311 Carole Linder Anderson, 11/14/1948.
    22c2b312 Erick Fred Anderson, 2/10/1951.

22c2b34 Carolyn Cook m. 8/20/1950, Etha A. McKee, Jr. They live at 165 Avant St., Spartanburg, S. C. They have one child:
    22c2b341 Gregory Lynn McKee, 6/20/1952.

22c2b4 Charles Stewart Cook m. 7/2/1939, Carolyn Wright, 8/18/1910. They live at Brevard, N. C. They have four children:
    22c2b41 Carolyn Virginia Cook, 7/4/1942.
    22c2b42 Charles Stewart Cook, 1/17/1945.
    22c2b43 Janice Cook, 12/28/1946.
    22c2b44 Anne McFall Cook, 12/3/1951.

22c2b5 Frank Abraham Cook m. 7/4/1935, Beatrice Petty, 7/19/1914. They live at 611 Northridge St., Greensboro, N. C. They have three children:
    22c2b51 Frank Abraham Cook, Jr., 5/25/1938.
    22c2b52 Gloria Mayson Cook, 10/11/1941.
    22c2b53 Mary Jane Cook, 9/13/1948.

22c2b6 Fred Martin Cook m. 9/5/1931, Louise Galdman, 1/10/1916. They live at 522 E. Faris, Greenville, S. C. They have one child:
    22c2b61 Fred Martin Cook, Jr., 11/27/1939.

22c2b8 Mildred Cook m. 7/20/1943, Thomas Calvin Hawkins, 12/7/1910. They live at Fountain Inn, S. C. They have three children:
    22c2b81 Joyce Ann Hawkins, 3/19/1945.
    22c2b82 Mary Jean Hawkins, 3/1/1947.
    22c2b83 Marsha Lee Hawkins, 8/4/1951.

22c2d Lillie May Stewart m. 12/12/1901, Perry Newton Gresham, 4/22/1877. They live at Simpsonville, S. C. They have three children:
    22c2d1 Martha Carolyn Gresham, 10/25/1903.
    22c2d2 Agnes Gresham, 2/19/1905.
    22c2d3 Edna May Gresham, 9/26/1906.

22c2d1 Martha Carolyn Gresham m. 8/14/1929, Price Howard, 11/25/1899. They have two children:
    22c2d11 Andy Swofford Howard, 2/26/1932.
    22c2d12 Eddie Price Howard, 9/16/1936.

22c2e Robert Raiker Stewart m. 9/6/1911, Sallie Mae Cook, 7/16/1881-11/30/1928. They had one child:
    22c2e1 Bobbie (nee Robbie) Stewart, 10/19/1912. She m. 6/27/1933, Bruce Harrison Richardson, 12/13/1913-10/13/1944. She lives at Simpsonville, S. C. They had two children:
        22c2e11 Sallie Richardson, 12/6/1936.
        22c2e12 Lawrence Richardson, 2/25/1940.

22c2g Mattie Maude Stewart m. 12/26/1906, Rev. James Preston Coleman, 2/22/1871-3/20/1929. She lives at 1411 E. North St., Greenville, S. C. They had nine children:
    22c2g1 Cecile Ernestine Coleman, 10/1/1906.
    22c2g2 Christine Nannie Coleman, 12/10/1907.
    22c2g3 Walter Stewart Coleman, 10/5/1909.
    22c2g4 Lucile Woodson Coleman, 5/24/1911; m. 8/12/1939, Robert W. Taylor, 3/9/1892. They live on Woodgate Ave., Greenville, S. C. They have no children:

22c2g5 John Preston Coleman, 6/7/1914.
22c2g6 Lois Shirley Coleman, 7/24/1916.
22c2g7 Rachel Frances Coleman, 7/25/1918; m. 7/5/1941,
James Fowler, 10/22/1916. They live on Carolina Ave.,
Greenville, S. C. They have no children.
22c2g8 Martha League Coleman, 8/8/1920.
22c2g9 Robert Earl Coleman, 3/3/1925.

22c2g1 Cecile Ernestine Coleman m. 6/5/1937, George Cleveland Weaver, 9/18/1909. They live at Moonville, S. C. They
have three children:
      22c2g11 Maude Kenielle Weaver, 5/2/1938.
      22c2g12 James Thomas Weaver, 10/10/1940.
      22c2g13 George Richard Weaver, 9/18/1941.

22c2g2 Christine Nannie Coleman m. 11/23/1934 James Lee
Gilstrap, 6/24/1908. They live on Waite St., Greenville, S. C.,
Rt. 6. They have one child:
      22c2g21 Mary Lou Gilstrap, 5/21/1938.

22c2g3 Walter Stewart Coleman m. 8/12/1939 Eva McRainey,
1/22/1913. They live at Box 722, Salisbury, N. C. They have
two children:
      22c2g31 Walter Stewart Coleman, Jr., 8/12/1942.
      22c2g32 Kenneth McRainey Coleman, 1/7/1945.

22c2g5 James Preston Coleman m. 5/17/1937 Jane Hunter, 12/
31/1915. They live at 215 Hillcrest Drive, Greenville, S. C. They
have four children:
      22c2g51 Carol Hunter Coleman, 9/19/1939.
      22c2g52 Lillian Stewart Coleman, 9/16/1940.
      22c2g53 James Preston Coleman, III, 2/19/1945.
      22c2g54 Mary Gwendolyn Coleman, 4/18/1950.

22c2g6 Lois Shirley Coleman m. 6/19/1943 Donald Nobson
Warne, 10/8/1913. They live at 23 Garreux, Greenville, S. C.
They have two children:
      22c2g61 Robert Preston Warne, 11/29/1944.
      22c2g62 Agnes Patricia Warne, 4/8/1949.

22c2g8 Martha League Coleman m. 10/2/1943 Roger Lowell
Gill, 12/1/1920. They live at 511 N. 8th St., Opelika, Ala. They
have two children:
      22c2g81 Daniel Ross Gill, 4/11/1948.
      22c2g82 Alan Stewart Gill, 3/7/1950.

22c2g9 Robert Earl Coleman m. 8/..../1952 Sarah Williams.
They live at Rome, Ga.

22c2h Thomas Thaddeus Stewart m. 12/22/1915 Mamie Cros-

well. They live at Mt. Pleasant, S. C. They have two children:
22c2h1 Janice Stewart, 1/7/1916.
22c2h2 Marian Stewart, 2/17/1918.

22c2h1 Janice Stewart m. 9/14/1940 Jack Monroe Smith, 1/17/
1913. They live at Florence, S. C. They have two children:
22c2h11 Stewart Monroe Smith, 6/10/1947.
22c2h12 Susan Jacque Smith, 6/11/1952.

22c2h2 Marian Stewart m. 2/27/1947 Richard Stanley Merritt,
1/1/1907. They live at Charleston, S. C. They have one child:
22c2h21 Janis Elizabeth Merritt, 4/30/1951.

22c2i Ben Price Stewart m. 12/20/1917 Sallie Boozer, 2/27/1895.
They live at Belton S. C. They have five children:
22c2i1 Frank Boozer Stewart, 12/1/1919.
22c2i2 Ben Pressley Stewart, 1/27/1922.
22c2i3 Martha Emma Stewart, 12/4/1923; m. 9/16/1951
James L. Dominick. They have one child:
22c2i31 Martha Gale Dominick, 9/3/1952.
22c2i4 Blanche Stewart, 6/27/1926.
22c2i5 Audrey Stewart, 6/26/1929.

22c2i1 Frank Boozer Stewart m. 9/21/1942 Estelle Steadman,
12/29/1921. They live at Chappels, S. C. They have three children:
22c2i11 Frank Donald Stewart, 3/12/1944.
22c2i12 Nina Ann Stewart, 7/1/1945.
22c2i13 ....?

22c2i2 Ben Pressley Stewart m. 11/28/1946 Gaynelle Harmon,
7/7/1921. They live at 1246 Jones St., Newberry, S. C. They
have two children:
22c2i21 Ben Pressley Stewart, Jr., 1/2/1948.
22c2i22 Gaynelle Harmon Stewart, 1/20/1951.

22c2i5 Audrey Stewart m. 12/24/1948 Charles William Coleman,
8/3/1917. They live at Belton, S. C. They have one son:
22c2i51 Charles William Coleman, Jr., 3/28/1950.

22c2k Walter Grady Stewart m. 11/22/1919 Azile Bozeman.
They live at Druid Hill Park Drive, Spartanburg, S. C. They have
one child
22c2k1 Walter Grady Stewart, Jr., 10/2/1926; m. 6/17/1949
Sibyl Creighton, 7/12/1927.

22c2L Maggie Grace Stewart m. 3/7/1925 Taro Toy Todd, Jr.,
12/1/1900. They live at Simpsonville, S. C. They have two
children:
22c2L1 Martha Jane Todd, 4/7/1926.
22c2L2 Jack Todd, 12/20/1930.

22c2L1 Martha Jane Todd m. 11/5/1945 Stanley J. Oldham, 8/3/1919.

22c3 James Addison Stewart m. 10/15/1874 Manta Lucinda Austin, 3/24/1857. They had seven children:
    22c31 Ina Pauline Stewart, 6/24/1875-6/24/1875 (twin).
    22c32 Minnie Ola Stewart, 6/24/1875 (twin).
    22c33 Eva Estelle Stewart, 1/13/1877.
    22c34 Fred Austin Stewart, 3/9/1879.
    22c35 Florence Margaret Stewart, 9/14/1882.
    22c36 Lola Fay Stewart, 6/4/1886-5/11/1887.
    22c37 Kate Walker Stewart, 7/9/1894.

22c32 Minnie Ola Stewart m. 4/5/1901 William Bonner Inglett, 12/11/1877. They had two children:
    22c321 Nellie Odessa Inglett, 1/7/1903.
    22c322 Houman Wade Inglett, 5/2/1905.

22c33 Eva Estelle Stewart m. 5/15/1905 Thomas Jefferson Dugard, 8/11/1879. They had one child:
    22c331 Mark Irvin Dugard, 8/5/1906.

22c34 Fred Austin Stewart m. 10/20/1902 Nancy Parker, 3/25/1885. They had two children:
    22c341 Thad Parker Stewart, 12/31/1902.
    22c342 Annie Lou Stewart, 2/24/1905.

22c35 Florence Margaret Stewart m. 6/1/1901 Ernest Benoit, 3/12/1887. They had three children:
    22c351 Ernest Theodore Benoit, 4/22/1902.
    22c352 Gladis Marie Benoit, 8/16/1903-2/6/1904.
    22c353 Ruth Estelle Benoit, 7/23/1905.

22c4 Margaret Linnie Stewart was buried at Clear Springs Baptist Church, Greenville County, S. C. She m. 11/24/1874 George H. Jones, 1/23/1853-10/30/1922. He was a brother to Mattie Jones who m. 22k Perry Franklin Templeton.) They had one son:
    22c41 William Stewart Jones, 12/8/1875-7/12/1910. He was a farmer. In attempting to mount a mule he frightened the mule which ran off with him. His feet were caught in the gear and he was dragged for nearly a mile. He lived only a few minutes after being rescued. He m. 11/24/1901 Nellie A. League, 7/17/1884. They had three children:
        22c411 Malcolm Stewart Jones, b. 4/4/1904 (the 4th hour of the 4th day of the 4th month of the 4th year).
        22c412 Margaret Agnes Jones, 12/1/1905.
        22c413 Ellen Louise Jones, 8/23/1908.

22c411 Malcolm Stewart Jones m. 7/23/1932 Thalia A. Neely,

10/16/1910. They live at Simpsonville. They have two children:

    22c4111 Margaret Louise Jones, 9/26/1933.
    22c4112 Nettie (Neels?) Eugenia Jones, 3/20 (30?)/1938.

22c412 Margaret Agnes Jones m. 6/18/1932 Curry Jasper Fowler, 3/1/1904. They live at Simpsonville S. C., R.F.D. They have five children:
    22c4121 William Cely Fowler, 2/20/1934.
    22c4122 Marilyn Joan Fowler, 3/26/1937.
    22c4123 Curry Jasper Fowler, Jr., 6/2/1940-6/4/1940.
    22c4124 Douglass Norman Fowler, 9/13/1942.
    22c4125 Michael Jeffry Fowler, 12/29/1944.

22c413 Ellen Louise Jones m. 6/29/1926 Ogelvie Pete (Dick?) Allen, 10/4/1898. They had one child:
    22c4131 Betty Jean Allen, 9/26/1929. She m. Dean Black.

22d James Clark Templeton was a mute. He was baptized in infancy at Rocky Springs Church. He married, 11/7/1854 Arena Bobo who was also a mute. They had three children:
    22d1 Jefferson Davis Templeton, who was living in Alabama at last account.
    22d2 Clayton Templeton, who moved to Lancaster County, S. C.
    22d3 Walker Templeton, who also moved to Lancaster County, S. C.

22e Samuel Taylor Templeton married, 1/5/1854, Elizabeth Ann Hutchinson. He moved to Georgia or Alabama.

22g Nancy Katherine Templeton married John Jones White, b. 1831 d. January, 1908. They had six children:
    22g1 Corrie E. White, b. 10/3/1857.
    22g2 Margaret Ida White b. 5/16/1859.
    22g3 Dr. James Ausker White, 4/15/1861-9/12/1924.
    22g4 John King White, 10/27/1862-4/11/1924.
    22g5 Robert Clark White, 3/12/1866-11/14/1927.
    22g6 Dr. Anthony White, 9/13/1869.

22g1 Corrie E. White married D. L. Jones. They live at Simpsonville S. C.

22g2 Margaret Ida White married S. T. Moore. They live at Simpsonville, S. C.

22g3 Dr. James Ausker White was buried at Greenville, S. C. He married Etta Putman.

22g4 John King White married Cynthia Smith. They had one son:
22g41 Alvin White, 7/11/1906. He m. 12/1/1929, 22c2ag Helen Gould Stewart, 1/29/1910 (See her line).

22g5 Robert Clark White married Eva Smith who was a sister to Cynthia Smith who married 22g4 John King White.

22g6 Dr. Anthony White married, July, 1899, Bessie Montgomery, b. 8/25/1880. They live at 8 Williams St., Greenville, S. C., where he has an extensive practice as a physician. They have one child:
22g61 Agnes Elizabeth White, b. 8/31/1900.

22h Robert Mitchell Templeton was received into Rocky Springs Church on profession Dec. 6, 1848. He "enlisted for 3 years at Newberry by Lieut. Herbert, March 19, 1862; not on any subsequent available muster roll. Unofficial compilation says he died of Disease at Williamsburg, Va., April 5, 1862." (This must have been an error, because 27i Robert Scott Templeton says that he moved to Talapoosa County, Ala. where he married and had two or more children:
22h1 Margaret Templeton,
22h2 Bob Templeton,
and at least two others, names unknown.
Also 22g6 Dr. Anthony White, his nephew, says that "He moved to Alabama when young man. Never came back. Raised a good sized family.")
It is interesting to note that 22i William Henry Templeton was a half brother of 22a William Templeton who had died in 1838. Their father, 22 Capt. James Templeton, probably had some sentimental reason for naming two of his children WILLIAM.

22j Isabella Adella Templeton married, Nov. 9, 1865, James M. Thackston, b. Oct. 16 1842, d. Nov. 29 1910. She was reared in the Fairview Presbyterian Church section of Greenville County, S. C., which church she joined in early childhood. She was a Sunday School teacher and an active member of the missionary society of this church. She was a good cook at anything from corn cake to pound cake. She was not only resourceful, but skillful in carding cotton, spinning it, and dyeing it in dye that she made of different kinds of bark. She would weave this yarn into cloth and make useful articles of clothing for the family. She could also spin and weave into cloth from which she made suits for the men in the family. During the long winter nights she would sit up and knit hosiery for the family. She also taught her daughters to do the same. When help was scarce on the farm she would go to the field and help with the crops. When she was about 45 years old she and her husband became dissatisfied with living on rented land and decided to buy a small home of their own, which they paid for from the income of the farm. Their children were:

22j1 Twynam B. Thackston, 8/6/1866-1/9/1869, buried at Fairview Presbyterian Church in Greenville County, S. C.
22j2 Henry M. Thackston, 2/10/1868-12/14/1873, buried at Clear Springs Baptist Church in Greenville County, S. C.
22j3 Mettie J. Thackston, 2/23/1870.
22j4 Nannie E. Thackston, 1/22/1872-11/29/1918, buried at Fairview Presbyterian Church, Greenville County, S. C.
22j5 Cannie H. Thackston, b. 1/29/1875.

22j3 Mettie J. Thackston married Jan. 24, 1889, John L. Sprouse who died Jan. 21, 1938, and was buried at Fairview Church in Greenville County, S. C. She lives at Fountain Inn, S. C., Rt. 3. They had six children:

22j31 Lucinda Adella Sprouse, b. 1/19/1890.
22j32 William Calvin Sprouse, b. 7/12/1892.
22j33 James L. Sprouse, b. 9/19/1897, living at Winsmith Ave., Spartanburg, S. C.
22j34 Mary Jane Sprouse, b. 9/19/1897, living on Beachwood Ave., Greenville, S. C.
22j35 J. Clyde Sprouse, b. 11/19/1899, living at 2 West Earl St., Greenville, S. C.
22j36 Bertha Sprouse, b. 8/27/1910.

22j31 Lucinda Adella Sprouse married Dec. 25, 1913, J. Russell Terry. They live at Fountain Inn, S. C. Their children are:

22j311 Lewis Terry, b. 9/13/1914.
22j312 J. W. Terry, b. 1/16/1917.
22j313 Sarah Terry, 5/13/1919-1921, buried at Pisgah Methodist Church.
22j314 J. Russell Terry, Jr., b. 7/15/1921.
22j315 Ansel Terry, b. 10/5/1923.
22j316 Frances Terry, b. 7/16/1926.
22j317 Lucy Terry, b. 10/16/1931.
22j318 Caroline Terry, b. 10/18/1933.

22j32 William Calvin Sprouse married April 27, 1918, Maggie Jenkins. They live at Fountain Inn, S. C. They have six children:

22j321 Infant son Sprouse, d. 2/3/1920.
22j322 Margaret Sprouse, b. 2/3/1921.
22j323 Hazel Sprouse, 1/6/1923.
22j324 Warren Sprouse, b. 12/17/1925.
22j325 James Sprouse, b. 2/25/1928.
22j326 Betty Sprouse, b. 5/2/1934.

22j4 Nannie E. Thackston married April 27, 1897, Jeff D. McKittrick, b. Dec. 27, 1861, d. Nov. 28, 1932, buried Fairview Presbyterian Church, Greenville County, S. C. They had one child:
22j41 ....McKittrick, d. 6/29/1909.

22j5 Cannie H. Thackston, married Aug. 27, 1913, John W. Woodside. They live at Fountain Inn, S. C. They have no children.

22k Perry Franklin Templeton was buried at Clear Springs Baptist Church, Greenville County, S. C. He attended a one-teacher school, though irregularly, because he had to work at home much of the time. He lived on a farm and followed that occupation all of his life. After he had attained a ripe old age he made a visit to Cross Anchor, S. C., one Sunday and knocked on the door of 14g6 Leumas B. Templeton, who was taken by surprise at the visit of an old bearded man who introduced himself with the following dialog: "My name is Templeton." "So is mine," replied 14g6 L. B. Templeton. "Well, I heard that there was an old codger by the name of Templeton down here, so I thought I would come down and look him over, and, if he looked like a pretty decent fellow, I might try to see if I was kin to him." "All right," replied 14g6 L. B. T., "come in and let me see if you deserve claiming kin with." After this and further sparring, they settled down in earnest to try to solve the question, "Are we akin?" At the end of the day's discussions they were both inclined to believe they were, but they were unable to establish the connections definitely. Their limited information was such a handicap to them in trying to solve the question that the writer's already keen interest in the subject was greatly stimulated. When 22k Perry Franklin Templeton was in his 79th year he was invited to the first Templeton reunion in 1929, at the home of 14g6 L. B. Templeton at Cross Anchor, S. C. In spite of his very poor physical condition he was determined to attend. He seemed to be enraptured all day, and on, his way home, he remarked that he was willing to die now that he had been to one Templeton reunion and found out so much about his family connections. Just nineteen days later he passed on to his reward.

On Nov. 21, 1871, he married Mattie Jones, b. Aug. 22, 1854, d. Nov. 1, 1925. To this union six children were born:
22k1 Samuel C. Templeton 10/14/1873-8/21/1934.
22k2 Carrie C. Templeton, 8/14/1875-3/30/1946.
22k3 Mary A. Templeton, 4/27/1878-1/3/1942.
22k4 Clark S. Templeton, 4/3/1880-10/1/1944.
22k5 Maggie D. Templeton, b. 2/1/1884.
22k6 James W. Templeton, b. 2/6/1891.

22k1 Samuel C. Templeton was a successful merchant. For

many years he was a major partner and manager of the firm of Cosby-Templeton, wholesale grocers, in Greenville, S. C. His friendly disposition won for him hosts of friends. He was a con-secrated Christian. During the later years of his life he suffered from a heart ailment and knew that he was likely to face a fatal attack at any time. On one occasion he remarked to the writer that he always carried a prescription of medicine with him in pre-paration for an attack. He added very calmly, but emphatically, that his real preparation was in his soul, that he was prepared to go on a moment's notice. He married 2/22/1899, Mattie Jane Bram-lett, 4/19/1875-2/9/1935. He died Aug. 21, 1934. A little less than a year later, Feb. 9, 1935, she also passed on to her reward. They were both buried at Bethel Methodist Church, Mauldin, S. C. They had five children:

    22k11 Ansel League Templeton, 12/4/1899-6/19/1902, bur-ied at Bethel Methodist Church, Mauldin, S. C.
    22k12 Bramlett Russell Templeton, b. 5/25/1902.
    22k13 Samuel Alvin Templeton, b. 5/23/1904.
    22k14 Myrtle Elizabeth Templeton, b. 2/21/1907.
    22k15 Mattie Lou Templeton, b. 3/8/1921.

22k12 Bramlett Russell Templeton married Agnes Gwendolyn White, b. Nov. 2, 1904. They live at 63 Augusta Court, Green-ville, S. C. They have two children:
    22k121 Eleanor Gwendolyn Templeton, b. 6/29/1925.
    22k122 Russell White Templeton, b. 10/7/1935.

22k13 Samuel Alvin Templeton married Mabel Louise Dilling-ham, b. March 25, 1906. They have three children:
    22k131 Samuel Lee Templeton, b. 11/3/1925.
    22k132 Betty Jane Templeton, b. 8/21/1927.
    22k133 John Alvin Templeton, b. 11/15/1932.

22k131 Samuel Lee Templeton m. 12/27/1952 Polly Glenn, b. 3/1/1931, of Union, S. C., who was graduated from Converse Col-lege, Spartanburg, S. C., in 1952.

22k14 Myrtle Elizabeth Templeton married John Milford Caugh-man. They have two children:
    22k141 Mary Jane Caughman, b. 7/24/1932.
    22k142 John Milford Caughman, b. 5/14/1939.

22k2 Carrie C. Templeton m. 2/13/1902 James C. Burdette. They live at Simpsonville, S. C., Rt. 1. They have eight children:
    22k21 Nora Burdette, b. ...., m. Clarence Gresham.
    22k22 Lucy Burdette, b. ...., m. J. F. Brockman.
    22k23 Willie Burdette, b. ...., m. Guy Bertram (?)
    22k24 James C. Burdette, Jr., b. ...., m. Ethel Thompson.

22k25 Pansie Burdette, b. ...., m. Stanley Martin.
22k26 Emma Burdette, b. ....
22k27 Robert Burdette, m. Ruth Vickory.
22k28 Ralph Burdette.

22k3 Mary A. Templeton, b. ...., m. John I. Wood. They live at 36 Hampton Ave., Greenville, S. C. They have five children:
  22k31 Roy Wood, b. ...., killed in a car wreck. He m. Symantha Vaughn.
  22k32 Wyman Wood, b. ...., m. Pearl Jones.
  22k33 Tessa Wood, b. ....
  22k34 Claude Wood, b. ...., m. Lois Kellett.
  22k35 Grady Wood, b. ...., m. Beulah Sue Smith.

22k4 Clark S. Templeton was born and reared on the farm in Greenville County, S. C. He received his education in a one-teacher school at Clear Springs. When he became old enough to do work on the farm he could attend school only every other year. He was a successful farmer and an upright citizen as well as a devoted Christian. On August 2, 1930, at the second Templeton reunion he was elected President of the Templeton Clan and served for one year. He m. 12/20/1903, Carrie League. She died September 14, 1952, and was buried beside her husband at Clear Spring Baptist Church, Greenville County, S. C. They had eight children:
  22k41 Bessie Lee Templeton, 10/23/1904. She m. C. C. McKinney and lives at Simpsonville, S. C., Rt. 1.
  22k42 Lucile Templeton, 1/7/1906. She m. Roy Fowler and lives at Simpsonville, S. C.
  22k43 Mae Templeton, 5/5/1907. She m. 3/23/1933 Earl Jackson and lives in Greenville, S. C.
  22k44 J. Frank Templeton, 1/5/1909, a Master Sergeant in the U. S. Army. He returned in 1952 from duty in Okinawa. He m. 9/6/1934 Leneva Fletcher.
  22k45 Arch League Templeton, 1/9/1913. He m. Mazel Broom and lives in Greenville, S. C.
  22k46 Grover Wilson Templeton, 11/25/1914-1/17/1915, buried Clear Springs.
  22k47 Ruth Margaret Templeton, 10/8/1918. She m. Ralph Taylor and lives in Columbia, S. C.
  22k48 Charles Morrison Templeton, 8/18/1931, A-3C, stationed at Hunter Air Force Base, Savannah, Ga.

22k5 Maggie D. Templeton m. 12/15/1907, True V. Snow. They operated a successful farm near Simpsonville, S. C. Since his death she has continued to supervise the farm efficiently. They had three children:

22k51 Ralph Perry Snow, 11/29/1909-6/22/1936.
22k52 Mattie Elizabeth Snow, 1/28/1914.
22k53 Paul Franklin Snow, 8/19/1919.

22k51 Ralph Perry Snow was buried at Clear Springs Baptist Church, Greenville County, S. C. He was a graduate of Simpsonville High School. He married, 1930, Pearl Cooper. They had one child:

22k511 William Zadie Snow.

22k52 Mattie Elizabeth Snow was graduated from Asheville Teacher's College, Asheville, N. C., and taught in the public schools for several years. Since her marriage, Sept. 19, 1937, to Rev. Charles A. Griffith, she has continued her studies, along with her husband, at the Southern Baptist Theological Seminary, Louisville, Ky. They moved to Lockhart, S. C., on April 1, 1953, where he is pastor of the Baptist Church. They have one daughter:

22k521 Alpha June Griffith, b. 7/7/1939.

22k53 Paul Franklin Snow attended the Simpsonville, S. C., High School, completing the ninth grade there. He m. Elizabeth Thompson.

22k6 James W. Templeton married Maude Cooper. They live at 15 Lucile Ave., Greenville, S. C. They have three children:

22k61 Wilma Templeton. She m. Lonnie League.
22k62 Leslie Templeton, m. Osie ... .
22k63 Joyce Templeton. She m. Rev. Alfred M. Smoak.

22L Clayton Walker Calhoun Templeton was buried at Fountain Inn, S. C. His father died when he was a little under three years of age, leaving his mother to provide for him and his five year old sister and his seven year old brother. By diligent reading and study at home he acquired a good common education. He lived and died on a farm in the Fountain Inn section of Greenville County, S. C. He was a successful farmer. On Nov. 21, 1872, he married Amanda C. Thackston who died May 2, 1891. They had no children. On July 30, 1891, he married a second time, Lora E. Thackston, b. June 23, 1871, d. Nov. 18, 1927. She was a sister of Amanda C. Thackston, his first wife. Their children were:

22L1 Annie Mae Templeton, 5/3/1892-8/3/1916, buried at Fountain Inn, S. C.
22L2 Lora Katherine Templeton, b. 5/12/1894.
22L3 Sarah Ellen Templeton, b. 12/25/1896.

22L4 Fay Adella Templeton, b. 7/6/1899. She lives at Fountain Inn, S. C.
22L5 Grace Elizabeth Templeton, b. 11/17/1901.
22L6 Ben Tillman Templeton, b. 12/9/1905.
22L7 James Clayton Templeton, b. 12/12/1908. He lives at Fountain Inn, S. C.
22L1 Annie Mae Templeton married, Dec. 8, 1912, Jesse Buchanan. They have one child:
    22L11 Ruby Lee Buchanan, b. 2/5/1915.

22L2 Lora Katherine Templeton married, December, 1915, H. B. Armstrong. They live at Fountain Inn, S. C. Their children are:
    22L21 Annie Nell Armstrong, b. 10/1/1917.
    22L22 James Bissel Armstrong, b. 1/30/1921.
    22L23 Benjamin Carl Armstrong, b. 8/6/1927.

22L21 Annie Nell Armstrong was graduated from college and is a successful teacher. She married Harold Smith. They live at Fountain Inn, S. C.

22L3 Sarah Ellen Templeton married, Dec. 12, 1915, F. A. Thomason. They live at Fountain Inn, S. C. Their children are:
    22L31 Henry Clayton Thomason, b. 1/12/1917. He lives at Fountain Inn, S. C.
    22L32 Douglass W. Thomason, b. 12/27/1919.
    22L33 Joe Thomason, b. 8/7/1921.
    22L34 Mary Ellen Thomason, b. and d. 11/23/1923.
    22L35 David Thomason, b. 10/23/1925. He lives at Fountain Inn, S. C.
    22L36 Lewis Thomason, b. 10/26/1928.

22L5 Grace Elizabeth Templeton married, Jan. 13, 1925, Harold Edward Thomason, cousin of F. A. Thomason, husband of 22L3 Sarah Ellen Templeton. They live at Greenville, S. C. They have three children:
    22L51 Harold Edward Thomason, Jr., b. 8/10/1925.
    22L52 Grace Elizabeth Thomason, b. 11/25/1928.
    22L53 James Franklin Thomason, b. 8/29/1934.

23 MARY TEMPLETON

23 Mary Templeton was born July 18, 1793, died May 23, 1864, and was buried at Rocky Springs Church, Laurens County, S. C. She was a life-long member of that church. She was never married.

24 SAMUEL TEMPLETON

24 Samuel Templeton was born Nov. 22, 1795, died July 8, 1888, and was buried at Rocky Springs Church. He married Elizabeth Hutchinson who was born August 25, 1795, died Dec. 31, 1872, and was buried at Rocky Springs. They had n ne children:

241 Elizabeth Templeton, 8/12/1817-2/13/1892, buried at Rocky Springs, NM.

242 Jane Lockridge Templeton, 8/4/1820-12/21/1879, buried at Rocky Springs, NM.

243 Margaret A. ("Peggy") Templeton, 8/4/1822-9/12/1876, buried at Rocky Springs, NM.

244 Mary Martha Templeton, 3/29/1824-1/21/1905, buried at Rocky Springs, NM.

245 Nancy Templeton, died in the S. C. State Hospital, buried at Rocky Springs.

246 Kate Templeton, buried at Rocky Springs.

247 Robert James Templeton, 1/6/1829-2/22/1908, buried at Rocky Springs, a Confederate veteran, NM.

248 Samuel Pharis Templeton, 9/13/1838-6/13/1915.

249 Abner Templeton, who was lost in the Battle of Gettysburg.

248 Samuel Pharis Templeton was buried at Rocky Springs. He was a Confederate veteran as is shown from the following quotation from "South Carolina Troops In Confederate Service" by Mr. A. S. Salley: "—Co. I, 3rd Regiment, enlisted at Clinton by Col. Preston July 1, 1862; wounded at Chicamauga Sept. 20, 1863; reported on muster roll of Dec. 31, 1863 as having been sent to general hospital; reported on muster roll of Dec. 17, 1864 as having been sent to hospital June 16, 1864, and since furloughed; paroled at Greensboro May 2, 1865." He married Sara C. Day, b. Sept. 9, 1846, d. Feb. 5, 1908, buried at Rocky Springs. She was a sister of Adaline Day who married 132 Col. David C. Templeton. They had five children:

2481 Claude Templeton, b. 1874.

2482 Beulah Templeton, b. 1877.

2483 Nathaniel Day Templeton, b. 8/3/1881.

2484 Carroll LaBorde Templeton, July, 1885-7/30/1939.

2485 Pearl Templeton, b. 1887.

2482 Beulah Templeton married Will F. Shockley and lives at Watts Mill, S. C.

2483 Nathaniel Day Templeton married Addie Snow and lives at Graycourt, S. C.

2484 Carroll LaBorde Templeton was buried at Rocky Springs. He married Effie Snow, b. 1889, sister of Addie Snow. Mrs. Effie S. Templeton lives near Laurens, S. C. They had one daughter:
  24841 .... Templeton, who married W. Talmage Babb. They live near Laurens, S. C. They have two children:
    28411 Coleman Babb, b. about 1938.
    28412 Patsy Babb.

2485 Pearl Templeton married John C. Jerry, who works at Laurens Glass Factory.

25 CAPTAIN JOHN TEMPLETON

25 Captain John Templeton was born July 31, 1800, died Oct. 28, 1858, and was buried at Rocky Springs Church. On Dec. 7, 1848, he was received into full fellowship of that church and later was made the ruling elder. His first wife was Martha. They had no children. He married, second, Elizabeth Speer, who was born July 26, 1798, died Sept. 14, 1842, and buried at Rocky Springs. They had eight children:
  251 Laura Evaline Templeton, a mute, who was "baptized in infancy (generally meaning in childhood) July 19, 1852" at Rocky Springs Church. She died, unmarried, and was buried in Georgia.
  252 Samuel Templeton.
  253 Mary Templeton, 5/16/1828-9/14/1903.
  254 Emmaline Templeton.
  255 John Oliver Templeton, 7/30/1833 (tombstone) 7/29/1833 (church records) - 1/10/1910.
  256 Margaret Jane Templeton.
  257 Caroline Templeton.
  258 Eunice Templeton.

252 Sam C. Templeton was received on profession into the Rocky Springs Church Dec. 6, 1848, and was dismissed June 19, 1867, along with his wife who was Araminta Putnam, whom he married May 3, 1855. They moved to Arkansas where they died and were buried. He was a Confederate veteran, having "—enlisted at Laurens April 14, 1861, mustered June 6, 1861; discharged by surgeon July 2, 1861." They had four children:
  2521 Mary Texanna Templeton, who was baptized at Rocky Springs Church Sept. 12, 1858.
  2522 Isabelle Caroline Templeton, who was baptized at Rocky Springs Church Sept. 12, 1858.
  2523 Hayne Templeton.
  2524 Henry Templeton.

253 Mary Templeton was buried at Rocky Springs. She married Matthew Benjamin who was born May 4, 1826, died Oct. 20, 1901, and was buried at Rocky Springs. They had two children:
2531 J. Elbert Benjamin, 12/25/1869-3/28/1953.
2532 Leila Benjamin, 6/4/1868-7/8/1943.

2531 J. Elbert Benjamin was an efficient plumber and repairman until his poor health forced him to retire a few years ago. He married, May 11, 1902, Janie Auld McQuon, a sister of Verona McQuon, who married 1321 J. Kemper Templeton. Mrs. Benjamin has, for many years, been interested and active in genealogy. She is one of the trustees of the Templeton Clan which was organized and registered with the South Carolina Secretary of State, Jan. 27, 1948. They lived at 88 Florida St., Clinton, S. C. They have six children:
25311 Roy Elbert Benjamin, b. 1/28/1904.
25312 Edwin Ralph Benjamin, b. 4/21/1906, who lives at Clinton, S. C.
25313 Mary Virginia Benjamin, b. 8/11/1908.
25314 Arthur Lee Benjamin, b. 1/2/1917, who runs a repair shop in Baltimore, Md.
25315 Paul McQuon Benjamin, b. 3/21/1918 (twin).
25316 Leila Pauline Benjamin, b. 3/21/1918 (twin).

25311 Roy Elbert Benjamin married, Jan. 22, 1932, Mary Lou Bagwell. They live at Clinton, S. C. They have one son:
253111 Roy Elbert Benjamin, Jr., b. 4/17/1936.

25313 Mary Virginia Benjamin was trained as a nurse at Mary Black Clinic, Spartanburg, S. C., and who was at last account at the Clear Lake Lodge Sanitarium, Orlando, Fla.

25315 Paul McQuon Benjamin is a mechanic in 29th Ordnance Co., U. S. Army, Fort Devans.

25316 Leila Pauline Benjamin was in training at General Hospital, Spartanburg, S. C.

2532 Leila Benjamin attended the public school of her native community, although the schools were not graded at that time, she completed what might be called the ninth grade. She married, Dec. 8, 1892, Jimmie Workman, b. June 20, 1861, died July 17, 1899, and was buried at Rocky Springs. They had three children:
25321 Metta Workman, b. 11/4/1893.
25322 Roy Workman, b. 7/22/1896.
25323 Jimmie Workman, 11/1899, d. (per tombstone) 1901, October, 1902.

109

25321 Metta Workman married Paul 'Quattlebaum. They live at 3016 River Drive, Columbia, S. C. They have seven children:
  253211 Thomas Quattlebaum, b. 1915.
  253212 William Allen Quattlebaum, b. 1917.
  253213 .... Quattlebaum.
  253214 Paul Quattlebaum, Jr., b. 1925.
  253215 Ralph Cecil Quattlebaum, b. 1928.
  253216 Joe Workman Quattlebaum, b. 1930.
  253217 Dorothy Lee Quattlebaum, b. 1934.

25322 Roy Workman married Adalaid Willard. They live on Florida St., Clinton, S. C., and have one son:
  253221 Roy Workman, Jr., b. 8/27/1924.

2532 Mrs. Leila B. Workman married, second, Sept. 8, 1902, James Young, b. Jan. 8, 1856. They had three children:
  25324 Belle Young, b. 9/5/1903.
  25325 Edgar Lee Young, b. 12/17/1905.
  25236 Lewis Anderson Young, b. 8/27/1911, married Josephine Logan.

25324 Belle Young married Fred Scott. They live on Carolina Ave., Clinton, S. C.

25325 Edgar Lee Young married Thelma Powers. They live on Sloan St., Clinton, S. C., and have two children:
  253251 Edgar Young, b. 1930.
  253252 Frances Jewell Young, b. 1932.

254 Emmaline Templeton married, first, Christopher Donnon. He was a Conederate soldier and died of fever in a hospital in Richmond, Va., during the war. She married, second, William Taylor. They have three children:
  2541 Wister Taylor, a tuberculosis patient for 20-25 years.
  2542 Zephia Taylor, who married and lived in Columbia, S. C.
  2543 Lester Taylor, who lived at Hyatt Park, Columbia, S. C.

255 John Oliver Templeton was buried at Rocky Springs. The church roll says "James Oliver Templeton was born July 29, 1833, and baptized 1833." (This being the only "Oliver Templeton" known in South Carolina at this time, variations evidently refer to one and the same man.)
  2532 Mrs. Leila B. W. Young wrote, June 29, 1939—"My mother had... and one brother, John Oliver Templeton ... John used to

raise the tunes at Rocky Springs church with a tune fork, but th
was over 60 years ago and now with pianos and pipe orga:
people would laugh at the tune fork and think it was silly. I c:
see him today just as well as I could 60 years ago. We had b(
ter singing in those days than we have today and the good o
tunes that we used to sing are not used as much."

255 John Oliver Templeton married first, Elizabeth Donnon,
Jan. 18, 1828 - Dec. 16, 1886, buried at Rocky Springs. They h;
six children:
> 2551 John Calvin Templeton, 9/18/1858-2/19/1926.
> 2552 Elbert Bordman Templeton, 10/14/1859-1724/1919.
> 2553 Emma Elizabeth Templeton, 7/12/1861-12/3/1864, b(
> ied at Rocky Springs. NM.
> 2554 Christopher Lee Templeton, 10/3/1866-7/31/1911.
> 2555 Ila Holmes Templeton, 7/30/1870—
> 2556 Sarah Frances Templeton, b. 11/11/1873, marri(
> James Arnold, and lives at 660 Ravenel St., Spartanbu;
> S. C. They have no children.

2551 J. Calvin Templeton was buried at Rocky Springs. I
married, first, Mattie Sloan (first cousin to Blakeley Sloan). Th(
had one child:
> 25511 Mattie Mae Templeton. She married J. T. Arnol
> They live at Fort Mill, S. C. They have seven children
> > 255111 James Arnold.
> > 255112 Johnnie Lee Arnold.
> > 255113 Joe Arnold.
> > 255114 Sarah Frances Arnold.
> > 255115 Robert T. Arnold.
> > 255116 Thomas Franklin Arnold.
> > 255117 Harry Arnold.

2551 J. Calvin Templeton married, second, Alice Lee Mila
She died, Jan. 19, 1945, and was buried at Rocky Spring;. The
had seven children:
> 25512 Oliver Milan Templeton, b. 10/3/1889.
> 25513 Robert Rhett Templeton, b. 6/22/1890.
> 25514 John Donnon Templeton, 5/11/1892-7/20/1944.
> 25515 Alice Montgomery Templeton, b. 7/1/1894, a gover;
> ment nurse at Washington, D. C.
> 25516 Jesse Rolph Templeton, 8/14/1898-7/25/1930, buried
> Rocky Springs.
> 25517 Frank McDuffie Templeton, b. 9/13/1900.
> 25518 Joseph B. Templeton, b. 5/28/1902.

25512 Oliver Milan Templeton married, September, 1907, Juli

111

Buchanan, who died July 8, 1950. He lives at Joanna, S. C. They had three children:
    255121 Lawrence LeRoy Templeton, b. 12/6/1910.
    255122 Louise Avenel Templeton, b. May, 1912.
    255123 Clisby Buchanan Templeton, b. 9/28/1920.

25513 Robert Rhett Templeton married Nellie Lewis. They have three children:
    255131 Beatrice Templeton, b. 1909, a nurse, living in Virginia.
    255132 William Cargill Templeton, b. 1917.
    255133 Frances Templeton, b. 1920.

25514 John Donnon Templeton was buried at York, S. C. For many years he was prominent in the textile industry in South Carolina. He was Superintendent of the Aragon-Baldwin Mills at Whitmire and Rock Hill. He married May 6, 1923, Susie Clair Hilton, b. Oct. 19, 1906. They lived at York, S. C. They had five children:
    255141 John D. Templeton, Jr., b. 3/14/1924. He m. Catherine Nivens. They live at York, S. C.
    255142 Joseph Hilton Templeton, b. 10/16/1925.
    255143 Billy McDufie Templeton, b. 9/30/1927.
    255144 Betty Claire Templeton, b. 3/28/1929.
    255145 Alice Montgomery Templeton, b. 1/27/1931.

25517 Frank McDufie Templeton married Cleo Robinson. They live at Joanna, S. C., where he is connected with the mill. They have two children:
    255171 Marian Jean Templeton, b. 11/27/1928.
    255172 Francis McDuffie Templeton, b. 12/1930.

25518 Joseph B. Templeton attended the Clinton Public Schools and Clemson College where he completed a special two-year course in textiles. He began a successful career in the textile industry first, with the Clinton Mills, and later with the Springs Mills at Fort Mill, Kershaw and Lancaster, as well as with the Aragon-Baldwin Mills at Whitmire. He was Superintendent of the Poinsett Mill in Greenville, S. C. He is now Vice President of the Clinton and Lydia Mills. He was President of the Templeton Clan for four years. He married, Dec. 24, 1928, Sarah McCarley, b. July 14, 1906. They live at Clinton, S. C. They have two daughters:
    255181 Elizabeth Ann Templeton b. 12/6/1929. She m. .... Mann, and lives at Lake Wales, Fla. They have one daughter, 2551811, born 11/..../1950.
    255182 Marian Allene Templeton, b. 3/14/1933.

2552 E. Bordman Templeton was buried at Rocky Springs. He married Frances McDowell, daughter of 262 Robert McDowell. They had six children:

25521 Mollie Templeton, who married Rev. John Marler and lives at Simpsonville, S. C.

25522 Robert Templeton, who lives at Watts Mill, S. C.

25523 Oliver Templeton, who lived at Watts Mill, S. C.

25524 Janie Templeton, who married Luther Patton and lived near Watts Mill, S. C.

25525 Fannie Belle Templeton, who married .... Riddle and lived at Laurens, S. C.

25526 Elbert Templeton, who is married and lived at Watts Mill, S. C.

2554 Christopher Lee Templeton was buried at Rocky Springs. He married Alice Compton. She died April 20, 1947, and was buried at Rocky Springs. They had five children:

25541 Elizabeth Templeton, 1/27/1898-7/1/1899, buried at Rocky Springs.

25542 Belle Templeton, who married .... of Honea Path, S. C.

25543 J. Warren Templeton, b. 1900, married Agnes Smith and lives at Laurens, S. C.

25544 James L. Templeton, b. 1906, married Sadie (per Poole History, page 132) Finley, and lives at Laurens, S. C. They have two or three children.

25545 Frances Templeton, b. 1906, married Earl Gauldin, lives at Laurens, S. C. and has one son:

255451 Earl Gauldin, Jr.

2555 Ila Templeton married Marcus Dillard and lives at Wrens, Ga. They have seven children:

25551 Ella Dillard, who married Lawrence Antley, lives at Wrens, Ga., and has one daughter:

255511 Ila Antley.

25552 Earl Dillard, now deceased.

25553 Viola Dillard, now deceased, married Traylor Wade and had one daughter:

255531 Mildred Wade.

25554 Gussie Dillard, who married Mamie Rhodes. They have no children.

25555 Roy Dillard, who is married.

25556 Marcus Dillard.

25557 Charles Dillard.

255 J. Oliver Templeton married, second, Nannie M. Rowland,

b. 1/20/1839, d, 3/13/1914, buried at Rocky Springs. They had no children.

256 Margaret Jane Templeton is listed on the roll "of Those Baptized in Infancy, Rocky Springs Church, Roll of Oct. 12, 1833", (and later) as "—Dar. John Templeton." Her name appears next to those of "Mary Templeton Dar Jno. T.," and "Samuel Templeton, son of Jno. T.," both of whom have been identified. 256 Margaret Jane Templeton's grave is evidently that one in Rocky Springs cemetery marked "Margaret Templeton, died Oct. 25, 1829, age 5 years, 10 months, 6 days," this grave being unaccounted for any other way.

257 Caroline Templeton (sister of 255 J. Oliver Templeton, per letter of 2532 Mrs. Leila B. W. Young, June 29, 1939) was born (as shown on tombstone next to that of "255 J. O. Templeton's) May 9, 1835, died Dec. 9, 1888, and was buried at Rocky Springs.

258 Eunice Templeton is identified as a sister of 255 J. Oliver Templeton by 2532 Mrs. Leila B. W. Young in her letter of June 29, 1939. Nothing further is known of her. (Rocky Springs Church rolls show Miss Eunica (e) Templeton received Sept. 24, 1858, baptized, infant;" also "Miss E. K. Templeton received Aug. 19, 1873, by examination, adult"). 271 Robert Scott Templeton claimed that 25 John Templeton had a daughter named Unicy, who was never married.

26 JANE TEMPLETON

26 Jane Templeton married John McDowell (also spelled McDowal) as shown by the records of the administration of the estate of 2 James Templeton. John McDowal's tombstone at Rocky Springs cemetery shows that he was born Jan. 14, 1798, and died March 14, 1826. On the Rocky Springs church roll of Oct. 12, 1833 (with corrections added at various times later) we find "Jane McDowal, widow;" and again on the roll of July 19, 1845 (with corrections added later), "Mrs. Jane McDowel dismissed in '58." Also, on the roll of Oct. 12, 1833, of those baptized in infancy, among the 184 names, we find the following:

"No. 17 James Anderson McDowal son of John"
"No. 18, Robert McDowal, son of John"
"No. 19, Emily McDowal, dau. " "
"No. 20, Jane McDowal, Dau. " "

Their names being near the head of the long list would seem to indicate that these four children were baptized soon after the roll was begun. Evidently they were the children of John and 26 Jane

Templeton McDowell, the oldest one probably being the one generally called 261 Anderson McDowell and the same one as we find on the Rocky Springs Church roll of 1851-52-53 as "Captain James Anderson McDowal," and also the same as we find on the roll of 1833 (containing corrections as late as 1873) as "James Anderson McDowal, joined the Baptists."

2612 Emily Catherine McDowell Senn (b. No. 17, 1848, d. Oct. 26, 1931) stated, in 1930, that her father, 261 Anderson McDowell, was lost in the Civil War having been last seen lying in a ditch by 255 Oliver Templeton who was in the same regiment. 2623 Rev. Henry C. McDowell, in a letter from Russellville, Ala., dated July 6, 1939, (questionnaire) says: "Pierce McDowel did not see his father after he went into the Army; was blown up in the St. Petersburgh mine." Mrs. Senn also said that her father, 261 Anderson McDowell, married, first, Nancy Word (the Rocky Springs Church rolls say: "Nancy McDowal died 1843"); and married, second, Katherine Ball and that they had one daughter:

   2611 Elizabeth McDowell who was burned to death, and who married Wash Taylor, and that they had two children:
      26111 Jimmie Taylor, who married .... Dill and lived at Monaghan Mill, Greenville, S. C. (Not there 1934 and 1939).
      26112 Ida Taylor, who also lived at Monaghan Mill, Greenville, S. C.

According to family Bible records in possession of 2612 Mrs. Emily Katherine McDowell Senn, 261 Anderson McDowell married, third, Sarah Ball. They had three children:
   2612 Emily Catherine McDowell, 11/17/1848-10/26/1931.
   2613 Robert Pierce McDowell, 11/29/1853-1934 or 1935.
   2614 Kemper Carlisle McDowell.

2612 Emily Catherine McDowell was buried at Rocky Springs. She married, Feb. 27, 1866, Thomas Fenson Senn, b. July 10, 1845, d. May 10, 1908, buried at Rocky Springs. They had seven children:
   26121 Miles Pierce Senn, b. 2/3/1867.
   26122 Hattie Gertrude Senn, 10/8/1870-9/10/1900.
   26123 Frederick Anderson Senn, b. 10/21/1873.
   26124 Sarah Isabella Senn, b. 6/7/1876.
   26125 Elizabeth Jane Senn, b. 11/7/1879.
   26126 Thomas McLee Senn, b. 5/27/1882.
   26127 James Kemper Senn, b. 12/1/1890.

26121 Miles Pierce Senn married, July 26, 1896, Sallie Traynum, b. June 7, 1876. They live at Princeton, S. C. They have five children:

261211 Katie Senn, who works for Nukasee Mfq. Co., Greenville, S. C.

261212 Thomas Senn, who lives at Ware Shoals, S. C.

261213 Ola Senn, who works for Nukasee Mfq. Co., Greenville, S. C.

261214 Miriam Senn who lives at Princeton, S. C., Rt. 1.

261215 Beatrice Senn who works at Ware Shoals, S. C.

26122 Hattie Gertrude Senn was buried at Rocky Springs. She married, 6/10/1888, Thomas Workman who was born 11/4/1847, died ...., buried at Rocky Springs. He claimed that he was the inventor of the telephone. The writer remembers hearing him relate his experience in developing his ideas and how he wrote to some electrical firm in New York for help in completing some detail, perhaps the diaphram. Instead of cooperating with Mr. Workman, it seems the firm took up the question with Mr. Alexander Graham Bell who soon came out with his invention. Mr. Workman had a variety of talents; among them were writing poetry, delving into religious history, teaching school, farming, saw-milling, threshing grain, etc. For many years before his health failed, Mr. Workman was a well known figure driving his steam tractor engine about over the country during harvest time threshing wheat and oats for the farmers. He was somewhat eccentric, in his old age in particular. He indulged himself freely in philosophical thought and was considered by some to be fanatical. His contemporaries, nevertheless, generally believed that he should have been given the credit for inventing the telephone. They had four children:

261221 Veda Workman, who died young.

261222 Lawrence Workman, who was born about 1897, was a soldier in World War I, stationed at Fort Snelling, Minneapolis, Minn., where he married and later made his home.

261223 Cora Workman.

261224 Melree Workman, born a cripple, who lived at Monaghan Mill, Greenville, S. C.

261223 Cora Workman married Leon Richardson, and was living, at last account, at Lavonia, Ga., where they have two children:

2612231 .... Richardson.

2612232 Jo Ann Richardson.

26123 Frederick Anderson Senn married, Sept. 16, 1894, Jessie Powers, who is dead and was buried at Rocky Springs. He lives at Watts Mill, S. C., where he operates a hardware store and lunch room. They had two children:

261231 Tommie Senn.

261232 Frank Senn.

26124 Sarah Isabella Senn was born in Laurens County, S. C. She married, May 5, 1897, James A. Traynum, a farmer of Greenville County. They had three children:
      261241 J. K. Traynum.
      261242 Viola Traynum
      261243 John Traynum.

26125 Elizabeth Jane Senn married, Nov. 3, 1912, Robert Bagwell. They live at Honea Path, S. C., Rt. 1, and have two children:
      261251 Robert Ernest Bagwell, 10/5/1913-2/8/1914, buried at Princeton, S. C.
      261252 Maxey Lee Bagwell.

26126 Thomas McLee Senn married Pluma Weeks. They live at Mills Mill, Woodruff, S. C., and have no children.

26127 James Kemper Senn married, Oct. 1, 1916, Sarah Pulley. They live at Laurens, S. C., Rt. 2. Their children are:
      261271 James Roy Senn.
      261272 Frances Catherine Senn.

2613 Robert Pierce McDowell married, first, Margaret Henry who died and was buried at Providence Church place near Clinton, S. C. He married, second, ... Garrett. They moved to Franklin County, Ala., in 1884. They had eight children:
      26131 Ora McDowell.
      26132 Minnie McDowell, d. 1907.
      26133 Rev. Henry C. McDowell, b. 1886.
      26134 T. Y. McDowell, d. 3/1939.
      26135 M. P. McDowell.
      26136 Will McDowell.
      26137 Mallie McDowell.
      26138 Callie McDowell.

26131 Ora McDowell married .... Bolding. They live at Leonard, Texas, and have four sons and two daughters, the eldest son a Baptist minister and graduate of Southwestern Seminary.

26132 Minnie McDowell married .... Reid. They have two children:
      261321 Elbert Reid.
      261322 Ruth Reid, who married .... Bishop and lives at Cherokee, Ala.

26133 Rev. Henry C. McDowell taught school in Franklin County, Ala., for ten years. He is a Baptist minister and is also the manager of the Lehman Furniture Store, Russellville, Ala. He has no children.

26134 T. Y. McDowell married and had three sons and two daughters.

26135 M. P. McDowell married .... He has five sons and one daughter. He lives at Russellville, Ala., where he has been Superintendent of the Methodist Sunday School at Isbel for years.

26136 Will McDowell married ...., He has two daughters and one son who is connected with the TVA in North Carolina.

26137 Mallie McDowell married M. J. Willis who is with the TVA.

26138 Callie McDowell married J. C. Johnson, master mechanic for the Alabama Mills Co., Haleyville, Ala.

2614 Kemper Carlisle McDowell was born in Laurens County, S. C. He married and moved to Franklin County, Ala., in 1885. Later he moved to Texas. He was an M. D. He died and was buried at Alvoid, Texas. He had two children:
   26141 .... McDowell, who married .... Copeland and lives in New Mexico.
   26142 Briggs McDowell who died and was buried at Alvoid, Texas.

262 Robert McDowell was born Dec. 25, 1822, died Nov. 15, 1904, and was buried at Rocky Springs. He married Sara Brown, b. Nov. 11, 1832, d. June 10, 1891, buried at Rocky Springs. She was a sister of Frances Brown who married 27 David Clark Templeton. They had two daughters:
   2621 Frances McDowell, who married 2552 E. Boardman Templeton. (See his line for their descendents.)
   2622 Ada McDowell, who married Jeff Summerall. She was buried at Rocky Springs (no tombstone). She had five children:
      26221 Will, lives at .... Mill, Gaffney, S. C.
      26222 Irwin, lives at Helena, Newberry, S. C.
      26223 Jim, deceased.
      26224 Elbert, lives at Watts Mill, S. C.
      26225 Hampton.

263 Jane McDowell was born Sept. 23, 1826, died Dec. 12, 1881, and was buried at Rocky Springs. The rolls of this church show that she was received by profession Oct. 29, 1848. She married, Nov. 13, 1851, William J. Taylor, b. Jan. 6, 1828, d. 1864, buried at Rocky Springs. He was a confederate soldier. When he came home from the war in 1864 he was seriously sick and died during the year. His widow then had to carry on with the children.

She was a good manager and did very well.   They had six children:

2631 An infant son, 11/22/1852-1852.
2632 John Telford Taylor, b. 4/6/1855-7/9/..........
2633 Emma Alice Taylor, 1/6/1857-4.............
2634 Thaddeus Boardman Taylor, 10/15/1858-12/15/1905.
2635 Ada Frances Taylor, 1/29/1860-1878, who was deaf and attended school at Cedar Springs, S. C.
2636 Infant daughter, 7/3/1861-1861.

2634 Thaddeus Boardman Taylor was born in Laurens County, S. C. He married, Dec. 14, 1882, Olive D. Duvall (first), b. 11/3/ 1859-5/29/1899. They had seven children:

26341 George Ernest Taylor, b. 7/12/1883.
       Infant son, 5/14/1885-1885.
26342 Claud Duvall Taylor, 8/23/1886-3/6/1889.
26343 Lewis Hayne Taylor, b. 5/24/1890.
26344 Ada Duvall Taylor, b. 6/23/1892.
26345 William Algie Taylor, b. 11/25/1894.
26346 Arthur T. Taylor, b. 1/7/1897.
26347 Infant son, 5/1899-6/5/1899.

2634 Thaddeus Boardman Taylor married, second, May, 1903, Maybelle Caldwell. They had two children:

26348 Ollie Belle Taylor, b. 1/1905.
26349 Thad B. Taylor, Jr., b. 2/2/1906.

26341 George Ernest Taylor lives at Laurens, S. C., where he is connected with the Southern Cotton Oil Mill.

26343 Lewis Hayne Taylor lives at Laurens, S. C., where he is manager of the Southern Cotton Oil Co. He is one of the outstanding citizens of his city and state. He has been mayor of the city for three terms. He takes an active part in civic, social and religious affairs. He is not only a leader in these matters, but he is also a devoted Christian and a leader in church and Sunday School work. He has always taken an active and leading part in promoting the Templeton re-unions. He served for two years as Vice President of the Templeton Clan. He married June 30, 1915, 27jb Avie Templeton. She was born Dec. 23, 1892. They have three children:

263431 Lewis Hayne Taylor, Jr., b. 2/4/1918.
263432 Evelyn Louise Taylor, b. 12/10/1924.
263433 Sarah Josephine Taylor, b. 12/31/1927.

263431 Hayne Taylor, Jr., is a practicing physician and surgeon in Greenville, S. C. He married Frances Anderson, and they have one child:

2634311 Ada Janet Taylor.

263432 Evelyn Louise Taylor is deaf and is a graduate of Cedar Springs Institute, Cedar Springs, S. C., and Gallaudet College, Washington, D. C. She now teaches in the School for the Deaf, Knoxville, Tenn.

263433 Sarah Josephine Taylor is also deaf and a graduate of Cedar Springs Institute, Cedar Springs, S. C. She attended Kendall School and Gallaudet College, Washington, D. C. She m. Fred Collins. They live in Washington, D. C. They have one child:
    2634331 Cathy Collins, 1/..../1950.

26344 Ada Duvall Taylor, being one of three small children left motherless when their mother died, was reared at Thornwell Orphanage, Clinton, S. C. She was graduated from Thornwell College in 1914, and taught school for seven years. She married, Aug. 25, 1921, C. A. Workman. They live at Marion, N. C., where they own and operate a department store. She takes an active interest in civic and social affairs. They have no children.

26345 William Algie Taylor is a veteran of World War I, being in Battery C, 340th Field Artillery. He served about ten months overseas. He now lives at Laurens, S. C., where he is connected with the Southern Cotton Oil Company. He married Ola Hill of Laurens, S. C.

26346 Arthur T. Taylor is a veteran of World War I, having seen service in the U. S. Navy as an apprenticed seaman. Upon being discharged from the service he resumed his education and his training for the ministry. He is now an active Presbyterian minister at Maxton, N. C. He married Janie Martin of Fountain Inn, S. C. They had no children.

26348 Ollie Belle Taylor married, 1930, Willie Sprouse. They live at Laurens, S. C., and have one daughter:
    263481 Mary Margaret Sprouse.

26349 Thad B. Taylor, Jr., married, 1926, Lois Bobo, daughter of Clarence Bobo. They live at Laurens, S. C., and have one daughter:
    263491 Marjorie Taylor.

264 Emily McDowell, as mentioned before, was baptized in infancy at Rocky Springs Church. Nothing more is known of her.

27 DAVID CLARK TEMPLETON

27 David Clark Templeton was the seventh and youngest child of 2 James Templeton, Sr. He was born in Laurens County, S. C., August 10, 1805, died April 22, 1880, and was buried at Rocky Springs Church in Laurens County. He was educated in private schools. He was a farmer, his farm, which consisted of some 600 acres, extending from what is now the Laurens Country Club to the Laurens City limits. Some years after the War Between the States the larger part of this estate was sold to take care of numerous loans made to friends and neighbors which were never repaid by them. He owned fifteen or twenty slaves. After these slaves were set free he deeded five acres of land to one of them June Kennedy, for a church site. He furnished the lumber to build the church which is now known as the New Grove Baptist Church, near the Laurens-Clinton highway. June Kennedy became the first preacher in this church. June, being unable to read, would go to the home of his former master, 27 David Clark Templeton, listen to him read the Scripture and make remarks on a text. June would then go to church and preach the sermon, reciting the Scripture from memory.

27 David Clark Templeton's name is on the roll of Rocky Springs Church as of October 12, 1833 (and later) of those baptized in infancy, being listed as "—son of James." The records of this church show that he was elected one of the deacons March 13, 1858, and was ordained March 27, of the same year.

On February 13, 1834, he married, first, Margaret Hanna Hitch, daughter of "Squire" John Hitch of near Sandy Springs Church, and Katherine Hanna (daughter of Robert and Mary Hanna) Hitch. She was a sister of Anne Elizabeth Hitch, who m. 22 Capt. James Templeton. She (Margaret H. Templeton) was born March 23, 1813, died June 4, 1844, 17 days after her youngest child was born, was buried at Rocky Springs. 27 David Clark Templeton and Margaret H. Templeton had five children:

27a Thaddeus McDuffie Templeton, 12/20/1834-10/19/1861.
27b John Pulaski Templeton, 5/11/1836.
27c James Ludy Templeton, 4/3/1837-5/30/1863.
27d Dr. Henry Tyler Templeton, 6/29/1841-11/10/1903.
27e Margaret Jane Templeton, 5/18/1844-5/29/1891.

27 David Clark Templeton married, second, Frances Brown, 10/9/1823-11/19/1880, buried at Rocky Springs. They had five children:

27f W. Rhett Templeton, 2/26/1852-11/19/1922.
27g Callie Catherine Templeton, received Rocky Springs Church by examination 9/17/1867, dismissed 10/16/1870.
27h Corrie Elizabeth Templeton, 5/10/1854 6/2/1896.

27i Robert Scott Templeton, 3/28/1857-11/11/1935.
27j Samuel Hood Templeton, 9/14/1864-7/31/1939.

27a Thaddeus McDuffie Templeton was received into Rocky Springs Church "on profession, Sept. 1, 1855." He was elected a deacon, along with his father, 27 David Clark Templeton, 3/13/1858, and ordained 3/27/1858, and was buried at Rocky Springs Church. His wife was Marthy Caroline Peden, b. July 2, 1838, d. Jan. 27, 1917, of near Fountain Inn, S. C. They had one child:
27a1 Lawrence Hayne Templeton, 1/31/1861-8/23/1934. He was buried at Fairview Church, Laurens County. He lived in the Fairview Church community (but in Greenville County) all of his life. He was engaged in farming until a few years before his death. He married Molly Alercy Howard, b. May 5, 1863. They had five children:
27a11 Ludie McDuffie Templeton, b. 10/30/1883.
27a12 Mary Lula Templeton, b. 9/21/1886.
27a13 James Howard Templeton, 4/25/1889-11/27/1952.
27a14 David Peden Templeton, b. 6/10/1893.
27a15 Carrie Elizabeth Templeton, b. 9/19/1895.

27a11 Ludie McDuffie Templeton married, first, Feb. 24, 1909, Itayline Scruggs, 3/24/1893-7/21/1918. They had three children:
27a111 Lawrence Holmes Templeton, b. 1/27/1910, who married Ethel Grimes.
27a112 Mable Lavonia Templeton, b. 5/23/1912, who married 12/23/1938, Charles Roosevelt Brown (of Piedmont, S. C.?)
27a113 Jones Howard Templeton, b. 10/13/1914.

27a11 Ludie McDuffie Templeton married, second, Mary Kathleen Scruggs, b. 2/25/1898. They live at 114 Laurens Road, in Greenville, S. C., where he has been associated with the Battery and Electric Company.

27a12 Mary Lula Templeton married, 12/26/1906, William Duard Rodgers. They live at Fountain Inn, S. C., Rt. 1, and have nine children:
27a121 Vernon DeWitt Rodgers, b. 6/10/1908, who lives at 831 Virginia Ave., Follensbe, W. Va.
27a122 James Harry Rodgers, b. 4/21/1910, who lives at Fountain Inn, S. C., Rt. 1.
27a123 Ralph Howard Rodgers, b. 5/9/1912.
27a124 Yonnie Britt Rodgers, b. 9/8/1914, who married, 12/26/1938, Lewis Capers Terry.
27a125 Nancy Caroline Rodgers, b. 6/22/1917.
27a126 Margaret Elizabeth Rodgers, b. 11/3/1919.
27a127 Mollie Frances Rodgers, b. 7/2/1922.

27a128 William Duard Rodgers, Jr., b. 9/28/1924.
27a129 Catherine Asbill Rodgers, b. 12/22/1927.

27a122 James Harry Rodgers married, 1/1/1934, Helen Garrett. They have two children:
27a1221 Ethel Carolyn Rodgers, b. 1/6/1935.
27a1222 James Harry Rodgers, b. 8/9/1938.

27a13 James Howard Templeton was a member of Fairview Presbyterian Church, Greenville County, S. C. He married, Oct. 12, 1914, Flora Ethel Nelson. They lived at Fountain Inn, S. C. They have five children:
27a131 Eudora Virginia Templeton, b. 8/28/1915.
27a132 Lula Grace Templeton, b. 4/9/1917.
27a133 Guynel Templeton, b. 12/18/1918.
27a134 James Davis Templeton, b. 9/16/1921.
27a135 John Hayne Templeton, b. 12/11/1923.

27a131 Eudora Virginia Templeton married, Nov. 18, 1934, John Russel Owings. They live at Fountain Inn, S. C. They have one son:
27a1311 Russell Ted Owings, b. 5/23/1936.

27a132 Lula Grace Templeton m. .... Wham. They live at Owings, S. C.

27a133 Guynel Templeton m. .... Taylor. They live at Greer, S. C.

27a134 James Davis Templeton is married and lives at Columbia, S. C.

27a135 John Hayne Templeton m. Olive Thomason. They live at Fountain Inn, S. C. They have one daughter:
27a1351 Ruby Flora Templeton.

27a14 David Peden Templeton is a veteran of World War I. He married, Dec. 30, 1922, Kathleen Hunter. They live at 1001 Maryland Ave., Bristol, Tenn. They have two children:
27a141 Virginia Lee Templeton, b. 9/22/1924.
27a142 David Peden Templeton, Jr., b. 2/7/1929.

27a15 Corrie Elizabeth Templeton married, Nov. 28, 1916, Claude Allen Parsons. They live at Fountain Inn, S. C., and have two children:
27a151 Alta Allen Parsons, b. 6/18/1919.
27a152 Billie Parsons, b. 11/26/1923.

27b John Pulaski Templeton was received by baptism into Rocky Springs Church June 29, 1839. He was a Confederate veteran as shown by the following quotation from Vol. 2, p. 486,

list of S. C. Confederate soldiers, compiled by Mr. A. S. Salley, Jr.:
"John P. Templeton joined for duty and was enrolled at Laurens, June 1, 1861; mustered into Confederate service at Columbia June 6, 1861; re-enlisted May 13, 1862; reported on muster roll of October 31, 1862, as having been sent to hospital July 28, 1862; reported on muster roll of Dec. 31, 1862, and Feb. 28, 1863, as in hospital at Columbia; returned to duty prior to May 3, 1863; wounded at Chancellorsville May 3, 1863, and sent to hospital; reported on muster roll June 30, 1863, as having been furloughed home for 30 days from June 1, 1863; reported on muster roll of Aug. 31 and Dec. 31, 1863, as having been sent to hospital and as having been furloughed home; reported on muster roll of June 30, 1864, which was not turned in until the end of the year. as absent in hospital at Columbia since July 1, 1864; not on muster roll at the surrender."

He followed Amelia Barksdale (of near Fountain Inn, S. C.) to Tennessee. Her father had taken her there to prevent their marriage. They were married, however. They both died in Tennessee. They had one daughter:

27b1 Irene Templeton, who married a lumber dealer. They were living in Tennessee at the last account.

27c James Ludy Templeton's name appears on the roll of Oct. 12, 1833, (and later) of Rocky Springs Church of those baptized in infancy. He was a Confederate veteran as shown by the following quotation from Mr. Salley's compilation of S. C. Veterans, Vol. 2, p. 315:

"James L. Templeton enlisted at Laurens April 14, 1861; mustered into Confederate service June 6, 1861; wounded at Fredricksburg Dec. 13, 1861, and sent to hospital; reported on muster rolls of Dec. 31, 1862 and Feb. 28, 1863, as at hospital; died at the general hospital, Charlottesville, Va., May 30, 1863."

He was buried at Rocky Springs. He was never married.

27d Dr. Henry Tyler Templeton was a Confederate veteran as shown by the following quotation from Mr. Salley's list of S. C. Confederate veterans, Vol. 2, p. 315:

"Pvt. H. T. Templeton enlisted for the war at Columbia by Col. Preston July 1, 1862; reported on muster rolls of June 30 and Aug. 31, 1863, as having been sent to the general hospital, Richmond, Va.; reported on muster roll of Dec. 31, 1863, and Feb. 29 and June 30, 1864, as having been left behind on the march from Knoxville; not on muster roll at the surrender April 26, 1865."

He was a physician at Laurens, S. C., with a wide practice. He was buried at Rocky Springs. He married Sara Friddle, b. March 22, 1844, d. April 23, 1904. They had seven children:

27d1 Clarence Ford Templeton, 8/4/1867-12/8/1940.
27d2 Susan Effie Templeton, 4/5/1869-9/26/1873, buried at Rocky Springs.

27d3 Corrie Alma Templeton
27d4 Edgar Templeton
27d5 Catherine Stewart Templeton.
27d6 Fannie Clark Templeton, 1/2/1880-2/15/1953.
27d7 Oscar Templeton, 11/19/1884-10/21/1916, buried at Rocky Springs Church, NM.

27d1 Clarence Ford Templeton lived in Greenville, S. C., at 120 Laurens Road. He was, for many years, license inspector for the City of Greenville. He was, until his death, 12/8/1940, keenly interested in the Templeton Clan and the reunions. He married, Dec. 4, 1895, Carrie Huff (daughter of Elmore Huff.) They had eight children:

27d11 Infant daughter, 3/6/1897, buried at Rocky Springs Church.
27d12 T. Huff Templeton, 11/12/1898.
27d13 Harriett Aughtry Templeton, 4/24/1902.
27d14 Clarence Ford Templeton, Jr., 9/21/1904.
24d15 Eugene Fenton Templeton, 10/22/1906.
22d16 Barron Elmore Templeton, 7/28/1909.
27d17 Clark Templeton, 10/8/1911.
27d18 Sarah E. Templeton, 2/21/1914.

27d12 T. Huff Templeton attended North Greenville Academy, Tigerville, S. C., where the writer was his teacher. He is married and lives at Ann Arbor, Mich., where he is employed by the Ford Motor Co.

27d13 Harriett Aughtry Templeton m. 12/19/1926, A. C. Vance. They live at Keystone Heights, Fla.

27d14 Clarence Ford Templeton, Jr., m., 5/6/1926, Evelyn Mc-Donald. They live at Long Beach, Cal.

27d15 Eugene Fenton Templeton m. 12/28/1926, Louise Bannister.

27d16 Barran Elmore Templeton lives at Brookside Way, Marshall Forest, Greenville, S. C.

27d17 Clark Templeton lives on Ebo Ave., Greenville, S. C.

27d18 Sarah E. Templeton m. Robert Swartzwelder and lives at Jacksonville Beach, Fla.

27d3 Corrie Alma Templeton m. Bud Russell who is Superintendent of a cotton mill in Mobile, Ala.

27d4 Edgar Templeton was, at last account, connected with the South Carolina Highway Department.

27d5 Catherine Stewart Templeton m. first, 5/___/1897, Ralph

Gore, 4/12/1875-5/2/1899 (son of Norman and Mildred Prather Gore). They had one son:

27d51 Ewart Ralph Gore, Jr., 5/11/1898-5/1/1899, who was buried at the Presbyterian Cemetery, Clinton, S. C.

27d5 Catherine Stewart Templeton Gore m. second, 12/23/1903, Will Sloan, who was, for a long time, manager of the Coca Cola Bottling Co., Anderson, S. C. He lived at 520 Broad St., Clinton, S. C. Died February, 1953.

27d6 Fannie Clark Templeton m. 7/31/1898, Edmond Martin. They live at Chappells, S. C. They have six children:
 27d61 Effie L. Martin, 7/6/1899-9/21/1899, buried at the Laurens Cemetery, Laurens, S. C.
 27d62 Eunice Martin, b. 8/3/1900.
 27d63 Beatrice Martin, b. 10/30/1903.
 27d64 Edmond M. Martin, Jr., b. 6/26/1906. He lives at Chappells, S. C.
 27d65 Doris (male) Martin, b. 2/17/1912. He lives at Elberton, Ga.
 27d66 David Martin, b. 2/15/1915.

27d62 Eunice Martin married, first, March 6, 1918, I. W. Sproles, Jr. They had three children:
 27d621 Freck Sproles, who attended Agnes Scott College, Decatur, Ga.
 27d622 James Sproles, who lives at Rt. 4, Box 476, Charlotte, N. C.
 27d623 Pat Sproles, who was in fifth grade in school in 1939.
27d62 Mrs. Eunice Martin Sproles married, second, Sept. 27, 1939, Bert L. Patterson. They live at Rt. 4, Box 476, Charlotte, N. C., and have one daughter:
 27d624 Shirley Patterson.

27d63 Beatrice Martin married, July 24, 1924, J. C. Smith. They live at Chappells, S. C.

27d64 Edmond M. Martin, Jr., married, Aug. 27, 1927, Elizabeth Purcell.

27e Margaret Jane Templeton was buried at Rocky Springs Church. She married April 17, 1869, Ellie W. Dendy, b. Sept. 14, 1837, d. Aug. 16, 1935, a Confederate veteran who was in Co. F, 14th Regiment, S. C. V. along with 14g3 Ben P. Templeton and others. In 1930 he attended the second Templeton re-union at Cross Anchor, S. C., and was given recognition as the oldest member of the Clan present, being nearly 93 years old. It is believed that he was the next to the last surviving member of his Company (F), being survived only by 14g3 Ben P. Templeton of Delvalle, Texas, who died about four months later.

27e Margaret Jane Templeton Dendy and Ellie W. Dendy had five children:

27e1 Margaret Elizabeth Dendy, 3/25/1870-9/14/1870, buried at Rocky Springs.
27e2 Mary Eulala Dendy, b. 1/8/1874.
27e3 Eugene Wilkerson Dendy, 1/18/1876-1880.
27e4 Minnie Estelle Dendy, 1/24/1878.
27e5 Whitfield Clark Dendy, 4/26/1880-1935.

27e2 Mary Eulala Dendy married, Feb. 4, 1892, Downs Casey, b. 9/28/1872. They live at Woodruff, S. C., R.F.D. They have seven children:

27e21 Lucas Dewey Casey, b. 11/16/1901.
27e22 Annie Margaret Casey, b. 6/28/1903.
27e23 Evan Wilkerson Casey, b. 5/14/1905.
27e24 Lula Estelle Casey, b. 9/13/1907.
27e25 James Downs Casey, b. 1/15/1910.
27e26 Callie Lillian Casey, b. 6/11/1913.
27e27 Conway Clark Casey, b. 11/2/1918.

27e21 Lucas Dewey Casey, married, 1930, Essie Bailey. They have two children:

27e211 Fred Marshall Casey.
27e212 James Milford Casey.

27e22 Annie Margaret Casey, married, Feb. 8, 1932, Dewey Woodruff. They have one child:
27e221 Dewey Evaline Woodruff.

27e23 Evan Wilkerson Casey married, Nov. 15, 1930, Grace Inez Woodruff. They have one child:
27e231 Donald Evan Casey, 9/13/1931-9/15/1931.

27e24 Lula Estelle Casey married, Dec. 31, 1927, Lewis Bailey and lived on South Liberty St., Spartanburg. S. C.

27e25 James Downs Casey married, Sept. 1, 1932, Mary Littlefield, b. July 20, 1913. They live at Woodruff, S. C., and have one child:
27e251 Ruskin Winnifield Casey, b. 12/1933.

27e4 Minnie Estelle Dendy married, Sept. 17, 1899, Alvin Jones Lawrence, b. May 23, 1880. They lived at Enoree, S. C. They have five children:
27e41 Maggie Leola Lawrence, b. 6/20/1900-10/1928.
27e42 John Elliott Dow Lawrence, b. 2/28/1902.
27e43 Lottie C. Lawrence, 5/2/1904-5/2/1904.
27e44 Alvin Eugene Lawrence, b. 6/6/1905.
27e45 Charles Grover Vincent Lawrence, b. 10/30/1913. He lives at Woodruff, S. C., Rt. 2.

27e41 Maggie Leola Lawrence was buried at Cedar Shoals Church, near Enoree, S. C. She married Guy Scott. Their children were:

    27e411 Belton Vernon Scott, b. 9/29/.....
    27e412 Myrtle Lucile Scott.
    27e413 Mary Estelle Amelia Scott.
    27e414 Floy Frances Scott.
    27e415 Minnie Ruth Scott, 1/9/1928-1/27/1934, buried, Cedar Shoal Church, Enoree, S. C.

27e42 John Elliott Dow Lawrence married Leona Mae Cantrell. They have two children:

    27e421 Allie V. Lawrence.
    27e422 A. B. Lawrence.

27e5 Whitfield Clark Dendy married, Dec. 25, 1904, Eva Cannon, b. Sept. 1, 1886. They lived at Shelby, N. C. They had six children:

    27e51 Mary Edna Dendy.
    27e52 Homer Dendy, who married Janette Thompson and lives at Shelby, N. C.
    27e53 Marcelle Dendy.
    27e54 Margaret Dendy.
    27e55 Catherine Dendy.
    27e56 Mildred Dendy.

27 David Clark Templeton married, second, Frances Brown, b. Oct. 9, 1823, d. Nov. 19, 1880, who was buried at Rocky Springs Church. The church records show that she was received for baptism at Rocky Springs Church July 9, 1843. They had five children:

    27f William Rhett Templeton, b. 2/26/1852.
    27g Callie Catherine Templeton.
    27h Corrie Elizabeth Templeton, b. 4/10/1854.
    27i Robert Scott Templeton, 3/28/1857-11/11/1935.
    27j Samuel Hood Templeton, 9/14/1864-7/31/1939.

27f William Rhett Templeton was baptised as an infant and received by examination into Rocky Springs Church Aug. 22, 1871, and later dropped from the roll. He had the usual childhood of those days of boys who were too young to go to the War Between the States, romping over the farm with younger boys of the countryside and the usual escapades of such boys. He had long desired to have a pair of spurs with which to ride the mules on the farm. Being unable to get them, he made a leather contraption and inserted a long thorn in the heel of each and mounted the mule, an old lazy one, bare-backed. He no sooner stuck his heel to the side of the mule than he suddenly found himself being taken for a wild exciting ride. Although he was "scared to death" during this wild ride, he always enjoyed telling about it in later years. He had a common school education. He was very fond of reading, especially the Bible. He was a shoemaker of the old school and was an expert craftsman in hand made shoes, making shoes for people with club feet and other deformities, that called for special-made shoes. He was in charge of the shoe shop at Thornwell Orphanage at Clinton, S. C., and taught the art of shoe-making to several boys at the orphanage. On Dec. 18, 1886, he married Ellen Valeria Prather, daughter of Wattie and Pernice Puckett Prather of near Duncan's Creek, Clinton, S. C. She was born Jan. 26, 1856, and died Jan. 9, 1929. They were both buried in the Presbyterian Cemetery at Clinton, S. C. They had four children:

2711 Fannie Lou Templeton, b. 10/18/1888.
2712 Joe Clark Templeton, b. 9/3/1892.
2713 George LaFayette Templeton, b. 9/29/1894.
2714 Hubert Lionel Templeton, b. 10/31/1896, who was a telegraph operator in Augusta, Ga.

2711 Fannie Lou Templeton married a Mr. Farmer and was living at 303 South Fielding Ave., Tampa, Fla.

2712 Joe Clark Templeton was for a number of years engaged in the marble business at Gaffney and Greenville, S. C. He is now the proprietor of a filling station on South Boulevard, in Charlotte, N. C. He married .... from Georgia. They have three children.

2713 George LaFayette Templeton was a soldier in World War I, having served in the National Guard and in the U. S. Army for about three years. He was a corporal and spent about eleven months in the A. E. F. He married, March 28, 1918, Annie Belle Brown, b. Sept. 18, 1893. They had one child that died at birth. They live at 3800 14th Street, N. W., Washington, D. C. She is a clerk in the Enlisted Division of the War Department and he is a statistician (statistical clerk) in the Budget and Statistical Section of the Veterans' Administration.

27h Corrie Elizabeth Templeton was received by examination as an infant into Rocky Springs church Aug. 23, 1871. She married Dec. 25, 1883, J. Lawrence Sloan, b. Feb. 16, 1854, d. April 23, 1906, a brother of Mattie Sloan who married 2551 J. Calvin Templeton. They were both buried at Rocky Springs Church. They had four children:

27h1 William D. Sloan 9/17/1884-5/19/1945.
27h2 Daughter Sloan, 1886-1887, buried at Rocky Springs.

27h3 Rhett Sloan, 9/26/1888-12/17/1952. Buried at Rocky Springs.
27h4 George L. Sloan, 12/9/1891-9/21/1931.
27h1 William D. Sloan was the express agent at Charlotte, N. C. He married, Feb. 26, 1908, Lucy McDowell, b. Nov. 18, 1888. They had no children. She lived at 2105 Dartmouth Place, Charlotte, N. C.

27h3 Rhett Sloan married, April 27, 1915, Beatrice Bennett, b. Oct. 3, 1893. They lived at Clinton, S. C., and had no children.

27h4 George L. Sloan was buried at Oaklawn Cemetery, in Charlotte, N. C. He married, June, 1921, Ruth White, who lives at 3330 Plaza Road, Charlotte, N. C., with their three children:
27h41 David Lawrence Sloan, b. 4/5/1922.
27h42 Ruth White Sloan, b. 7/31/1923.
27h43 Mary Allen Sloan, b. 9/12/1925.

27i Robert Scott Templeton was reared in Laurens County, S. C. He was baptized as an infant in Rocky Springs Church, Sept. 11, 1858. He was educated in his native county where he lived all of his life. In his early life he was a successful farmer. After reaching middle age he moved to the Old Mill at Laurens where he worked in the mill for about 40 years. He was highly esteemed by all who knew him. He showed a keen interest in the Templeton Clan when it was first organized in 1929, and was elected the first president. He was twice married; first, on Feb. 23, 1882, to Alma Ramage, 3/11/1860-8/7/1895. Their children were:
27i1 Frank Templeton, b. 12/20/1882.
27i2 Robert E. Templeton, 3/1/1884-10/27/1948.
27i3 J. Grace Templeton, b. 3/28/1885.
27i4 Charlie K. Templeton, b. 8/15/1886.
27i5 Anna D. Templeton, 10/22/1888-1/7/1921.

27i Robert Scott Templeton married, second, July 12, 1900, Margaret Reeves. They had no children. He was buried at Holly Grove Baptist Church, Laurens County, S. C. She has since remarried, Mr. Fox.

27i1 Frank Templeton attended Bailey School in Laurens County, S. C. He is now superintendent of the Laurens Country Club. He married, March 2, 1904, Ethel Arnold. They have five children:
27i11 Rolfe Allen Templeton, 11/11/....-7/6/1906.
27i12 Mary E. Templeton, b. 2/4/1909.
27i13 James Edwin Templeton, b. 3/9/1912.
27i14 Jack Templeton, b. 8/16/1914.
27i15 Robert Allen Templeton, b. 10/18/1920.

130

27i12 Mary E. Templeton attended the Clinton High School. Her pleasing manners and attractive personality have won for her hosts of friends. She has always been an active leader in the Templeton Clan, having served most efficiently as President for two years and as Secretary for several years. For a number of years she has been connected with the Jacobs Printing Co., Clinton, S. C. She m., Feb. 18, 1953, Pierre Ramage.

27i13 James Edwin Templeton lives at Laurens, S. C., Rt. 2. He married, July 23, 1937, Miss Nancy Adair, b. Sept. 23, 1916. They have two children:

    27i131 Sarah Alice Templeton, b. 11/14/1939.
    27i132 .... Templeton.

27i14 Jack Templeton m. Miriam Bobo. They live at 518 Greenville Road, Laurens, S. C. They have two daughters.

27i2 Robert E. Templeton lived at 405 Holmes St., Laurens, S. C. He worked in the Laurens Mill for fifty or more years. He was a member and deacon of the Todd Memorial Presbyterian Church as well as choir director. He served the church and his community faithfully, devoting much of his time and energy to helping his friends and neighbors. He married December 14, 1902, Carrie Powell, b. May 18, 1886. They had five children:

    27i21 Rufus Scott Templeton, 9/6/1904-5/11/1905.
    27i22 Harry Templeton, b. 9/5/1905.
    27i23 Alma Theresa Templeton, b. 1/26/1913.
    27i24 Edith Boling Templeton, b. 11/7/1916.
    27i25 Bruce Ramage Templeton, b. 7/22/1920.

27i22 Harry Templeton m. Eva Barnett. They are presently living at Ninety Six, S. C., where Harry is connected with the Greenwood Mills. They have three children:

    27i221 Joel S. Templeton, b. 2/23/1939.
    27i222 Darlene Templeton, b. 8/8/1944.
    27i223 Diana Templeton, b. 9/1948.

27i23 Alma Theresa Templeton is connected with the Watts Division of J. P. Stevens Co. She has served as president of the Laurens Business and Professional Women's Club, of which she is now a member. She also served two years a hostess for the Teen-Age Club and on the recreational program. She is a member of the First Presbyterian Church of Laurens and a member of the church choir. She is a member of the American Legion Auxiliary and is active and interested in other civic club activities. She is keenly interested in the Templeton Clan and is now serving her fourth year as the efficient secretary and treasurer of the

Clan. She married, December 26, 1936, Louis Wham, b. Dec. 17, 1912.

27i24 Edith Boling Templeton married May 1 1949, William Joseph Fix. They have one son:
27i241 William Edward Fix, b. 12/25/1949.

27i25 Bruce Ramage Templeton is a veteran of World War II, having served in the Marine Corps. He is presently enrolled at the University of South Carolina in the School of Business Administration, where he is studying toward a law degree. His excellent scholarship has placed him on the Dean's List and the Honor Roll. He married Carolyn Smith of Rock Hill. S. C., Jan. 17, 1948, and they are living in the Veterans Apartments. Coumbia, S. C. After his military service, Bruce was for several years connected with the Ford Automobile Agency in Laurens, S. C., and the George Motor Company there.

. 27i3 J. Grace Templeton married, Dec. 29, 1901, John Madden who died 1947. They had three children:
27i31 Roy Madden, b. 11/3/1902.
27i32 Charlie Madden, b. 12/5/1905.
27i33 Mary Grace Madden, b. 2/26/1908.

27i3 J. Grace Templeton Madden married, second. 1950, Shell Benjamin. They live at Madden Station near Laurens, S. C.

27i31 Roy Madden is married and has two children:
27i311 William Roy Madden, Jr., b. 7/12/1929.
27i312 Rebecca Jane Madden, b. 3/15/1932.

27i32 Charlie Madden is married and has two sons:
27i321 John L. Madden, b. 3/9/1934.
27i322 Charles Madden, Jr., b. 7/30/1936.

27i4 Charlie K. Templeton lives at Madden Station, S. C. He is not married. He has been active in the interest of the Templeton Clan.

27i5 Anna D. Templeton was buried at Holly Grove. Church in Laurens County. She married, Dec. 23, 1909, T. Plus Brown. They had one son:
27i51 Eugene Brown, who married, 6/7/1935, May Will Suddeth. They have three sons:
27i511 William Plus Brown, b. 3/31/1942.
27i512 David Brown, b. 7/27/1944.
27i513 Frank Templeton Brown, b. 4/28/1947.

27j Samuel Hood Templeton was educated in a private school taught by Rev. Z. L. Holmes, who was the president of the Laurens Female College. Classes were held in what is now the Guy Watson home on East Main Street, in Laurens, S. C., one of the few octagon shaped houses in the United States. Classes were held for girls at the Laurens Female College. After his father's death, 27j Samuel Hood Templeton was left, at the age of 16, with the support of his mother and two sisters. After the marriage of the sisters and the death of his mother he lived, until 25 years of age, at the family farm home as a young bachelor and until a year or two after his marriage. The farm was located between Laurens and the present Laurens Country Club. Thereafter he was engaged in textile work until January, 1938, when, at the age of 73, ill health caused him to retire. In January, 1939, it became necessary to have his right leg amputated. He recovered from this operation in a miraculously short time, but he was closely confined at home thereafter until his death, July 31, 1939.

The following are extracts from the account of his death and funeral as taken from The Laurens Advertiser, dated August 3, 1939: "—S. Hood Templeton, 74, retired textile overseer, died at 7 o'clock Monday evening at the home of his son-in-law and daughter, Mr. and Mrs. James Donnan, Lee Street, after an illness of a few days. Last January he lost one leg as the result of blood poisoning, but apparently had recovered. He became ill Friday night from a heart attack and never recovered. Funeral services were conducted from the Donnan residence at 5 o'clock Tuesday afternoon by his pastor, the Rev. E. P. Moye; a former, pastor, the Rev. M. G. Woodworth, D. D.; and the Rev. Adlai C. Holler, pastor of the First Methodist Church. Interment followed in the Laurens Cemetery. . . . Mr. Templeton was overseer in the Laurens Cotton Mill for about 40 years, having been connected with the company practically since its organization and until his retirement several years ago. He was known as a man of sound judgment and sympathetic interest, his counsel being frequently sought on questions affecting the welfare of his community. Since 1902, he had been a member of Todd Memorial Presbyterian Church and had served as deacon from 1906 until 1918, when he was made an elder, and served until his death. He was also treasurer of the church, clerk of the Session and secretary-treasurer of the Sunday School. In 1928, he was honored by the South Carolina Presbytery by being sent as one of the commission to the General Assembly of the Southern Presbyterian Church held that year in Atlanta."

He took an active, leading part in the Templeton re-unions. In 1931 he was elected President of the Clan and re-elected in 1932. During both terms his capable and sympathetic leadership was outstanding. He was always modest but efficient. He married, Feb. 20, 1890, Annie Leola Martin, b. May 1, 1870, d. June 3, 1930. They had ten children:

27ja Althea Floy Templeton, b. 12/19/1890.
27jb Avie Inez Templeton, b. 12/28/1892.
27jc Maxcy Hood Templeton, 3/12/1894-8/11/1942.
27jd Vera Sue Templeton, b. 12/28/1896.
27je Larry Leo Templeton, b. 5/7/1899-1/24/1948.
27jf Samuel Clark Templeton, b. 10/26/1901.
27jg Gary Scott Templeton, b. 5/25/1904.
27jh Ruby Louise Templeton, b. 4/16/1906.
27ji Harold Merritt Templeton, b. 3/21/1909.
27jj Sarah Helen Templeton, b. 11/25/1914.

27ja Althea Floy Templeton was educated in the Laurens City
Schools and in private schools. The experiences and responsi-
bilities that come with being the oldest of a family of ten children
formed a sterling character, sweetness of disposition and nobility
of mind not often found in the possession of one person. That
"she is my idea of a perfect lady" is the tribute of one brother.
To others who love her she is a perfect wife, sister, mother, and
daughter. Her service and devotion to family, friends and church
are untiring and utterly unselfish. She married, Nov. 23, 1915,
James M. Donnan, who has been active in the interest of the Templeton Clan, having served two years as President of the Clan.
They now live on the site of the old home place of the family in
Laurens, S. C. They have two children:
    27ja1 Frances Floy Donnan, b. 7/6/1916. She m. Stewart
O. Brown. They have three children:
        27ja11 Patricia Brown.
        27ja12 Stewart O. Brown, Jr.
        22ja13 David Brown.
    27ja2 James M. Donnan, Jr., b. 12/18/1920. He m. Runette
Dendy. They have one child:
        27ja21 James M. Donnan III.

27jb Avie Inez Templeton attended the Laurens City Schools.
She tells of how her grandfather, 27 David Clark Templeton, after
the War Betwen the States, found himself left with much useless
Confederate money which he divided among some of the children as souvenirs of a once valuable estate. She says that her
father inherited a bureau drawer full of such money and that she
used to amuse herself by counting this now worthless money
and day-dreaming of what might have been if—. She married,
June 30, 1915, 26343 Lewis Hayne Taylor. See his line for their
descendents.

27jc Maxcy Hood Templeton attended the Laurens City Schools.
When a small boy he became an apprentice in a printing office,
and was, for many years, associated with L. B. Blackwell, and later,
with The Laurens Advertiser office and with the Life Insurance

Company of Virginia. Among his hobbies were sketching, painting, coats-of-arms, playing the guitar, etc. He married, March 28, 1917, Mary Martin. Their children are:

27jca Maxcy Hood Templeton, Jr., b. 1/28/1918.
27jcb Virginia Templeton b. 9/10/1920.
27jcc Agnes Templeton, b. 10/14/1922.
27jcd Robert Wayne Templeton, b. 6/4/1924.
27jce Jack Martin Templeton, b. 12/21/1925.
27jcf Samuel Frank Templeton, b. 8/9/1927.
27jcg Betty Lee Templeton, b. 1/19/1930, married Harold Power.
27jch Margaret Ann Templeton, b. 9/4/1931.
27jci Mary Jane Templeton, b. 3/9/1933.
27jcj Nancy Templeton, b. 7/28/1934. She lives on Lee St., Laurens, S. C.

27jcb Virginia Templeton married Frank Lyon. They live on Lee St., Laurens, S. C. They have two children:
27jcb1 Michael Lyon, b. 12/23/1942.
27jcb2 Janice Claire Lyon, b. 11/6/1946.

27jcc Agnes Templeton married Frank Armfield. They have three children:
27jcc1 Mary Ruth Armfield, b. 4/3/1947.
27jcc2 Agnes Carol Armfield, b. 6/7/1948.
27jcc3 Steven Franklin Armfield, b. 6/.../1950.

27jcd Robert Wayne Templeton married Ruby Cogdill. They have two children:
27jcd1 Lynn Templeton, b. 11/20/1946.
27jcd2 Robert Wayne Templeton, Jr., b. 8/.../1949.

27jce Jack Martin Templeton married June Tunstall. They have one child:
27jce1 Samuel Templeton, b. 2/1/1950.

27jcg Betty Lee Templeton married Harold Power. They have two children:
27jcg1 Stanley Power, b. 1/9/1949.
27jcg2 Timothy Power, b. .../.../1951.

(An exceptionally interesting observation in connection with this family is that:

27 David Clark Templeton had ten children all of whom lived to be grown. His youngest son, 27j Samuel Hood Templeton, had ten children, all of whom lived to be grown. His son, 27jc Maxcy Hood Templeton, had ten children, all of whom lived to be grown.)

27jd Vera Sue Templeton attended Laurens City Schools. She married, June 8, 1921, Pet Boyd Holtzclaw. They live at Arcadia,

S. C., where he was the manager of the Mayfair Mill Store, and is now paymaster and filling station owner and operator. They have three children:

27jd1 Pet Boyd Holtzclaw, Jr., who died, 1923.
27jd2 Kenneth Leon Holtzclaw, b. 6/14/1924, d. 11/9/1944, Dakar, West French Africa, in an airplane crash, World War II.
27jd3 Barbara Louise Holtzclaw, b. 6/23/1928.

27je Larry Leo Templeton attended the Laurens City Schools. He also had instruction in interior decoration in New York City. He was a veteran of World War I, having served as seaman, 2nd class, in the U. S. Navy. For many years he was engaged in interior decorating and painting. He married April 29, 1929, Velma Lineberger of Fitzgerald, Ga. They had two children:

27je1 Thomas Nathaniel Templeton, b. 4/6/1930.
27je2 Annette Templeton, b. 6/26/1933.

27jf Samuel Clark Templeton attended the Laurens City Schools, and the School of Interior Decorating, New York City. He is now a building contractor and interior decorator, living at 1703 Ione St., in Jacksonville, Fla. He married Mable Williams of Fitzgerald, Ga. They have one child:

27jf1 Jimmie Lee Templeton, b. 8/15/1929. She m. L. M. Green, Jr., of Jacksonville, Fla. They have two children:
27jf11 Marsha Green.
27jf12 Gregory Green.

27jg Gary Scott Templeton attended the Laurens City Schools. His chief occupation at present is city fireman and special deputy police. He lives at 214 Clemson St., Laurens, S. C. However, he has experimented as a carpenter, painter, electrician, cotton ginner, etc. He is a great lover of dogs and has owned several German police dogs, the favorite one being Mike who, some years ago, fought off a mad dog and protected two of the children until they could get safely into the house. Eye witnesses declare the dog really saved the lives of these two small children. 27jg Gary Scott Templeton married, 1926 (?) Mary Boyd. They have five children:

27jg1 Gary Wofford Templeton, 9/1/1927.
27jg2 Gerald Neil Templeton, 12/5/1929
27jg3 Sanford Merritt Templeton, 2/14/1935.
27jg4 James Robert Templeton, 7/6/1937.
27jg5 David Boyd Templeton, 4/17/1939.

27jh Ruby Louise Templeton was graduated from the Laurens High School with honors, being the salutatorian of her class. She then entered a local newspaper contest and won a handsome new Buick automobile which she promptly sold for $1495 in order that she might continue her education. At Winthrop College she used this $1495 along with other scholarship incomes to pay her way. She was awarded a service scholarship in one of the business offices of the college and, later on, served for two years as a stenographer in the office of the college president, Dr. D. B. Johnson. These services were not only valuable sources of income to her but were excellent preparation for a career which she is still enjoying with brilliant success. She has served as secretary to the County Superintendent of Education, Laurens, S. C.; secretary of the Laurens City Schools; Secretary of the Board of Education of the Upper South Carolina Conference of the Methodist Church; Director of Public Welfare, Laurens, S. C.; Secretary to the Assistant Commissioner of Public Welfare, Columbia, S. C.; one year in Washington, D. C., with the Veterans Administration; and now, with the Social Security Board in Greenwood, S. C. She also served one year in the Women's Army Auxiliary Corps during World War II, stationed at Fort Des Moines, Iowa. Even while in the midst of these duties she has found time to give most valuable services to the Templeton Clan. As an example of her loyalty to the Clan, although she was out of the State of South Carolina, she carried on most of the duties while secretary of the Clan by mailing out notices of the re-union and carrying on other vital correspondence. She has been, and still is, one of the staunchest supporters of the Clan. In 1949, she was elected President of the Clan for a term of two years. In 1951, in recognition of her outstanding interest and leadership she was re-elected President for another term of two years.

27ji Harold Templeton was graduated from the Laurens High School and attended Presbyterian College, Clinton, S. C. He served in the armed services in World War II, 16th Armored Division, 216th Armored Engineers, with combat duty in the European Theatre. He is now employed by the Southern Cotton Oil Company, Laurens, S. C. He is a member of the Medical Corps of the S. C. National Guard. He married, 12/25/1938, Margaret Mims. This marriage was later terminated by divorce. His favorite hobby is fishing. He lives with his sister, Mrs. J. M. Donnan.

27jj Sarah Helen Templeton was graduated from the Laurens High School with highest honors. She also attended Anderson College. While in school she was a member of the glee club. She still plays the piano beautifully. While in college she took a business course. She is married and lives at Lexington, N. C., where she is a leader in the social, civic and church (Methodist) life of the community. She married, June 22, 1934, Earl Riddle, who is Vice President and General Manager of the Wenonah Cotton Mill at Lexington, N. C. They have one son and two daughters:

27jj1 Earl Edward Riddle, Jr., b. 1/19/1938.
27jj2 Sarah Elizabeth Riddle, b. 2/19/1942.
27jj3 Suzanne Riddle, b. 5/25/1948.

Another interesting observation in connection with the line of 2 James Templeton is the fact that he, a soldier of the Revolution, had a grandson, 27j Samuel Hood Templeton, surviving as late as 1939, thereby creating a span of 191 years of life (1748-1939) for 2 James Templeton and his grandson, 27j Samuel Hood Templeton.

2 James Templeton, b. 1748, was 57 years old when his youngest son, 27 David Clark Templeton, was born in 1805, who was 59 years old when his youngest son, 27j Samuel Hood Templeton, was born in 1864.

3 ROBERT TEMPLETON, SR., 1762-1845

The earliest record we have of 3 Robert Templeton, Sr., is in the form of a land grant. In the office of Secretary of State, Columbia, S. C., we find recorded a grant of "—250 acres in Craven (now Laurens) County, on the waters of Enoree River—to Robert Templeton, March 17, 1775." In this same office we find that the survey for this tract of land was "—certified for 16th day of December, 1772, per me, Pat Cunningham, D. S. (district surveyor)— 250 acres Irish."

In the office of Clerk of Court, Laurens, S. C., we find this record (abstract): "Indian Territory, Dearborn County—we, Robert Templeton and Mary Templeton, his wife, of Dearborn County, and state aforesaid—for $100—sell to Samuel Hanna—two tracts of land joining each other—granted to William Hanna, Sr.,—150 acres each, one granted by Charles Greville Montague, Oct. 2, 1766, the other by His Excellency Benjamin Guerard, Esq., Jan. 21, 1785—which the said William Hanna, deceased, surveyed—situate in Laurens District, S. C., Duncan's Creek" (a branch of Enoree River); signed by Robert Templeton and Mary Templeton; witnessed by Robert Hanna; dowry signed by Mary Templeton; probated by John Templeton, J. P. (Justice of Peace).

From this deed it seems that Mary, wife of Robert Templeton, was, very probably, the daughter of William Hanna, Sr. It would certainly be a logical procedure for Mary Hanna Templeton to inherit the land from her father and find it convenient to sell it after she had moved to Indiana to live.

The next record we have of 3 Robert Templeton, Sr., is that of his military services in the Revolutionary War as found in the office of the South Carolina Historical Commission, Columbia, S. C., a part of which is reproduced here.

In addition to this record (Fig. 6), the office of Bureau of Pensions, Washington, D. C., shows that, on Oct. 16, 1832, Robert Templeton applied for a pension. In this application he stated that, at the time of his enlistment, his residence was "—near Musgrove Mill, Ninety Six District, S. C." (This mill was on Enoree River in Laurens County). The application shows that his services included:

Dates of Enlistment	Officer Under Whom Services Rendered
February, 1780—3 Mo.	Kilgour (Kilgore)
1780—2 Mo.	"
December 1780—2 Wks.	Lard (Laird)
1781—2 Wks.	"
October, 1781—I Mo.	Kilgore
Siege of Ninety Six	

139

(Fig. 6)

Part of Military Record of 3 Robert Templeton, Sr., in the Revolutionary War,
Reproduced From Original In Office of South Carolina Historical Commission.

According to an article in the Brookville, Ind., Democrat, dated
April 15, 1915, "—Robert Templeton—was one of the pioneer settlers who visited the White Water Valley in 1804. He, in company with General Robert Hanna, came from South Carolina in
1802, leaving their families in camp on the Dry Fork of the White

Water near Harrison, Ohio, while they surveyed the lands of the East White Water Valley that was opened for settlement in 1804. Selecting sites for their homes these pioneers built cabins on their claims and, returning, brought their families to this wilderness home in the Valley 3½ miles north of Brookville in 1805. The Robert Templeton cabin, built on a plateau east of Battle Point, was the first house erected by the Carolina pioneers, he having entered the northwest quarter of Section 38, Oct. 16, 1804."

According to 3691 Mrs. Bessie Templeton Johnson, of Liberty, Ind., this house was built in 1808.

The Brookville Democrat article continues: "This patriarchal pioneer served the county in the capacity of surveyor, was one of the first Grand Jurymen in 1811 and, in 1817, was appointed Treasurer of Franklin County. In many ways he made his country more desirable as a habitation, and was often honored in positions of trust in early affairs, and he was classed among the prominent citizens.—Robert Templeton, Sr., paternal grandfather of the Templeton generation, was born Sept. 6, 1762. He was united in marriage to Mary Hanna in Laurens District, South Carolina, on February 17, 1785.

WILL OF ROBERT TEMPLETON, SR.

"IN THE NAME OF GOD, AMEN! I, Robert Templeton, Sr., County of Franklin, State of Indiana, being somewhat indisposed and weak of body, but of sound and disposing mind, memory and understanding, cosidering the certainty of death, and the uncertainty of the time thereof, and being desirous to settle my worldly affairs and thereby to be better prepared to leave the world when it shall please God to call me hence, I do, therefore make and publish this, my last will and Testament, in manner and form following, that is to say:

FIRST: and principally, I commend my soul into the hands of the Almighty God and my body to the earth, to be decently buried by my executors herein named and after debts and final charges are paid, I divide and bequeath as follows, to-wit:

ITEM 1: To my well beloved wife, MARY TEMPLETON, Two Hundred Dollars $(200.00) in money, together with so much of the household and kitchen furniture as she may think proper to select at my death, also the roan mare which I now own, and the light wagon with the harness thereunto belonging; also one cow which she may select from among the stock on hand at my death.

I wish it to be known and understood that she, my wife, MARY TEMPLETON, is before or at her death to have the full and free right to dispose of all her clothes, also all the beds and bedclothes which we are possessed of at my death.

ITEM 2: I give and bequeath to Mary Templeton, widow of William Templeton, deceased, One Dollar ($1.00).

ITEM 3: I leave and bequeath to my children and other heirs all my property, both real and personal, which I may be possessed of at my death, to be disposed of at public sale by my Executors, and the proceeds of the sale to be divided among my heirs as follows, to-wit: Between ROBERT TEMPLETON, JAMES TEMPLETON, JENNET HANNA BAUCKMAN (BARRICKMAN), wife of Jacob Baukman (Barrickman), Jr., AGNES TEMPLE-

141

TON, ALSO AGNES TEMPLETON, OLIVER G. TEMPLETON, JAMES M. TEMPLETON, heirs of William Templeton, deceased. It is to be divided into seven equal shares after clearing all expenses, each one of our children now living is to have one share and one share to be equally divided among the above named heirs of William Templeton, deceased, which my Executors shall pay to those who may still be minors, pay to their guardians; my Executors will pay to the other six heirs above mentioned their equal dividends. Also all notes and amounts which I may have as my own right at the time of my death, all money recoverable on them after clearing all expenses, is to be equally divided among the above named heirs, i. e. ROBERT TEMPLETON, DAVID TEMPLETON, JAMES TEMPLETON, MARY REED, wife of John Reed, JENNET H. BAUKMAN (Barrickman), wife of Jacob Baukman (Barrickman), Jr., and the four children of William Templeton, deceased, also to AGNES TEMPLETON, my child, to her must be paid seventy dollars ($70.00) in place of a horse (creature) which each of my other children received of me—the seventy dollars is to be paid her before the dividend (division) of the whole is made.

It is to be noted that the First and Second Items are to be satisfied before any other division is made.

I DO HEREBY CONSTITUTE AND APPOINT JOHN REED AND JAMES TEMPLETON to be Executors of this my last Will and Testament, revoking and annulling all former wills that may have been heretofore made by me, ratifying and confirming this, and none other to be my last Will and Testament.

IN TESTIMONY WHEREOF, I have hereunto set my hand and fixed my Seal this 7th day of October A. D. 1829.

ROBERT TEMPLETON (Seal)

Signed, sealed, published and delivered by the said ROBERT TEMPLETON, as and for his last will and Testament, in the presence of us, who, at his request, in his presence and in the presence of each other have subscribed our names as witnesses thereunto.

ROBERT TEMPLETON, JR. (Seal)
DAVID TEMPLETON (Seal)

Probated .... Day of November, 1845.
John M. Johnson, Clerk of Probate Court"

3 Robert Templeton, Sr., died November 10, 1845. He and his wife, Mary Templeton, had nine children:

31 William Templeton, 4/30/1786-2/21/1826.
32 Mary Templeton, 2/7/1788-8/24/1863.
33 Robert Templeton, Jr., 12/6/1789-1/8/1872.
34 David Templeton, 12/15/1791-11/22/1863.
35 Jane Templeton, 9/12/1794-2/21/1797.
36 James Templeton, 4/29/1797-6/16/1848.
37 Elizabeth Ann Templeton, 3/31/1799-9/25/1821, who m. Isaac Crist.
38 Jennet Templeton, 3/24/1803-12/8/1865.
39 Nancy Agnes Templeton, 4/6/1805-3/18/1867.

31 William Templeton m., about 1810, his first cousin, 41 Mary Hanna Templeton, daughter of 4 John and Mary Hanna Templeton. They had one daughter:

311 Agnes Templeton, b. 8/5/1811, who m., first, James Wright and, second, George Miller.

32 Mary Templeton m. John Reed. This was the first marriage in the valley. They had one daughter:

321 Elizabeth ("Betsy") Jane Reed who m. Sam Clark. They had three sons and one daughter, names unknown.

33 Robert Templeton, Jr., m. 2/14/1811, Mary Adams. They had one son:

331 George W. Templeton who m. Ellen Ross.

34 David Templeton m., 6/30/1814, Jane Barrickman, 10/8/1794-7/31/1889, daughter of Jacob and Jane Swàn Barrickman. 34 David Templeton and his wife, Jane Templeton, were both charter members of the U. B. Church, the building known as "Old Franklin." She died at the ripe old age of 94 at the home of her daughter, 346 Catherine Templeton Crist, near Adams, Decatur County, Indiana. They had eight children:

341 John Templeton, who m.................
342 Betty Ann Templeton.
343 Mary Jane Templeton, who m. Sears Carter. They had two children, names unknown.
344 Sarah ("Sallie") Templeton, who m. Sam Fry. They had two daughters, names unknown.
345 Martha Templeton, who m. John Murphy.
346 Catherine Templeton.
'347 (Name unknown).
348 (Name unknown)

In letters, dated 1/30/1930, and 2/5/1930, from 522 Walnut St., Kokomo, Ind., Mrs. W. A. Easter says that her father Charles Robert Templeton, was one of 14 children (only 3 of whom she ever saw) of David Templeton, 9/14/1794 9/10/1874, and his wife, Elenor Clanton Templeton; that her grandfather, David Templeton, came from South Carolina and lived in Henry County, Indiana, and was the son of Robert Templeton, a Revolutionary soldier, and his wife, Anna Templeton. The writer regrets his inability to correlate this properly with other data.

36 James Templeton m., 8/23/1832, Keturah Barrickman, 1/16/1803-12/4/1900 (a sister of Jane Barrickman who m. 34 David Templeton). They had nine children.

361 Oliver Goldsmith Templeton, 8/18/1833-1/29/1921.
362 Martha Jane Templeton, 9/9/1834-4/28/1839.
363 Mary Eliza Templeton, 4/30/1836-__/__/1896.
364 Ann Elizabeth Templeton, 10/13/1837-10/18/1881.
365 William Jacob Templeton, 3/7/1839-1927, who m. Sarah E. Ward.

366 Robert Dudley Templeton (twin), 11/27/1841-2/13/1896, who m. Nina Burris.

367 James Wiley Templeton (twin), 11/27/1841-11/25/1926.

368 Keturah Jennie Templeton, 10/30/1843-2/7/1927, who m., first, Lewis Quick, and second, Frank Stanton.

369 David Winfield Scott Templeton 5/8/1846-7/22/1913.

The Brookville Democrat article continues:

"361 Oliver Goldsmith Templeton was in his fifteenth year when his father died. Being the oldest child, he stepped into his father's shoes, metaphorically speaking, and, with his mother's aid and advice, and the help of younger brothers, they reared the family to manhood and womanhood and made a success and respectable standing that was commendable. He volunteered as a private soldier at Fairfield, Ind., on the 11th of August, 1862—was mustered into Company G of the 68th Indiana Regiment, Volunteer Infantry, under Captain V. C. Lynn, Colonel King commanding, at Greensburg, Ind., and was duly sworn in at Indianapolis on August 19, 1862. He saw service in the Sunny South at Hoover's Gap and, with his company, followed General Bragg's Army across Elk River to University Heights when he was sent to the Convalescent Camp near Cowan's Station and from that place he was removed to the Field Hospital on the Nashville and Chattanooga Railroad. His condition continuing to grow worse, he was sent to General Hospital No. 7, at Nashville, Tenn. He received his honorable discharge and was mustered out on Sept. 30, 1863. For 14 years after his return home he remained on the farm until about 1877. On June 28, 1887, he married Elizabeth Myrtle Robinson who died June 6, 1909. They had two children:

    3611 Audrey Keturah Templeton, b. 12/22/1890.

    3612 Eva Elizabeth Templeton, b. 7/1/1893."

3611 Audrey Keturah Templeton m. Sylvester Jarrell. They live at Connersville, Ind. They have one daughter:

    36111 Eva Louise Jarrell who m. Edward Cain. They have one daughter:

        361111 Pamelia Cain.

3612 Eva Elizabeth Templeton m. Charles Higgs. They live at Connersville, Ind. She has the old tar bucket that hung on the side of the wagon and which held the tar for lubricating the axles of the wagon that brought her great-grandfather, 3 Robert Templeton, and his family on their long journey from South Carolina. They have one son:

    36121 Carroll Higgs, who m. _____.

363 Mary Eliza Templeton m. Jacob Erwin. They had two sons:

    3631 Scott Erwin, 3/28/1860-9/22/1912.

3632 Oliver Ellsworth Erwin, b. 10/7/1863-d........, who m. .... They had two sons, names unknown.

3631 Scott Erwin m. .... They had two daughters:
    36311 Edna May Erwin, 8/30/1885-11/1/1914.
    36312 Mamie Erwin, 2/24/1888-1/13/1915.

364 Ann Elizabeth Templeton m., 1857, William H. Likely. They had seven children:
    3641 James T. Likely, b. 4/4/1859, d.............. .
    3642 William Oliver Likely, 1/5/1861-8/..../1939.
    3643 Laura Ann Likely, b. 1/8/1863, d.............
    3644 Mary A. Likely, b. 1/18/1864, d.............
    3645 Cora Keturah Likely, b. 4/20/1866. :
    3646 Margaret E. Likely, b. 6/10/1868, d.............
    3647 Annabell Likely, b. 2/16/1870, d.............., who m. Clint Waltz.

3642 William Oliver Likely m. Lizzie Beasley. They live at Muncie, Ind. They have two children:
    36421 Raymond Likely.
    36422 Esther Likely who m. Ralph Guiler. They have one son:
        364221 Charles Guiler.

367 James Wiley Templeton m., 1871, Kate W. Skinner. They had one daughter:
    3671 May Pearl Templeton, b. 7/29/1878, who m. John C. Leffler. They live at Liberty, Ind., Rt. 1, and have one son:
        36711 Marlin T. Leffler, b. 2/28/1911, who m. Martha Driscol. They have three children:
            367111 Susan Leffler, b. 4/26/1937.
            367112 Mary Elizabeth Leffler, b. 1/25/1941.
            367113 Martha Ann Leffler, b. 6/20/1947.

369 David Winfield Scott Templeton m., 1881, Phoebe Dorrell. They have two children:
    3691 Bessie Edith Templeton, b. 5/24/1882.
    3692 Infant son, still born 11/..../1895.

3691 Bessie Edith Templeton lives at Liberty, Ind. She has been intensely interested in the history of the Templeton family and has been most generous and cooperative in supplying and correcting data. Among the items of information furnished by her were the copy of the will of 3 Robert Templeton, Sr., and a copy of the picture of 4 John Templeton, Sr., which is reproduced herein. She has the old wagon hammer used by her great-grandfather, 3 Robert Templeton, and others on their migration journey from South Carolina. She also has the old tin bucket which he used to carry the county funds between his office and his home when he served as the first treasurer of Franklin County, Ind. She m., 8/23/1905, Albert D. Johnson. They have two children:

    36911 Lloyd Denman Johnson, b. 4/18/1908, who m. Mae Bailey.

    36912 Hazel Fay Johnson, b. 6/2/1911, who m. Murhl S. Rogers. They have one adopted daughter, Carrol Fay Johnson, b. 5/1/1940.

38 Jennet Templeton m., 1820, Jacob Barrickman. They had one daughter:

    381 Sarah Augusta Barrickman, 1827-1860, who m., 10/5/ 1842, Joseph Barnard, 1818-1900. They had one daughter:

        3811 Ella Barnard, 1845-1920, who m., 6/10/1868, Altus M. Harding, 1844-1914. They had four children:

            38111 Augusta Harding, who d. 7/.../1937.

            38112 Isadore Harding, b. 1872.

            38113 Alice Harding, 11/25/1875-12/31/1939.

            38114 Horace Harding, b. 1877, who was living in Los Angeles in 1933.

38111 Augusta Harding m. Cornelius Browder. She lived at 308 Northern Ave., Indianapolis, Ind. In 1933 she was joint hostess to the writer, his wife and daughter while on their way to the Century of Progress, World Fair in Chicago. Their cordial hospitality made the visit and tour of the city of Indianapolis a most pleasant occasion. Mr. and Mrs. Browder had one daughter:

    381111 Mary McEnaney Browder, b. 1927.

38112 Isadore Harding lives at Brookville, Ind. She is the proud possessor of the old spinning wheel "used in the (3) Robert Templeton family years and years ago." She is an active member of the Daughters of the American Revolution as a descendent of 3 Robert Templeton, Sr. She has manifested a keen interest in the Templeton genealogy. She m. Charles L. Masters. They have one daughter:

    381121 Mildred Masters, b. 1907, who m., 6/..../1933, Wayne Listerman, a graduate of .... College with Phi Beta Kappa honors. They were living in Philadelphia, Penn., in 1933, where he was connected with the Department of Justice.

38113 Alice Harding was an active member of the D. A. R. as a descendent of 3 Robert Templeton, Sr. It was through her enthusiastic interest and cooperation that most of the information about the Templetons in Indiana was made available. She was the first one of the Indiana Templetons to attend one of the Templeton reunions in 1930 at Cross Anchor, S. C. While visiting in South Carolina she endeared herself to many of her kinfolks by her agreeable manner and pleasing personality. She m. W. E. Erwin. After their divorce she made her home with her sister, 38111 Mrs. Augusta Harding Browder, at 308 Northern Ave., Indianapolis, Ind.

39 Nancy Agnes Templeton m. Jefferson Colescott. They had one son:

    391 John Colescott, who m. Emma Jarard. ,They had four children:

        3911 Adah Colescott who m. G. E. Demett. They live at Brookville, Ind.

        3912 May Colescott who m................... Gifford.

        3913 Cora Colescott who m. Charles Hutchinson. They live at Laurel, Ind.

        3914 Perry Colescott who m .... He lives in Chicago.

4 JOHN TEMPLETON, SR. (1766-1837)

This picture of 4 John Templeton, Sr., was furnished by 3691 Mrs. Bessie Johnson of Liberty, Ind. She says: "We cannot find a date on the picture. It is not a daguerreotype. We think it is a drawing. It is 14 x 17 inches and the drawing is on paper pasted to cloth."

According to the old family Bible in possession of 4321 Mrs. Julia Templeton Miller of Brookville, Ind., "Judge John Templeton was born in County Antrim, Ireland, cn 21st of January, 1766, died April 30, 1837. Mary Hanna Templeton, his wife, was born March 22, 1770. William Templeton was born April 30, 1786. Mary Templeton, his wife, was born Dec. 8, 1789. Agnes Templeton, daughter of William and Mary Templeton, was born August 5, 1811."

Here we find more authentic evidence that these Templetons came from Ireland.

In a letter from Aurora, Ill., dated Dec. 27, 1938, 4211 Mrs. Lillian Fullmer says: "My great-grandfather, John Templeton, was born in Ireland. . . . When a small boy he came to America . . . and settled in the Laurens District . . . . They moved to what is now Hamilton County, Ohio, near the village of Harrison. There were six members in his family, other than heads of families, that came to Ohio with John Templeton. They were: Robert Templeton, Sr., Robert Hanna, Sr., Joseph Hanna, George Lewiston, William Logan, John Ewing or Erwin and Robert Swan. They brought their families to Union County Indiana, on April 7, 1805. The party was under the leadership of Robert Templeton and Robert

Hanna. John Templeton married Mary Hanna, daughter of Robert and Mary Parks Hanna."

The Indianapolis Star recently published a picture of: "one of the oldest buildings in Eastern Indiana is the log cabin built at Liberty in 1810 by John Templeton, member of the Constitutional Convention. The house is now owned by the Union County Historical Society."

According to 3691 Mrs. Bessie Johnson, of Liberty, Ind.: "This house was built by John Templeton. I am not sure the date, 1810, is correct but it was near that time, possibly three years earlier. It now stands near the jail in our town, having been moved to Liberty about 1939, or earlier."

4 John Templeton, Sr., was a member of the Territorial Legislature of Indiana in 1811 and subsequently. He is said to have given the name to Franklin County. Records show that he was Judge of Common Pleas Court on Feb. 11, 1811, and later.

As stated on page 1, we find no record of any military services or land grants to 4 John Templeton, Sr., in South Carolina, although we do find in the office of Clerk of Court, Laurens, S. C., a deed by James Puckett for 100 acres of land on the waters of Enoree River to John Templeton, dated Oct. 22, 1795. This was evidently 4 John Templeton, Sr. since we have been unable to find a trace of any other John Templeton in Laurens County who was of legal age at that time. The only other John Templeton known of in Laurens County at that time was 15 John Templeton, born 3/9/1787, son of 1 David Templeton, Sr. We find further that this same tract of land was sold to George Gordon on Oct 12, 1801 by "Captain John Templeton of Laurens District, S. C.," and the dowry was signed by "Mary Templeton, wife of Capt. John Templeton."

In the U. S. Census of 1790 we find John Templeton listed in Laurens County, S. C., as the head of a family with no other male 16 years of age. This census report shows also that there were in this family 3 females, including heads of families. Evidently these were Mary Templeton, his wife, 41 Mary Templeton, b. 12/8/1789, his daughter and one other female.

From family Bible and other records we find that 4 John Templeton Sr., and his wife, Mary Templeton, had nine children:

41 Mary Hanna Templeton, b. 12/8/1789.
42 Nancy Templeton
43 Alexander ("Sandy") Templeton.
44 David Clark Templeton, b. 1/21/1800.
45 John ("Jack") Templeton.
46 Jane Templeton.
47 Catherine H. Templeton, b. 7/16/1805.
48 James Madison Templeton, who m. Mary Burns.
49 Julia Templeton.

41 Mary Hanna Templeton married her first cousin, 31 William Templeton, son of 3 Robert Templeton, Sr. See his line for their descendents.

42 Nancy Templeton m. James Lewiston. They had two daughters:
    421 Nancy Lewiston.
    422 Mary Hanna Lewiston who m. Henry King.

421 Nancy Lewiston m. Stephen Farlow. They had one son:
    4211 James Madison Farlow who m. Christine Hunt Meek. They had one daughter:
        42111 Lillian Farlow, who m., 11/18/1896, Percy F. Fullmer in chicago. They live at 100 Main St., Aurora, Illinois.

43 Alexander ("Sandy") Templeton m. Margaret T. Moore. They had five children:
    431 Martha Templeton who m. Samuel Henderson.
    432 Simon Bolivar Templeton.
    433 Francis Templeton.
    434 Mary Templeton who m. .... Welsh.
    435 Irene Templeton who m., first, Samuel Diggins. They had one son:
        4351 Edward Diggins.

435 Irene Templeton Diggins m. second, Wilson Carter.

432 Simon Bolivar Templeton m. Susan Collier. They had one daughter:
    4321 Julia Templeton who m. Charles Miller. She lives at Brookville, Ind. She has the old family Bible which records the birth of 4 John Templeton, Sr., and others.

In a letter from Brookville, Ind., Rt. 4, dated July 21, 1930, 44211 Mrs. Stella Hill says: ". . . My great-grandfather (44 David Clark Templeton) built the first log cabin on East White Water River Valley just 2 miles south of Quakertown. This primitive colony consisted of nine family cabins that were occupied in 1805 on tracts of fertile land from the historic Battle Point at Templeton's Ford 3½ miles north of Brookville up the Valley to near Brookville in Union County. Ind. David Clark (Templeton) was two years old when his parents established the Templeton home near Quakertown. The log house is still standing. My grandfather was past his eightieth milestone when he died. His son, David C. Templeton, is living near Brookville, Ind. My mother is living at 129 North Grand Ave., Connersville, Ind."

44 David Clark Templeton m. Matilda Baxter. They had five children:

150

441 Julia A. Templeton who m. Thomas Bond.
442 James Madison Templeton.
443 Lydia Templeton who m. Jackson Brandenberg.
444 Cynthia Templeton who m. James Brandenberg.
445 Mary Templeton.
446 Sarah Templeton who m. .... McAlister. They had
two children. names unknown.
447 Ulysses Templeton.
448 Nancy Templeton.

442 James Madison Templeton m. Elizabeth Minson. They had
two children:
    4421 David C. Templeton.
    4422 Addie Jones Templeton.

4421 David C. Templeton m. .... They had one daughter:
    44211 Stella Templeton who m. .... Hill. She lives at
Brookville, Ind., Rt. 1.

445 Mary Templeton m. Fenton Brookbank, a Captain in the
War of Secession. They had six children:
    4451 Bruce Brookbank.
    4452 Chase Brookbank.
    4453 Ida Brookbank.
    4454 Nevada Brookbank.
    4455 Arizona Brookbank.
    4456 Matilda Brookbank.

447 Ulysses Templeton m. Mary Moore. They had one son:
    4471 Abner Templeton.

448 Nancy Templeton m. James Barrickman. They had five
children:
    4481 James Barrickman.
    4482 Bart Barrickman.
    4483 Clark Barrickman.
    4484 Scott Barrickman.
    4485 Nina Barrickman

45 John ("Jack") Templeton m. Lucinda Snodgrass. They lived
at Quakertown, Ind. They had five children:
    451 Benjamin F. Templeton (twin), who m. Rose Miller.
    452 Thomas J. Templeton (twin).
    453 Helen Templeton.
    454 Mary Templeton.
    455 Anna Templeton who m. Theodore Miller.

452 Thomas J. Templeton was a Union soldier during the entire War Between the States. He m. Mary Sample. They had
three children:

4521 Alpha Templeton who m. Lieut. Frank Dawson.
4522 Katherine Templeton, a teacher in Union County, Ind.
4523 Elizabeth Templeton who m................

453 Helen Templeton visited 29i Scott Templeton in Laurens, S. C., about 1910-1920. She m. Edwin Beckett. They had four children:
    4531 Clementine Beckett.
    4532 Cora Beckett.
    4533 Grace Beckett.
    4534 Frederick Beckett.

454 Mary Templeton was a supervisor, Prep. Civil Service School, Washington, D. C . She m. Kosciusco Kelly. They had one daughter:
    4541 Bessie Kelly.

46 Jane Templeton m. Abner McCarty. They had six children:
    461 Catherine McCarty who m. Theodore Purcell and lived in California.
    462 John McCarty who m. .... He died in California.
    463 Indiana McCarty who m. Mrs. .... Burriss.
    464 Mary Hanna McCarty who m. Henry Galleon. They had one daughter, who lived at Brookville, Ind., name unknown.
    465 Jane McCarty who m., first, Abner Bennett, and, second, Lee Yaryan.
    466 Ben McCarty.

47 Catherine Templeton m. George Newland.. He ran a flat boat selling whiskey. They had eight children:
    471 Thompson Newland.
    472 Abner Newland.
    473 James Newland.
    474 John Newland.
    475 Jane Newland.
    476 Herod Newland.
    477 Dallas Newland.
    478 Robert Newland.

49 Julia Ann Templeton m., first, James Addison, and, second, Judge Enoch McCarty. They had one son:
    491 Thomas Jefferson McCarty.

APPENDIX

The earliest authentic records we have of Templetons living in what is now the United States are found in the Pennsylvania Archives. There we find recorded a grant of 200 acres of land in that colony to David Templeton on August 9, 1738. Another grant to him was dated February 6, 1744. We also find there the record of a grant to James Templeton dated February 20, 1748 (9).

In the Land Grant Office in Raleigh, N. C., we find records of land grants on Catawba River to one David Templeton as early as 1752. We also find here a record of a grant of 400 acres to him "—in Anson County on the South Side of Enoree River joyning Walter Caruth's survey on Duncan's Creek." This 400 acres was supposed to have been in North Carolina, but when the line between North and South Carolina was completely surveyed the land was found to be in South Carolina. Walter Carruth's land was on the head waters of Duncan's Creek and David Templeton's was on Rocky Creek, now known as Warrior Creek, in Laurens County, S. C. This David Templeton died in 1761. His will is recorded at Wadesboro, N. C. He willed the 400 acres on Rocky (now Warrior) Creek to his son, Archibald Templeton, who sold it in 1788 to James Templeton of Abbeville District, S. C. This David Templeton was, for a long time, mistaken by Thomas Workman and other bonafide genealogists, as the ancestor of the Templetons who later lived in Laurens County. However, no authentic record of kinship between them has yet been established.

In Foote's Historical Sketches of Virginia and in Howe's History of the Presbyterian Church in South Carolina records are found of one Rev. James Templeton, a Presbyterian minister, who served vaious churches in Laurens, Abbeville, Greenville, Spartanburg and York Counties from 1776 until 1810. No kinship between him and the other Laurens County Templetons has been established.

Other Templetons with whom no kinship with those of Laurens County, S. C., has been established include:

Hugh Templeton, whose patents are recorded in the office of Secretary of State, Columbia, S. C., for "— a carding machine that will card 80 pounds of cotton per day," and "—a spinning machine with 84 spindles that will spin one man's attendance ten pounds of good cotton per day," dated March 13, 1789; William Templeton, who was given a grant of 150 acres of land on the south side of Broad River on the waters Cannon Creek, May 5, 1773; Andrew Templeton, who was given a grant of 100 acres in "Colleton County," June 16, 1769; Henry Templeton, who was given a grant of 350 acres "in Boonsborough Township at a place where the Cherokee Road crosses the head branch of Long Cane, April 1, 1763;" "_____ Templeton," who married James M. Calhoun as recorded on page 96, Vol. VII, S. C. Historical magazine;

James Templeton of York District and Margaret Templeton in Lancaster District, who were heads of families as shown by the U. S. Census report of 1790; Aaron Templeton who was listed as the head of a family in Spartanburg District in the first Census report of 1790, a brief sketch of whose line may be found elsewhere in this volume; scores of other Templetons in nearly all of the states from New England to Georgia left records, most of which were authentic, but many of which were meager records, and dating as early as the 1730's and 1740's.

AARON TEMPLETON

Aaron Templeton (also spelled Templeman) evidently settled in what is now Spartanburg County, S. C., and lived there until his death.

In the office of the South Carolina Historical Commission, Columbia, S. C., we find that he was a soldier of the Revolution. His indent, dated October 1, 1784, showed that he was a"—private in McKenzie's Troop, Hill's Regiment, Sumter's Brigade, state troops." It showed that he was due "—94 pounds sterling being the amount due him for services in that troop together with interest thereon from the first April, 1782, to date hereof; Agreeable to a resolution of the General Assembly of the 11th of March last—."

In the census of 1790 we find that, in Spartanburg District, Aaron Templeton was listed as the head of a family with one male 16 years old and upward (evidently Aaron Templeton himself); no males under 16; 3 females (evidently his wife and two oldest daughters).

In the office of Secretary of State, Columbia, S. C., we find the record of a grant of land, 230 acres, to Aaron Templeton "—in the district of Ninety Six—," and dated November 27, 1792.

In the office of Register of Mesne Conveyance, Greenville, S. C., we find that, in 1803, "—Aaron Templeton of Spartanburg District" sold to "—John Wheeler, Sr., 300 acres on the waters of Pacolet and Saluda Rivers—" This land must have been in Greenville County on the mountain ridge since this would have been the only place that could lie on the waters of both Pacolet and Saluda Rivers.

In the same office we find also that, in 1814, Aaron Templeton sold "—to Charles Gosnell 20 acres adjacent to Glassy Rock."

In the office of Register of Mesne Conveyance, Spartanburg, S. C., we find that, in 1816, Aaron Templeton sold to "—Lewis Cannon 150 acres on Thickety Creek."

In the office of Probate Judge, Spartanburg, S. C., we find that on April 12, 1822, Lee Lindler, John Lindler and William Tracy signed the administration bond in the settlement of the estate of Aaron Templeman (also spelled Templeton).

In the History of Spartanburg County by J. B. O. Landrum (The Franklin Prtg. & Pub. Co., Atlanta, Ga., 1900), page 391, we find that "His (Captain Romulus Lee Bowden's) mother (Nancy Linder who m. Reuben Bowden) was, as previously stated, the daughter of Mary Templeton Linder, his descendents on both sides being English." In this same history, page 390, we find "—Reuben Bowden—married August 21st, 1823, to Nancy Linder, daughter of the elder Lee Linder, who was born Oct. 27th, 1809."

In the office of Probate Judge, Spartanburg County, S. C., we find that, on Oct. 10, 1844, in the settlement of the estate of Lee Linder, the widow's share was $5,450.78, while Reuben Bowden and his wife's share was $1,429.12½. Besides Reuben Bowden's wife ten other legatees were named.

Thus we see that Aaron Templeton evidently lived and died in Spartanburg County, leaving a long line of descendents there. Whether he was closely related to the Templetons in Laurens County or not we are unable to say. However, his descendents should be proud of the fact that he had a part in the War for Independence.

THE END

155

CORRECTIONS

TEMPLETON FAMILY HISTORY

Page 7: Caption for Fig. 3 should read:
"—by her Grandfather, JOHN TEMPLETON—"

Page 10: 111d Jane Sabema Templeton Boggs and Joseph Addison Boggs had only three children:
111d1 John Thomas Boggs
111d2 Ella Catherine Boggs
111d3 George Leland Boggs

Page 11: 1123 Eunice Pauline Stewart Boggs and Joseph Addison Boggs had six children. Their names and correct identification numbers should be on

Page 14: 11231 Lizzie Jane Boggs
11232 Mary Josephine Boggs
11233 Walter Lewers Boggs ⎫ Identification numbers
11234 Sarah Ada Boggs   ⎬ of these four persons
11235 Louise Florence Biggs ⎨ should be revised ac-
11236 Corrie Addison Boggs ⎭ cordingly.

Page 18: 11411 William Perry Lyles
"—lived at Drayton Mill—."

Page 21: 1142432 "Louis Templeton—He lives—."

Page 38: 13645 Bessie Smith who m. John Dulin."

Page 50: 14g1114 Danner Watkins.

Page 67: "—He married, May 26, 1915,
Kathryn Childs, b. June 5, 1891."

156

APPENDIX

By

Ronald H. Templeton

L. B. Templeton did an excellent and time consuming job in his publication of the Laurens County, SC, Templetons. His research in finding and documenting the various Templeton descendant lines helps modern day descendants in their research for ancestors. Over the years since the publication of his book additional information has been found which aids in correcting some original assumptions. Also, the current use of DNA in genealogical research now provides us with the ability to more firmly determine our connection to various Templeton lines.

In addition to the first Templeton (David Templeton) in Laurens County, L. B. also provides information on the Templetons who arrived in November 1772 from Ireland. Based on land grants issued in 1772, these were Robert, James, Martha, and Agnes. Robert received a land grant of 250 acres. James, Martha, and Agnes each received a grant of 100 acres. Grants were awarded based on heads of households (100 acres), other members of the household (50 acres for each member), and 100 acres for single individuals over the age of 16.[1] This means Robert was a household head with three family members. James, Martha, and Agnes were all over 16 and unmarried. L. B. made an assumption the Robert who received the 250 acres was the Robert born in 1762. This Robert was too young (10 years of age) to receive a land grant and too young to have had a family consisting of three members. The following explains the Robert of 250 acres was much older and the apparent patriarch of the Templetons who came over from Ireland in 1772.

On page 120 of Brent Holcomb's book[2] there is a record of the session for Laurens County held on 8 December 1788. It shows the names of the men selected for the petit court and the second name on the list is "Rob't Templeton, Jun'r." This cannot be the Robert Junior listed by L. B. since that Robert Junior had not been born (born a year later on 6 December 1789). Since the records show a Robert Junior in 1788, then there must have been an elder Robert still alive at the time.

On page 9 of *"Laurens County SC Wills 1784-1840"* by Colleen Elliott we find the following:

---

[1] Walter Edgar, *South Carolina A History,* pages 53/54

[2] Brent Holcomb, *Laurens County SC Minutes of the County Court, 1786-1789*

"8 Mar 1794 Appraisal of estate of Robert Templeton dec'd by Robt. Hanna, James Adair & Thomas Logan."

The Robert Templeton who was granted the 250 acres brought his family to SC in 1772 and died in SC between 1790 and 1794. Based on the land grants we have this family makeup: Robert the Elder, his wife (name unknown), James, Agnes, Martha, Robert Junior and John.

There were Templetons in York County and Spartanburg County, SC, with one being the possible father of the David Templeton who died in Laurens County, SC, in 1817. A James Templeton appears in the census records for York County for 1790, 1800 and 1810. In the 1810 census he is listed as over 45 years of age, giving a birth year of 1755 or earlier. James' birth year would be close to the birth year of the Laurens County David. On 20 April 1771, James was granted 90 acres of land on Bullock's Creek. In a deed transaction on 22 November 1771, he purchased 240 acres on Bullock's Creek.[3] [4] In 1811 James moved to Missouri with his family and settled on Buffalo Creek in Pike County.[5] Per one genealogy record, James died in 1822 in Pike County. He is listed as being born in the New Acquisition District, SC, around 1750-1755. His children are listed as being born in SC, with one daughter being born in the New Acquisition District.[6] When the border between North and South Carolina was corrected by a new survey in 1772, land previously allocated to NC counties fell into SC. Present day counties, all or part, which were originally in NC include: Spartanburg, Cherokee, York, Lancaster, Greenville, Laurens, Union, Newberry and Chester.

Of particular note related to James of York County, his parents had to have been living in the "New Acquisition District" area in the 1750s. The 1790 census for James has two males over 16. The older male in James's household was not James' son since the son was under 16 at the time. Two possibilities for the other older male would be a brother of James or his father. At any rate, we have the parents of James in the area who may have also been the parents of the David of Laurens County.

From the online SC archives there is 20 February 1773 plat action for an Andrew Brown on Ferguson's Creek of the Tyger River. The plat for Brown shows its northern border was adjacent to land owned by a David Templeton. A later action on 13 September 1784 for 200 acres on Ferguson's Creek states it was surveyed for a David Templeton on 23 December 1772. It appears this David owned 200 acres adjacent to Andrew Brown in 1773.

[3] Jay Norwalk, *The Genealogy of John Templeton 1755-1822 of Iredell County, NC*, page 199

[4] Brent Holcomb, *North Carolina Land Grants in South Carolina*

[5] Louis Houck, *History of Missouri*, page, 158

[6] www.familysearch.org

Turning attention to the DNA results we find family relationships not only between the Robert and David of Laurens County but with a Templeton family line in Iredell County, NC. David Templeton and Robert Templeton of Laurens County were very closely related. A descendant of David's son Robert tested out to 67 markers, and a descendant of Robert's (who arrived in 1772) son James tested out to 25 markers. A comparison of the values for the first 25 markers shows a perfect match between the two individuals. Using the 25 markers means the two individuals have a 65% probability of a most recent common ancestor (MRCA) 5 generations back, 73% for six generations back, and about 78% for seven generations back.[7] DNA results also show the Laurens County Templetons are related to a Templeton line in Iredell County, NC. I have a paper trail to a James Templeton who was in Iredell County, NC, as early as 1748 when he was listed by name as a chain carrier for a survey team. I have tested out to 67 markers. When comparing my DNA with the descendant of David of Laurens the probability of MRCA 5 generations back is 75%, for 6 generations back it is 85%, and for 7 generations it is 90%. Putting this in perspective, the seventh generation back from me would be the father of my ancestor James Templeton of Iredell County. The James Templeton of Iredell County did not have a son named David so we must go at least one more generation back for the Laurens County Templetons. Based on the previous discussion for the "New Acquisition District" the father of the David of Laurens County may have been the same father of the James Templeton of York County.

In summarizing, we have the following possible scenario based on the DNA results. Three brothers lived Antrim County, Ireland, in the early 1700s. My ancestor James Templeton and a brother, possibly named David, came to the colonies in the late 1730s or early 1740s. James settled in Iredell County, NC, and the brother settled in what became York or Spartanburg County, SC. In 1772, the third brother, Robert, came to SC with his family and settled in Laurens County.

---

[7] MRCA calculations are based on the Infinite Alleles Model.

INDEX

Index prepared by James D. McKain, Tucson, AZ

161

(BAGWELL) Robert 117
Robert Ernest 117
BAILEY, Essie (Casey) 127
Lewis 127
Lula Estelle (Casey) 127
Mae (Johnson) 146
BALL, Alice Deveaux (Templeton)
23, 24
Charles 24
Cornelia 24
David Edward 24
Gertrude (Towe) 24
James 24
Joseph 24
Katherine (McDowell) 115
LeRoy 24
Margaret 24
Sarah (McDowell) 115
BANNISTER, Louise (Templeton)
125
BARKSDALE, Amelia (Templeton)
124
Lilly (Templeton) 27, 28, 30
William Dale 28
BARNARD, Ella (Harding) 146
Joseph 146
Sarah Augusta (Barrickman) 146
BARNETT, Eldridge C. 93
Eva (Templeton) 131
Frances (Stewart) 93
Robert Layne 93
BARRICKMAN, Bart 151
Clark 151
Jacob 141-143, 146
James 151
Jane (Swan) 143
Jane (Templeton) 143
Jennet (Hanna) 141
Jennet (Templeton) 142, 146
Jennet H. 142
Keturah (Templeton) 143
Nancy (Templeton) 151
Nina 151
Sarah Augusta (Barnard) 146
Scott 151
BAUCKMAN, Jennet (Hanna) 141
BAUKMAN, Jacob 141, 142
Jennet H. 142
BAXTER, Matilda (Templeton) 150
BEAN, P. T. 26
BEARD, 72
BEASLEY, Ed 79
Inez (Mullikin) 79
Lizzie (Likely) 145
Susan T. (Templeton) 21

BEAUFORD, Katie (Stewart) 93
BECKETT, Clementine 152
Cora 152
Edwin 152
Frederick 152
Grace 152
Helen (Templeton) 151, 152
BELL, Alexander Graham 116
BENJAMIN, Arthur Lee 109
Edwin Ralph 109
Elbert 109
J. Grace (Templeton) (Madden)
130, 132
Janie Auld (McQuon) 109
Leila (Workman) (Young) 109, 110
Leila Pauline 109
Mary (Templeton) 108, 109
Mary Lou (Bagwell) 109
Mary Virginia 109
Matthew 109
Paul McQuon 109
Roy Elbert 109
Shell 132
BENNETT, Abner 152
Amanda (Templeton) 33, 34
Beatrice (Sloan) 130
Esther 34
Jane (McCarty) (Yaryan) 152
Sam 34
BENOIT, Ernest 98
Ernest Theodore 98
Florence Margaret (Stewart) 98
Gladis Marie 98
Ruth Estelle 98
BERDIE, Flora (Boggs) 11
Louise 11
Willie 11
BERTRAM, Guy 103
Willie (Burdette) 103
BILTON, Ivy May (Templeton) 34
BIRD, W. D. 15
BISHOP, Bobby Joe 60
Catherine (Crook) 60
Harold Davis 60
Mamie Robinson Watkins 50, 51
Patton 51
Ruth (Reid) 117
Victor 60
BLACK, Betty Jean (Allen) 99
Dean 99
BLACKWELL, L. B. 134
BLAKELEY, Nannie (Mullikin) 80
BLAKELY, Mattie (Watkins) 50
BOBO, Arena (Templeton) 99
Clarence 120

(COLEMAN), Rachel Frances
(Fowler) 96
Robert Earl 96
Sarah (Williams) 96
Sarah Georgia (Templeton) 29, 30
Walter Scott 30
Walter Stewart 95, 96
COLESCOTT, Adah (Dernett) 147
Cora (Hutchinson) 147
Emma (Jarard) 147
Jefferson 147
John 147
May (Gifford) 147
Nancy Agnes (Templeton) 142, 147
Perry 147
COLLIER, Susan (Templeton) 150
COLLINS, Cathy 120
Fred 120
Sarah Josephine (Taylor) 119, 120
COMPTON, Alice (Templeton) 113
Charles 22
Cornelia Emmaline (Templeton) 22
Nancy (Poole) 22
CONN, Ida (Puckett) 47
CONNALLY, John 46
Mamie (Templeton) (White) 46
CONNELLY, Alice (Hopkins) 81, 82
Beulah (Monroe) 82
Blanch (Ellison) 82
Lula (Templeton) 46
Mae 82
Oleina (Jarvis) 82
Pearl (Sligh) 82
Pierce 82
COOK, Anne McFall 94
Beatrice (Petty) 95
Carolyn (McKee) 94
Carolyn (Wright) 94
Carolyn Virginia 94
Carrol 94
Celeste (Morrison) 94
Charles Stewart 93, 94
Doris (Anderson) 94
Ernest Glenn 93
Frank Abraham 93, 95
Fred Martin 93, 95
Gloria Mayson 95
Janice 94
John Breckenridge 93, 94
Louise (Galdman) 95
Lucile (Jackson) 94
Madge (Drummond) 93, 94
Mary Ann (Stewart) 92, 93
Mary Jane 95
Mildred (Hawkins) 93, 95

Nell 93, 94
Sallie Mae (Stewart) 95
COOPER, Averil 58
Billy 58
Doris E. (Jennings) 65
Frances (Prather) 59
Francis 65
Jerry 65
Maude (Templeton) 105
Pearl (Snow) 105
Ruth (Puckett) 57, 58
Terry 65
COPELAND, 118
CORE, Mildred (Prather) 126
CRADDOCK, Dorothy Jane
(Templeton) 43
Jane Simpson (Campbell) 78
CRAIG, 63
Creek William 5
Eleanor 2
William 5
CRANE, 73
CRAWFORD, Owen (Giles) 29
CREIGHTON, Sibyl (Stewart) 97
CRIST, Catherine (Templeton) 143
Elizabeth Ann (Templeton) 142
Isaac 142
CROOK, Alma (Dunaway) 60
Ben 60
Bennie Celestine (Langley) 59
C. B. 60
Catherine (Bishop) 60
Cullen 58
Edith (Hughes) 60
Edna Frances 60
Edward 58
Emily 57, 58
Ethel (Prather) 57, 58
Hallie (Hadock) (Howard) 60
Hugh (Willard) 60
Isabella A. (Templeton) 48, 57
James 57
James Ed 57, 60
Jim 60
Le Grand 58
Mattie Belle (Brown) 60
Merle (Brakefield) 58
Minnie (Brewington) 59
Narcissa (Puckett) 57
Rebecca (Lawson) 60
Virginia (Ivey) 60, 61
W. Ben 57, 59
CROSWELL, Mamie (Stewart) 96
CROW, 15
Jimmie Leila (Templeton) 71

166

CULLOM, Smith 15
CUMMINGS, Sallie (Stewart) 92
CUNNINGHAM, 54
 Frances 63
 John Stewart 53
 Jonnie 53, 55, 63, 74
 Laura Ann Frances (Templeton)
  48, 49, 53
 Pat 85, 139
DANDY, Ellie W. 127
 Eugene Wilkerson 127
 Margaret Elizabeth 127
 Margaret Jane (Templeton) 127
 Mary Eulala (Casey) 127
 Minnie Estelle (Lawrence) 127
 Whitfield Clark 127
DARNELL, Grace (Clark) 52
DAVIS, 78
 Billy 80
 Calvin C. 50, 53
 Florrah (Woodruff) 50, 51
 Frank 80
 Giles Jerome 50
 Homer 80
 Ione (Clark) 50, 52
 James 80
 Jimmie 88
 Joe Hill 50
 Johnnie 80
 Kate (Watkins) 50
 Lottie 80
 Mamie (Davis) 50
 Marie (Mullikin) 79, 809
 Marjorie (Templeton) 48, 50
 Mary 80
 Mary Susan (Templeton) 20
 Mildred (Rhoades) 24
 Nellie Dee 80
 Pearl (Holman) 50, 51
 Walter 50
DAWSON, Alpha (Templeton) 152
 Frank 152
DAY, Adaline (Templeton) 33, 34,
  107
 Sara C. (Templeton) 107
DEAN, Adelia (Campbell) (Morris)
  78, 81
 James Walter 81
 John 81
 William Albert 81
DEASON, Ida (McCoy) 45
DENDY, Catherine 128
 Ellie 22
 Ellie W. 126
 Eva (Cannon) 128

 Homer 128
 Janette (Thompson) 128
 Marcelle 128
 Margaret 128
 Margaret Jane (Templeton) 121,
  126
 Mary Edna 128
 Mildred 128
 Runette (Donnan) 134
 Whitfield Clark 128
DERNETT, Adah (Colescott) 147
 G. E. 147
DESSAUSURE, W. D. 25
DICKSON, Leila Ada (Templeton)
  29
DIGGINS, Edward 150
 Irene (Templeton) (Carter) 150
 Samuel 150
DILDAY, Essie (McCoy) 45
 S. 45
DILL, 115
DILLARD, Charles 113
 Earl 113
 Ella (Antley) 113
 Gussie 113
 Ila (Templeton) 113
 Mamie (Rhodes) 113
 Marcus 113
 Roy 113
 Viola (Wade) 113
DILLINGHAM, Mabel Louise
  (Templeton) 103
DISBROW, Charles 23
 Estelle Elliott (Harding) 23
 Sybil 23
DODD, Dooley L. (Templeton) 76
DOMINICK, James L. 97
 Martha Emma (Stewart) 97
 Martha Gale 97
DONNAHOE, Earl 24
 Lottie (Rhoades) 24
DONNAN, Althea Floy (Templeton)
  134
 Frances Floy (Brown) 134
 J. M. 137
 James 133
 James M. 134
 Runette (Dendy) 134
DONNON, Christopher 110
 Elizabeth (Templeton) 111
 Emmaline (Templeton) (Taylor)
  108, 110
DORRELL, Phoebe (Templeton)
  145
DORROH, 52

DRAPER, Cora Delia 81
Sadie (Campbell) 80, 81
Samuel M. 81
DRISCOL, Martha (Leffler) 145
DRUMMOND, Barbara (Fisher) 94
Charles Max 94
Deborah Irene 94
Fred Owings 94
Madge (Cook) 93, 94
Suzanne 94
DUCKETT, Thomas 49
DUCKWORTH, Frances (Lyles) 19
DUFFIE, John 43
Mary (Templeton) 43
DUGARD, Eva Estelle (Stewart) 98
Mark Irvin 98
Thomas Jefferson 98
DUKE, Ben 80
Willie Irene (Mullikin) 80
DULIN, Bessie (Smith) 38, 156
John C. 38, 156
DUMPHY, James Day 23
Lydia (Karp) 23
Martha Elizabeth (Templeton) 22,
23
DUNAWAY, Alma (Crook) 60
Nora (Lynch) 84
DUPREE, J. W. 14
Lizzie Jane (Boggs) 14
DURRAH, 49
DUVALL, Olive D. (Taylor) 119
EASLEY, Floyd 44
Jewell L. (Templeton) 44
EASTER, W. A. (Templeton) 143
EDGAR, Walter 157
EICHELBERGER, Margaret Joyce
(Templeton) 67
ELFORD, Mamie Spriggs
(Templeton) 61
ELLIOTT, Colleen, 157
Sallie (Templeton) 61
ELLIS, Verdie (Templeton) 44
Will 44
ELLISON, Blanch (Connelly) 82
Joe 82
ERWIN, Alice (Harding) 146
Edna May 145
Jacob 144
John 148
Mamie 145
Mary Eliza (Templeton) 143, 144
Oliver Ellsworth 145
Scott 144, 145
W. E. 147
EVATT, Alma (Templeton) 68

EWING, John 148
FAIRBURNE, Catherine
(Templeton) 10
FARLOW, Christine Hunt (Meek)
150
James Madison 150
Lillian (Fullmer) 150
Nancy (Lewiston) 150
Stephen 150
FARMER, Fannie Lou (Templeton)
129
FARROW, Samuel 18
FAULCONNER, Irene M. (Stewart)
12
FEW, Billie Margaret (McKain) 58
FINLEY, Sadie (Templeton) 113
FISHER, Barbara (Drummond) 94
FIX, Edith Boling (Templeton) 131,
132
William Edward 132
William Joseph 132
FLEMMING, Samuel 85
FLETCHER, Leneva (Templeton)
104
Margaret (Howard) 92
FLOYD, Ann (Templeton) (Martin)
(McCoy) 43, 47
Pomp 47
FOLGER, Ethel (Stewart) 12
FORTUNE, Pauline (Bradley) 91
FOWLER, Clara (Simpson) 37
Curry Jasper 99
David Donald 93
Douglass Norman 99
Estelle (Templeton) (Jones) 76, 77
J. Donald 93
James 96
Kathleen Stewart 93
Lucile (Templeton) 104
Margaret Agnes (Jones) 98, 99
Marilyn Joan 99
Mary Alice (Stewart) 93
Michael Jeffry 99
Nannie Hunter (Stewart) 92
Rachel Frances (Coleman) 96
Roy 104
Wade D. 92
Will 77
William Cely 99
FOX, Margaret (Templeton)
(Reeves) 130
FOY, Horace N. 13
Lucius Barrington 13
Sarah Louise (Templeton) 13

FREDERICKSON, Minnie
(Martindale) 17
FRIDDLE, Sara (Templeton) 124
FRY, Sam 143
  Sarah "Sallie" (Templeton) 143
FULLER, Annie Lee (Lockman) 75
FULLMER, Lillian (Farlow) 150
  Lillian 148
  Percy F. 150
FURR, Edna Lawson 64
GAFFNEY, Tessie (Ramsey) 57
GALDIN, 63, 70, 71
GALDMAN, Louise (Cook) 95
GALLEON, Henry 152
  Mary Hanna (McCarty) 152
GALLMAN, Alma Mae (Templeton)
  21
  Buron 21
  Eva 22
  Geneva 22
  Rufus 21
  Sybil 21
GALLOWAY, Corrie Addison
  (Boggs) 15
  Pauline 15
  T. H. 15
GARLAND, Ellen (Arnold) 91
GARRETT, 117
  Elizabeth (Lynch) 83
  Helen (Rodgers) 123
  Joseph 83
  Mary Elizabeth (Templeton) 83
  Priscilla 7, 31, 83
GASTON, William 36
GAULDIN, Earl 113
  Frances (Templeton) 113
GAULT, Dora Louise (Templeton)
  73, 74
  Joseph David 74
  Virginia Kathryn 74
GAUSE, Sara (Stewart) 93
GENTRY, Bessie (McCoy) 45
  Is 43
  Louisa (Templeton) 42
  Louisa Templeton 43
GIFFORD, May (Colescott) 147
GILES, Elizabeth Ann (Templeton)
  27, 28
  Ellen Emeline (Rittenburg) 29
  George Wesley 29
  George White 29
  Ira Alexis 29
  James Mabry 29
  James Mason 28
  John Archie 29

Josiah Patterson 29
Lucile (Muckenfus) 29
Lucile 29
Mary Graham (Hollis) 29
Owen (Crawford) 29
Sarah Wilson (McCully) 29
Susan Emma (Templeton) 24, 28
Willamena Glenn (Phifer) 29
William Templeton 28, 29
GILL, Alan Stewart 96
  Daniel Ross 96
  Martha League (Coleman) 96
  Roger Lowell 96
GILLESPIE, Cora (Smith) 90
  Tom 90
GILSTRAP, Christine Nannie
  (Coleman) 95, 96
  James Lee 96
  Mary Lou 96
GIMPEL, Carl 45
  Leila Lee (Templeton) 45
GLASGOW, John 17
  Venus (Martindale) 17
GLENN, Ada Gilliland (Humbert)
  35
  Amanda (Smith) 35
  Anna (McCown) 35
  Annie (Carter) 81, 82
  Arthur 82
  Ben 82
  Bessie M. (Smith) 35
  Calla (Chapman) 35
  David 36, 37
  Emma (Little) 37
  F. M. 35
  Flora 36
  Frank M. 35
  Harrison Kennedy 35
  J. P. 36, 37
  J. Perry 35
  Jessie N. (Shelor) 35
  John M. 35
  John Perry 35
  Mamie (McCollough) 35
  Margaret 35
  Mary (Sheldon) 35
  Mary (Simpson) 36
  Mary G. (Templeton) 34
  Polly (Templeton) 103
  Robert 35
  S. D. 32
  Sarah A. (Templeton) 32, 36
  Sarah Cornelia (Smith) 35
  Simpson Dunlap 36
  Thomas Knox 35

(SIMPSON), Rebecca Ryan 74
Sue (McHugh) 37
T. C. 37
Tom 37
William Van 73
SKINNER, Kate W. (Templeton)
145
SLIGH, Hubert 82
Pearl (Connelly) 82
SLOAN, Beatrice (Bennett) 130
Blakeley 111
Catherine Stewart (Templeton)
(Gore) 125, 126
Corrie Elizabeth (Templeton) 128,
129
David Lawrence 130
George L. 130
J. Lawrence 129
Lucy (McDowell) 130
Mary Allen 130
Mattie (Templeton) 111, 129
Rhett 130
Ruth (White) 130
Ruth White 130
Will 126
William D. 129, 130
SMALLWOOD, Jess (Templeton) 43
Leo 43
SMITH, Addie Hollingsworth 38
Agnes (Templeton) 113
Amanda (Glenn) 35
Anna Pearl (Robinson) 36
Annie Nell (Armstrong) 106
Archie Henry 38
Beatrice (Martin) 126
Bessie (Dulin) 38, 156
Bessie M. (Glenn) 35
Beulah Sue (Wood) 104
Carolyn (Templeton) 132
Charles Butler 38
Cora (Gillespie) 90
Cynthia (White) 100
Dorothy (Prather) 59
Elizabeth (Arnold) 90
Elizabeth (Richardson) 36
Elizabeth Jane (Templeton) 89
Estelle (Stewart) 92
Eugenia (Templeton) 45
Eva (White) 100
Frank Monroe 36
George David 38
George T. 38
Grace (Howe) 38
Harold 106
Herbert Glenn 36

J. C. 126
Jack Monroe 97
James Noah 38
Janice (Stewart) 97
Jennie (Lewis) 38
Jephtha 35
John Clark 90
Joshua A. 18
Kate (Carter) 82
Lois Amanda (Taylor) 36
Margaret (Rutherford) 90
Margaret Anderson (Templeton)
18, 22
Marion Glenn 36
Martha Elizabeth 38
Mary Catherine (Arnold) 90
Mary Ella McCravy 38
Mary Hester 36
Mattie (Hollingsworth) 38
Maude (Hass) 38
Minnie (Pickens) 38
Nancy (Templeton) 38
Paul 45
Sarah Cornelia (Glenn) 35
Sarah Evaline (Morgan) 38
Stewart Monroe 97
Susan Jacque 97
Thelma (Puckett) 58
Thomas Lewers 38
W. M. 35
W. Turner 89
Walter Marie Glenn 35
SMOAK, Alfred M. 105
Joyce (Templeton) 105
SNEAD, Martha Ann (Templeton)
22
SNODGRASS, Lucinda (Templeton)
151
SNOW, Addie (Templeton) 107, 108
Effie (Templeton) 108
Elizabeth (Thompson) 105
Maggie D. (Templeton) 102, 104
Mattie Elizabeth (Griffith) 105
Paul Franklin 105
Pearl (Cooper) 105
Ralph Perry 105
True V. 104
William Zadie 105
SPARKS, Eula (Templeton) 56
SPEER, Elizabeth (Templeton) 108
SPROLES, Eunice (Patterson)
(Martin) 126
Freck 126
J. W. 126
James 126

(TEMPLETON), Agnes (Wright)
    (Miller) 143
Agnes 1, 85, 141, 142, 148, 157
Agnes Gwendolyn (White) 103
Alexander "Sandy" 149, 150
Alexis Everette 30
Alexis Holtzclaw 24, 29, 30
Alice (Compton) 113
Alice (Martin) 44
Alice Deveaux (Ball) 23, 24
Alice Lee (Milan) 111
Alice Montgomery 111, 112
Alma (Evatt) 68
Alma (Middlestadt) 67
Alma (Ramage) 130
Alma Mae (Gallman) 21
Alma Theresa (Wham) 131
Alpha (Dawson) 152
Althea Floy (Dorman) 134
Amanda (Bennett) 33, 34
Amanda (Bowen) 43
Amanda (Williams) 42
Amanda 33
Amanda C. (Thackston) 105
Amelia (Barksdale) 124
Amelia (Puckett) 43, 47
Andrew 153
Ann (Floyd) (Martin) (McCoy) 43,
    47
Ann Elizabeth (Likely) 143, 145
Anna (Miller) 151
Anna 143
Anna D. (Brown) 130, 132
Anne Elizabeth (Hitch) 89, 121
Annette 136
Annie (Rampey) 46
Annie Belle (Brown) 129
Annie Leola (Martin) 133
Annie Mae (Buchanan) 105, 106
Ansel League 103
Araminta (Putnam) 108
Arch League 104
Archibald 153
Arena (Bobo) 99
Arroane (Shamby) 77
Audrey Keturah (Jarrell) 144
Avie (Taylor) 119
Avie Inez (Taylor) 134
B. E. (Perkins) 44
B. W. 44
Barbery (Burke) 83
Barbery 83
Barran Elmore 125
Batty Jane 103
Beatrice 112

Belle 113
Ben P. 126
Ben Preston 56, 57
Ben Tillman 106
Benjamin Archie 20
Benjamin Clark 5, 6, 39, 42, 48-50,
    72
Benjamin F. 151
Benjamin P. 42
Benjamin Preston 22, 48, 55
Bernard Allison 20
Berry J. 21
Bessie (Johnson) 141
Bessie Edith (Johnson) 145
Bessie Lee (McKinney) 104
Betty Ann 143
Betty Claire 112
Betty Lee (Power) 135
Beulah (Adderson) 46
Beulah (Shockley) 107
Billy McDufie 112
Blondell 21
Bob 100
Borman 20
Bramlett Russell 103
Briggs 21
Bruce 77
Bruce Ramage 131, 132
Callie (McBride) 77
Callie Catherine 121, 128
Callie Stone 20
Callie Vesta 20
Captain John 108, 149
Carl 76, 77
Caroline (Peden) 88
Caroline 30, 108, 114
Carolyn (Smith) 132
Carrie (Huff) 125
Carric (League) 104
Carrie (Powell) 131
Carrie C. (Burdette) 102, 103
Carrie Elizabeth (Parsons) 122, 123
Carroll LaBorde 107, 108
Catherine (Crist) 143
Catherine (Fairburne) 10
Catherine (Newland) 152
Catherine (Nivens) 112
Catherine 143
Catherine H. 149
Catherine Stewart (Gore) (Sloan)
    125, 126
Charles Morrison 104
Charles Robert 143
Charlie K. 130, 132
Chester 21

(TEMPLETON), Mary A. G.
  (Hopkins) 39, 81
Mary A. G. 42
Mary Alice (Bowen) 44
Mary Ann (Goodwin) 48
Mary Ann (Stewart) 89, 91
Mary Ann (Templeton) 19, 20, 83
Mary Ann 18, 89
Mary E. (Ramage) 130, 131
Mary E. 33, 34
Mary Eliza (Erwin) 143, 144
Mary Elizabeth (Garrett) 83
Mary Ellie (Lockman) 49, 74
Mary Ellie (Simpson) 73
Mary Ellie 63
Mary Etta 45
Mary Eunice 10
Mary Frances (Carr) 71
Mary G. (Glenn) 34
Mary G. 32
Mary Hanna (Templeton) 142, 149,
  150
Mary Jane (Carter) 143
Mary Jane 135
Mary Kathleen (Scruggs) 122
Mary Lula (Rodgers) 122
Mary Martha 107
Mary Ruth 33
Mary Susan (Davis) 20
Mary T. (Jester) 46
Mary Texanna 108
Masby M. 33, 34
Mascy 32
Massie (Laird) 9, 10, 14, 15, 17, 24,
  32, 36
Mat (Hopkins) 81, 82
Matilda (Baxter) 150
Mattie (Hopkins) 46
Mattie (Jones) 98, 102
Mattie (Sloan) 111, 129
Mattie Jane (Bramlett) 103
Mattie L. 47
Mattie Lou 103
Mattie Mae (Arnold) 111
Maude (Cooper) 105
Maxcy Hood 134, 135
May Pearl (Leffler) 145
Mazel (Broom) 104
Meurice 34
Minnie (Lorry) 77
Minnie Cornelia (Rhoades) 23
Miriam (Bobo) 131
Mittie Gertrude (Lawson) 62-64
Mollie (Marler) 113
Molly Alercy (Howard) 122

Murrell (Adcock) 77
Myrle (Thompson) 68
Myrtle Elizabeth (Caughman) 103
Nadine 45
Nancy (Adair) 131
Nancy (Barrickman) 151
Nancy (Lewiston) 149, 150
Nancy (Luke) 43, 83
Nancy (Smith) 38
Nancy 32, 107, 135
Nancy Agnes (Colescott) 142, 147
Nancy C. (Templeton) 83
Nancy Carolyn (Lyles) 18
Nancy Estelle (Harding) 22, 23
Nancy Katherine (White) 89, 99
Nannie M. (Rowland) 113
Nathaniel Day 107
Nellie (Lewis) 112
Niles G. 33
Nina (Burris) 144
Nora (Allison) 44
Olive (Thomason) 123
Oliver 1, 113, 115,
Oliver Ervin 20
Oliver G. 142
Oliver Goldsmith 143, 144
Oliver M. 52
Oliver Milan 111
Oneal 21
Ora Sophia 20
Orra Augusta 22
Oscar 125
Osker 76
P. C. 43
Pauline (Monroe) 47
Pauline 45
Pearl (Jerry) 107, 108
Peggy 49, 74
Perry Franklin 89, 98, 102
Phoebe (Dorrell) 145
Phonice 45
Polly (Glenn) 103
Pope 43
Rafe Orbey 20
Ralph 13
Reba 45
Robert 1, 4, 5, 39-43, 47, 48, 85,
  113, 139-146, 148, 150, 157-159
Robert Jr. 157, 158
Robert Allen 130
Robert Dudley 144
Robert E. 130, 131
Robert James 107
Robert Martin 89
Robert Mitchell 89, 100

WALTZ, Annabell (Likely) 145
  Clint 145
WARD, Sarah E. (Templeton) 143
WARNE, Agnes Patricia 96
  Donald Nobson 96
  Lois Shirley (Coleman) 96
  Robert Preston 96
WATKINS, Albert 50
  Christine (Riddle) 50, 51
  Danner 50, 156
  Frances (Powers) 50
  Irene (Allen) 50, 51
  Kate (Davis) 50
  Kate (Meadors) 50, 51
  Mamie Bishop Robinson 50, 51
  Mattie (Blakely) 50
  Raymond 50
  Robert 50
  Russie (Riddle) 50
  Ruth (Stewart) 50
WATSON, Claude D. 66
  Guy 133
  John Parham 66
  Margaret Elizabeth 66
  Ruby Altahlee (Parham) 65, 66
  Tom 54
WEAVER, Cecile Ernestine
  (Coleman) 95, 96
  George Cleveland 96
  George Richard 96
  James Thomas 96
  Maude Kenielle 96
WEEKS, Pluma (Senn) 117
WELBORN, Ann (Boggs) 11
WELLS, Gwen (Templeton) 21
  Jane Ellen (Griffin) 13
  Ora (McCoy) 45
  Walter Gay 13
WELSH, Mary (Templeton) 150
WERTZ, James Claudine 15
  Julian 15
  Sarah Ada (Boggs) 15
WHAM, Alma Theresa (Templeton)
  131
  Louis 132
  Lula Grace (Templeton) 123
WHEELER, John 154
WHITE, Agnes Elizabeth 100
  Agnes Gwendolyn (Templeton) 103
  Alvin 93, 100
  Anthony 89, 99, 100
  Bessie (Montgomery) 100
  Bud 46
  Corrie E. (Jones) 99
  Cynthia (Smith) 100

Cynthia Anita (Cannon) 93
Etta (Putman) 99
Eva (Smith) 100
George 93
Helen Gould (Stewart) 92, 93, 100
James Ausker 99
John Jones 99
John King 99, 100
John William 93
Kenneth Stewart 93
Mamie (Templeton) (Connally) 46
Margaret Ida (Moore) 99
Nancy Katherine (Templeton) 89,
  99
Robert Clark 99, 100
Ruth (Sloan) 130
WHITLOCK, 66
WHITMIRE, Winnie Mae
  (Campbell) 81
WHITTON, Levi 39, 78
  Sarah P. (Templeton) 39, 78
WILBANKS, 63, 64
  Cleala (Templeton) (Thomason) 76,
  77
  U. G. 77
WILLARD, Adalaid (Workman) 110
  Hugh (Crook) 60
WILLIAMS, Amanda (Templeton)
  42
  Annie 42
  Darthula (Arnold) 90
  James Clifton 23
  Mable (Templeton) 136
  Margaret Elliott (Templeton) 22, 23
  Mary (Templeton) 45
  Minnie Luva (Attaway) 42
  Pick (Carter) 82
  Pick 42
  Pres. 42
  Quincy 42
  Sarah (Coleman) 96
WILLIS, M. J. 118
  Mallie (McDowell) 117, 118
WILSON, Kathleen Lander 75
  President 38
WOFFORD, James Arthur 19
  Lillie Genelle (Lyles) 18, 19
WOOD, Beulah Sue (Smith) 104
  Claude 104
  Grady 104
  John I. 104
  Lois (Kellett) 104
  Mary A. (Templeton) 102, 104
  Pearl (Jones) 104
  Roy 104

www.ingramcontent.com/pod-product-compliance
Lightning Source LLC
Chambersburg PA
CBHW070914270326
41927CB00011B/2571

* 9 7 8 0 7 8 8 4 5 5 6 3 6 *